ASTROLOGICAL PREDICTION:

A Handbook of Techniques

Öner Döşer

EDITED WITH A PREFACE BY
BENJAMIN N. DYKES, PHD

The Cazimi Press
Minneapolis, Minnesota
2015

Published and printed in the United States of America

by The Cazimi Press
515 5th Street SE #11, Minneapolis, MN 55414

© 2015 by Öner Döşer

ISBN-13: 978-1-934586-42-6

ACKNOWLEDGEMENTS

I first met with predictive techniques through the astrology lessons of Hakan Kırkoğlu. Through my studies with Robert Zoller I later became more familiar with traditional predictive techniques, and had the opportunity to develop my skills in that area. I owe many thanks to these two teachers who guided me in understanding these predictive techniques. I would also like to thank my dear friend Benjamin Dykes, who edited this book and made valuable contributions to it; I am happy and honored to have his support.

Translating this book from Turkish to English took a great and long effort. Sibel Oltulu, who is familiar with these techniques as a graduate of AstroArt (our astrology school), accomplished this task very well. I would like to extend many thanks to her.

I would also like to thank Mustafa Konur, the editor of the Turkish edition, who helped with the book layout and artwork.

Finally, I give endless thanks to my dear wife Gaye, who never stopped giving me her support, patience, and tolerance, while I worked hard on both the Turkish and the English versions of this book.

Öner Döşer
Istanbul, Winter 2014

Also available at www.bendykes.com:

Designed for curious modern astrology students, *Traditional Astrology for Today* explains basic ideas in history, philosophy and counseling, dignities, chart interpretation, and predictive techniques. Non-technical and friendly for modern beginners.

The first volume of the new medieval mundane series, *Astrology of the World I: The Ptolemaic Inheritance* describes numerous techniques in weather prediction, prices and commodities, eclipses and comets, and chorography, translated from Arabic and Latin sources.

Two classic introductions to astrology, by Abū Ma'shar and al-Qabīsī, are translated with commentary in this volume. *Introductions to Traditional Astrology* is an essential reference work for traditional students.

The classic medieval text by Guido Bonatti, the *Book of Astronomy* is now available in paperback reprints. This famous work is a complete guide to basic principles, horary, elections, mundane, and natal astrology.

This first English translation of Hephaistion of Thebes's *Apotelesmatics* Book III contains much fascinating material from the original Dorotheus poem and numerous other electional texts, including rules on thought-interpretation.

The largest compilation of traditional electional material, *Choices & Inceptions: Traditional Electional Astrology* contains works by Sahl, al-Rijāl, al-'Imrānī, and others, beginning with an extensive discussion of elections and questions by Benjamin Dykes.

The famous medieval horary compilation *The Book of the Nine Judges* is now available in translation for the first time! It is the largest traditional horary work available, and the third in the horary series.

The Search of the Heart is the first in the horary series, and focuses on the use of victors (special significators or *almutens*) and the practice of thought-interpretation: divining thoughts and predicting outcomes before the client speaks.

The Forty Chapters is a famous and influential horary work by al-Kindī, and is the second volume of the horary series. Beginning with a general introduction to astrology, al-Kindī covers topics such as war, wealth, travel, pregnancy, marriage, and more.

The first volume of the *Persian Nativities* series on natal astrology contains *The Book of Aristotle*, an advanced work on nativities and prediction by Māshā'allāh, and a beginner-level work by his student Abū 'Ali al-Khayyāt, *On the Judgments of Nativities*.

The second volume of *Persian Nativities* features a The second volume of *Persian Nativities* features a shorter, beginner-level work on nativities and prediction by 'Umar al-Tabarī, and a much longer book on nativities by his younger follower, Abū Bakr.

The third volume of *Persian Nativities* is a translation of Abū Ma'shar 's work on solar revolutions, devoted solely to the Persian annual predictive system. Learn about profections, distributions, *firdārīyyāt*, transits, and more!

This compilation of sixteen works by Sahl b. Bishr and Māshā'allāh covers all areas of traditional astrology, from basic concepts to horary, elections, natal interpretation, and mundane astrology. It is also available in paperback.

Expand your knowledge of traditional astrology, philosophy, and esoteric thought with the *Logos & Light* audio series: downloadable, college-level lectures on MP3 at a fraction of the university cost!

Enjoy these new additions in our magic/esoteric series:

Astrological Magic: Basic Rituals & Meditations is a basic introduction to ritual magic for astrologers. It introduces a magical cosmology and electional rules, and shows how to perform ritual correctly, integrating Tarot and visualizations with rituals for all Elements, Planets, and Signs.

Available as an MP3 download, *Music of the Elements* was composed especially for *Astrological Magic* by MjDawn, an experienced electronic artist and ritualists. Hear free clips at bendykes.com/music.php!

Nights is a special, 2-disc remastering by MjDawn of the album GAMMA, and is a deep and powerful set of 2 full-disc MP3 soundtracks suitable for meditation or ritual work, especially those in *Astrological Magic*. Hear free clips at bendykes.com/music.php!

Aeonian Glow is a new version of the original ambient work mixed by Steve Roach, redesigned by MjDawn and Vir Unis from the original, pre-mixed files. This MP3 album is entrancing and enchanting: hear free clips at bendykes.com/music.php!

TABLE OF CONTENTS

Table of Figures iv

Editor's Preface 1

Author's Preface 3

Introduction: The Art of Prediction in Astrology 5

Chapter 1: The Ages of Man 13

Moon period (ages 0-4) 14

Mercury period (ages 4-14) 19

Venus period (ages 14-22) 22

Sun period (ages 21-41) 22

Mars period (ages 41-56) 23

Jupiter period (ages 56-68) 23

Saturn period (age 68 to end of life) 24

Chart distinctions according to the waxing and waning Moon 24

Chapter 2: Directing by Triplicities 29

The Method 29

Times of success and welfare in life 32

Chapter 3: *Firdaria* 37

The order of *firdaria* periods 38

Practical information on the use of *firdaria* 41

Examples: Princess Diana 41

Times of recognition 46

Chapter 4: Profections 49

The technique of profections 49

Example: George W. Bush 56

Handy rules for profections 57

Example: Öner Döşer, age 37 59

Chapter 5: Transits 65

Key issues in transits 67

Transits in traditional astrology 71

Eclipses, New Moons, and Full Moons 74

Retrograde motion of the planets 74

Pluto transits 75

Neptune transits 84

Uranus transits 92

Saturn transits 102

Jupiter transits 113

Mars transits 123

Sun transits 129

Venus transits 133

Mercury transits 137

Moon transits 141

Transits of the Nodes 144

Four examples 144

Transits and Solar/Lunar returns 150

Chapter 6: Solar Arc Directions **153**

The solar arc technique 153

Keywords and interpretation hints 154

Practice example 156

Chapter 7: Secondary Progressions **159**

Differences between secondary progressions and transits 159

The meanings of progressed planets 160

The progressed Sun 163

The progressed Moon 168

Progressed Mercury 173

Progressed Venus 175

Progressed Mars 176

The Moon-Sun relationship 178

Progressed retrograde planets 181

The progression of house cusps 182

Chapter 8: Directing by Bounds or Terms **185**

Interpreting the bound 187

Example chart 188

Chapter 9: Primary Directions **195**

Basic concepts 195

Terminology and symbols 201

Calculation examples 201

Interpreting primary directions 208

Chapter 10: Eclipses **211**

Basic principles of eclipses 211

Contacts between eclipses and planets 216

Practice example: two solar eclipses 219

Prenatal eclipses 221

Chapter 11: Solar and Lunar Returns..**227**

Rules for interpreting solar returns..227

Comparing the nativity and solar return.....................................231

Five examples..234

Planets in the solar return chart 247

Review of important principles of interpretation........................248

Lunar returns...252

Return charts of other planets...260

Chapter 12: Rectification **269**

Traditional rectification techniques 269

Modern Rectification Techniques..278

Important changes in life..285

Glossary...**294**

Bibliography..**297**

About AstroArt: The School of Astrology...................................**302**

TABLE OF FIGURES

Figure 1: Planetary ages of man 14
Figure 2: Öner Döşer nativity, Placidus houses 15
Figure 3: Öner Döşer nativity, Placidus houses 15
Figure 4: Dorothean triplicity lords 29
Figure 5: *Firdaria* periods 38
Figure 6: Bonatti's *firdaria* periods table 39
Figure 7: Table of *firdaria* sub-period lords 40
Figure 8: Length of *firdaria* sub-periods 40
Figure 9: Nativity for Princess Diana 42
Figure 10: *Firdaria* for Princess Diana 42
Figure 11: Table of ages and houses for profected Ascendant 50
Figure 12: George W. Bush nativity 50
Figure 13: George W. Bush profections for 1947 (age 1) 51
Figure 14: George W. Bush nativity and 1947 profections 52
Figure 15: George W. Bush nativity and 1981 profections 55
Figure 16: George W. Bush nativity and 2004 profections 57
Figure 17: Approximate transit cycles of the planets 66
Figure 18: Aspects as harmonics 70
Figure 19: Standard retrogradation periods 75
Figure 20: Öner Döşer, transits for June 21, 2003 145
Figure 21: Öner Döşer, transits for October 6, 2004 146
Figure 22: Gaye Döşer, transits for June 13, 2006 147
Figure 23: Öner Döşer, Saturn opposition 149
Figure 24: Aspects and phases in the Sun-Moon cycle 178
Figure 25: The Ascendant in the bound of Saturn in Libra 185
Figure 26: Table of Egyptian Bounds 186
Figure 27: Primary directions and secondary progressions 196
Figure 28: Square of Mars (promittor) directed to Moon (significator) 198
Figure 29: Table of right ascensions and declinations, Öner Döşer 203
Figure 30: Table of values for directing the Sun to Venus 206
Figure 31: Öner Döşer, 1979 eclipse 219
Figure 32: Öner Döşer, 1997 eclipse 221
Figure 33: Öner Döşer, 1965 solar eclipse 222
Figure 34: Öner Döşer, 1965 lunar eclipse 223
Figure 35: Öner Döşer, 2003 solar return 235
Figure 36: Öner Döşer, 2003 SR on nativity 238
Figure 37: Öner Döşer, nativity on 2003 SR 239
Figure 38: Öner Döşer, 2005 solar return 241
Figure 39: Öner Döşer, 1997 solar return 243
Figure 40: Öner Döşer, 2004 solar return 245
Figure 41: Gaye Döşer, 1992 solar return 246
Figure 42: Illustration of Ptolemy's *namūdār* 272
Figure 43: Nativity of Heinrich Rantzau 273

ESSENTIAL DIGNITIES

ESSENTIAL DIGNITIES		♈	♉	♊	♋	♌	♍	♎	♏	♐	♑	♒	♓
DOMICILE RULERSHIP	(+5)	♂	♀	☿	☽	☉	☿	♀	♂	♃	♄	♄	♃
EXALTATION	(+4)	☉ 19	☽ 3	☊ 3	♃ 15	—	☿ 15	♄ 21	—	☋ 3	♂ 28	—	♀ 27
TRIPLICITY RULERS (Trigon Lords / Dorotheus) — DAY	(+3)	☉	♀	♄	♀	☉	♀	♄	♀	☉	♀	♄	♀
TRIPLICITY RULERS — NIGHT		♃	☽	☿	♂	♃	☽	☿	♂	♃	☽	☿	♂
TRIPLICITY RULERS — COMMON		♄	♂	♃	☽	♄	♂	♃	☽	♄	♂	♃	☽
TERMS (Bounds / Egyptian)	(+2)	♃ ♀ ☿ ♂ ♄	♀ ☿ ♃ ♄ ♂	☿ ♃ ♀ ♂ ♄	♂ ♀ ☿ ♃ ♄	♃ ♀ ♄ ☿ ♂	☿ ♀ ♃ ♂ ♄	♄ ☿ ♃ ♀ ♂	♂ ♀ ☿ ♃ ♄	♃ ♀ ☿ ♄ ♂	☿ ♃ ♀ ♄ ♂	☿ ♀ ♃ ♂ ♄	♀ ♃ ☿ ♂ ♄
DECANIC FACES (Chaldean) — 1. DECAN (00° 00' – 9° 59')	(+1)	♂	☿	♃	♀	♄	☉	☽	♂	☿	♃	♀	♄
DECANIC FACES — 2. DECAN (10° 00' – 19° 59')		☉	☽	♂	☿	♃	♀	♄	☉	☽	♂	☿	♃
DECANIC FACES — 3. DECAN (20° 00' – 29° 59')		♀	♄	☉	☽	♂	☿	♃	♀	♄	☉	☽	♂

ESSENTIAL DEBILITIES

ESSENTIAL DEBILITIES		♈	♉	♊	♋	♌	♍	♎	♏	♐	♑	♒	♓
FALL	(-4)	♄	—	—	♂	—	♀	☉	☽	—	♃	—	☿
DETRIMENT	(-5)	♀	♂	♃	♄	♄	♃	♂	♀	☿	☽	☉	☿

EDITOR'S PREFACE

I am pleased to present this English translation of a handbook on predictive techniques by my Turkish colleague, Öner Döşer (*Uner Dusher*). After a long career in Istanbul's oldest and most prestigious bazaar, Öner followed his heart and turned fully to astrology, soon becoming one of the leading astrologers in Turkey, with numerous television appearances and books to his credit. His Istanbul-based astrology school, AstroArt,[1] is a popular and bustling hive of student activity, and his Astrology School Publishing has released 14 well-received books, not to mention his own articles in international astrological publications. Since 2012 he has been the organizer of the highly successful International Astrology Days in Istanbul.

Öner Döşer's work represents an important trend in contemporary astrology: the blending of traditional and modern techniques and attitudes. For example, for the most part he uses Placidus houses, but for certain techniques he focuses on whole signs. In terms of planets, he uses the three outers as well as Chiron. He employs out-of-sign aspects, and some features of the 12-letter astrological alphabet (for example, associating some meanings of Scorpio, Pluto, and the 8th). On the other hand, the reader will see a liberal use of the traditional terms "native" and "nativity," which refer to the person born and his or her birth chart, respectively. And his approach to astrology combines modern psychological and spiritual interests with realistic attitudes about determinism or fate. That is, astrological prediction works because of Divine creative and causal rules in the universe, which bring about events reflected in the nativity. In Döşer's view, free will operates within these rules, in things which we can control and respond to: like having free reign to paint on a canvas, but within certain lines and constraints put on us. The contemporary reader should understand his occasional references to fate in this spirit.

One central feature of this book (and of traditional astrology) is its presentation of time lords. As some modern readers are not familiar with this term, let me define it here. A time lord (Gr. *chronokratōr*) is normally a planet which has management responsibility over your life (or some aspect of life) for a specific amount of time: it is a way of making longer periods of life intelligible, as opposed to finding "hits" or particular days or weeks when

---

[1] www.astrolojiokulu.com/eng/.

some specific event is sought. The order of the planets, and the time period managed by each, are determined by the technique one is using. Moreover, what a time lord actually indicates for a particular person depends in large part on what it is doing in the nativity. For example, Venus means certain general things for everyone, but as a time lord for *this* person, she might indicate friends (if she is natally in the 11th) or mortality and fear (if in the 8th), and so on. Techniques in this book cover time spans anywhere from around one year to twenty-five years. Time lord systems are very valuable and I am sure you will find them fascinating and accurate.

In terms of editing, I have occasionally added an explanatory footnote (prefaced by **BD**). But for the most part have let Döşer's style and vocabulary speak for itself, so the reader may appreciate this leading voice from a dynamic country with one of the fastest-growing appreciations for both traditional and modern astrology. I would also like to thank Mustafa Konur and Maria Mateus for their help.

Finally, below I append part of an invocation by Guido Bonatti, the 13th Century Italian astrologer, from his Latin *Book of Astronomy*, which also appeared in the Turkish edition of this book.

"In the name of our Lord Jesus Christ, commiserator and holy one, true God and true man, to whom there is none equal nor like, nor could there be (and [in the name] of his most blessed mother Mary, ever glorious virgin, and of Saint Valerian the Martyr, captain and governor and defender of the community of Forlì), Who is supplicated and likewise glorified by the faithful (at once with the Father and the Holy Spirit, in a unity of essence and a Trinity of Persons, triune and one); nor is there another God besides Him, Who made and secured and produced (all together for the usefulness of man) the heaven and the earth, with all that is in them, and [Who] adorned the heaven with stars – illuminating lamps, so to speak – so that with their virtues they would dispose [all] inferior things together, and rule a command over men just as it was granted to them (likewise so they would exhibit it); and [Who] put what is rational over all living things together so that they might serve, and He made it their prerogative to [be able] to sense and understand; He even manifested to them the motions of the super celestial bodies and what is signified by them, and He extended the heavens over them like a tent, so that in it and through it (and with Divine Wisdom revealing and imparting [it]) they would be able to understand not only past or present things, but even so they might beware of, predict, and be able to announce future ones."

AUTHOR'S PREFACE

On the occasion of our third book published by the Astrology School Publishing House, we are proud to present another valuable resource for astrology students. The original edition of this book was in Turkish, but one of our aims is to educate the astrological public via books in their own native languages: hence this English edition by The Cazimi Press, which we hope will find wide acceptance.

Astrological Prediction: A Handbook of Methods is perhaps the most comprehensive manual currently available which includes both traditional and modern predictive techniques. It is an enlarged version of the Advanced Astrology textbook which we have used in our school since 2008, and offers a detailed overview of manifold techniques along with numerous example charts and explanations, in order to help practitioners make accurate predictions.

In addition to numerous familiar modern techniques, it introduces contemporary astrologers to essential and accurate traditional methods such as primary directions, *firdaria*, distributions or directions through the bounds, directing by triplicities, and the Ages of Man. These precious traditional techniques were developed, used, or explained by older masters of astrology, like Claudius Ptolemy, Vettius Valens, al-Qabīsī, Māshā'allāh, Abū Ma'shar, 'Umar al-Tabarī, Guido Bonatti, and Jean-Baptiste Morin. They have remained in the shadows of astrological practice for some time, due in part to different conceptions of astrology, some complicated calculations, and because psychological astrology gained so much acclaim in the 20th Century. Beginning in the 1980s, traditional astrology texts have been translated and compiled as reference books by contemporary astrologers such as Robert Zoller, Robert Hand, Robert Schmidt, James H. Holden, and more recently Dr. Benjamin Dykes.

In addition to traditional techniques, we introduce and explain more familiar modern methods: transits, secondary progressions, solar arc progressions, solar and lunar returns, and eclipses. In the last chapter, we explain how to use these techniques in rectification.

I would like to thank to the Astrology School tutors Dr. Barış Özkırış, Ebru Kart, Yeşne Karaca, and Mustafa Konur for their contributions in revising and compiling the existing textbooks of our school. I would also like to thank Mustafa Konur for his contribution in preparing the cover and page designs, and also for editing the Turkish edition.

This book is a gift to astrology readers from the Astrology School team.

Öner Döşer
April 30th, 2013 10:53 AM
The Astrology School, Istanbul

INTRODUCTION: THE ART OF PREDICTION IN ASTROLOGY

Predicting the future is an intuitive need in human nature. This is one of the main reasons why humans have always been interested in astrology. We want to know how events will develop and advance, and where they will arrive in the end; in response, we need to take necessary precautions and make decisions as accurately as possible.

Even if we are not aware of it, prediction exists in all areas of life. For example, when we want to make an investment, we need to predict how the stock market may change and what the future trends might be. When we plan a vacation, we need to know how weather conditions will change. When we are taking an important exam for admission to a university, we need to predict which university will be the best decision for our future.

Likewise, certain people in society are appreciated for having foresight; those with the ability to think beyond their time and foresee the future, are always successful in life. Astrology itself is a guiding light which shows us our path, what we may experience, when we might be successful (or not), and the best periods for any new endeavor. Undoubtedly, identifying such indicators beforehand provides an important advantage. We may avoid some negative events, or we may at least be mentally and emotionally prepared for their consequences. This, in fact, shows us that we do have some control over events, and do not have control over others.

Guido Bonatti, the 13th-Century Italian astrologer who compiled texts of Hellenistic and Arabic astrology, states that astrology is a unique science which helps us know and predict things.[1] According to Bonatti, wise men thought that they could prevent some negative events which were otherwise predicted, or at least they could be spiritually prepared for such things, by reading the astrological indications. Ptolemy also states that those familiar with the nature of the stars have the power to prevent some of their effects and get prepared before their manifestation takes place.[2] With the help of prediction, people may be prepared for the coming events, with calm and strength. Astrological prediction is one of the talents that raises humans to the level of wisdom.

---

[1] See *Bonatti on Basic Astrology*, Treatise 1, Ch. 11.
[2] *Tet.* I.2-3.

Predictive techniques in traditional astrology

Predictive techniques such as secondary progressions, solar returns, solar arc progressions, and especially transits, are widely used by modern astrologers. However, some of the predictive techniques of traditional astrology which should be known by all well-equipped astrologers are not as widespread and familiar.

In fact, the predictive techniques of traditional astrology have made a great contribution to astrology, with a high degree of accuracy. If we have enough information about the techniques of traditional astrology, we may be able to understand the source of modern techniques. I believe these predictive techniques should be used together with new trends in modern astrology and psychological concepts.

The most important contribution of traditional astrology's predictive techniques is to maintain an objective approach to the course of events that the native might experience. Traditional techniques help us to understand fate, and as fated events run in a systematic and orderly way, we are able to foresee both the details and general course of our life. We may easily observe this system in charts of the heavens, because in general the themes and events of our lives are out of our direct control. Likewise, the techniques of traditional astrology are systematic and orderly. They give us certain rules for analyzing the chart and making predictions. So, in principle we are able to predict future events accurately. The methods also offer a hierarchical approach when predicting the general course of life: first the life is divided into main, longer periods, and then these periods are divided into smaller subperiods.

There is no doubt that secondary progressions and solar arcs are crucial tools of modern astrology. But they were not used in the era of traditional astrology. For example, secondary progressions were first mentioned in the book *Primum Mobile* by Placidus di Tito, an astrologer from the Renaissance who lent his name to the house system he invented.[3] However, progressions have been particularly used in the modern age. Traditional astrologers mostly used primary directions, profections, directing by bounds or terms, and *firdaria*. Primary directions (one of the most common techniques) are not used very often by modern astrologers, because they can involve mathematical calculations that intimidate some people, and there are many conflicting

---

[3] Gansten, p. 20.

opinions as to the best way to make them. (We will explain how to perform Ptolemaic directions easily.)

Transits, which traditional astrologers used after studying all of the other techniques, are also widely used by modern astrologers. But one of the biggest problems with transits for modern astrologers, is that they sometimes seem to have no effect. Traditional astrology proposes a solution for this: the transits of planets which are already time lords[4] in *other* techniques, will be more important and effective than those of just any planet. That is, traditional astrology treats transits as the *triggers* for *firdaria*, profections, solar returns, primary directions, and other techniques, not as independent indicators of events.

Another reason why certain techniques are often not used correctly, is that not all planets in a chart are related solely to the native. Modern astrology tends to assume that the whole horoscope represents the native. This leads to the following: the 1st house represents *me*, the 2nd house represents *my* money, the 3rd house represents *my* ideas, etc... and everything seems to be "mine." This is an egocentric view which leads us to conclude that there are no outer conditions in life and no genuine "others." But we always have others in our lives, and much of our experiences are related to these others. In traditional astrology, the native is represented by the 1st house, the lord of the 1st house, and the planets in or in aspect to the 1st house (the Ascendant). The remaining houses and their lords are related to others in the native's life. When these other indicators are in aspect to transiting planets, the "I" alone may not necessarily be affected. Rather, external things are affected, such as family members, friends, career, money, etc. Thus, when the lord of my 11th house or a planet in my 11th house is in aspect to a transiting planet, I am not affected by that transit, but someone within my circle of friends is affected.

The predictions made by traditional astrological techniques are more accurate because they make certain distinctions (such as those above) which are not always present in modern or psychological astrology. In psychological astrology, predictions are not the backbone of practice, but they do play this role in traditional astrology. By drawing on these traditional techniques, we may make better chart interpretations and more accurate predictions. However, we cannot claim that the accuracy rate is 100%. As humans, we have only limited knowledge: we may predict, but absolute knowledge only be-

---

[4] See the Glossary.

longs to God. Everyone who is interested in astrology should know his place and his limits.

Beware of your language in predictions!

An important mission of astrology is to warn against possible negative outcomes, not making up disaster scenarios. When making these warnings and practicing this art for the service of humanity, the conscious astrologer should always be aware of the psychology of the people he is addressing, and take care never to give rise to fear and worries by exaggerating conditions. Some astrologers who know nothing about human psychology and make predictions freely fill the hearts of their clients with fear and suspicion; but if we are careful and knowledgeable, we may help people overcome their fears by showing how their choices can help actively shape the future. Otherwise people may feel scared, thinking that they are victims of the stars and planets, on which they have no control nor effect.

Particularly when interpreting the effects of transiting planets, we should always keep in mind that these planetary movements are predestined—but their precise effects as well as our final destination will be based on how we react to their effects through our free will and awareness. Donna Cunningham emphasizes that transits are not isolated events on which we have no control, but they are parts of our psychological process.[5]

Transits help us increase our awareness about our lives and existence. If you are aware that life is a learning process and everything you experience helps you know your highest being, then transits will never surprise you. Even the hardest transits help us develop our understanding. Instead, sorrow grows as a result of resisting changes, and sometimes difficulties assist our growth. We must be focused on creativity and the developmental process rather than on our sorrows: then we may be thankful for all the difficulties we face, as they have brought us from darkness to light and have helped us reveal our true potentials.

---

[5] Cunningham, Ch. 15 *passim*.

A short preview of the techniques

In this book, the predictive techniques we will explore are as follows:

The Ages of Man. This ancient technique described by Ptolemy assigns certain years of life to the basic meanings of the seven traditional planets. The specific meaning of any of these time lords depends on their situation and condition in the natal chart.

Directing by bounds or terms. This directs the degree of the ASC through subdivisions of each of the signs, called "bounds" or "terms." Each bound is worth a certain amount of time, and the planet ruling it becomes a general time lord over the associated period of life.

Directing by triplicities. Here, we take three planets called "triplicity lords," and associate each with roughly one third of life: this gives a broad sketch of the quality of that part of life and its chief issues.

Primary directions: This ancient technique is based on the daily rotation of the heavens, and is used for both individual natives and in mundane astrology. According to the method we will follow, seven significators can be directed: the ASC, MC, Sun, Moon, Lot of Fortune, and the degrees of pre-natal New Moon and Full Moon.

Solar arc directions: Each planet is advanced by as much as the Sun advances day by day, and each day's motion is associated with one year of life. For instance, if the native is 38 years old, all planets in his chart are advanced by as much as the Sun moves in the first 38 days from birth. The planets do not retrograde. This technique is related more to the outer conditions of life than to the native's psychological condition.

Secondary progressions: This technique equates the daily motion of each planet with one year of life. So, the secondary progressed chart of a native for age 30 is in fact a chart of the transits which took place 30 days after his birth (the progressed ASC and MC are handled differently). Secondary progressions explain the psychological development of the native, but since one's inner and outer conditions are often go together due to the principle of synchronicity, they also give some clues about outer dynamics.

Transits. This technique tracks the real-time motion of the planets in relation to the natal chart, particularly their conjunctions and aspects to sensitive natal points such as the axial degrees.

Eclipses. The charts of solar and lunar eclipses are important indicators of crisis and change, especially if the degree of the eclipse is closely associated with a key natal degree.

Firdaria. This Persian time lord system divides births into day and night births, and assigns the planets to different periods of life for a specific number of years. These long periods (such as 9 years for the Moon) are also subdivided into smaller periods. The general character of the planetary combinations is analyzed according to what those planets are doing in the nativity.

Profections: This traditional technique is based on equation of one year of life to each house. A point (usually the ASC) is advanced by one house for every year of life, beginning with the first house at birth.

Solar and lunar returns. Return charts are charts for the time a planet (especially the Sun or Moon) returns to its natal location. These charts are examined both by themselves and in relation to the natal chart, to make predictions about a particular year or month.

Rectification. Finally, many of these techniques are useful in the always-important area of rectification: determining a more accurate birth time when the true one is not known.

Some details on the charts and approaches in this book

Before continuing, it would be good to explain which planets and house system I use for both nativities and return charts.

First, I use the seven traditional planets, the three modern outer planets, and Chiron. I give priority to the traditional rulers of the zodiacal signs as the rulers of house cusps, but I also use the modern rulers as co-rulers. In addition, I use both the domicile or sign rules as well as the exalted rulers: for instance, Mars is the domicile or sign ruler of Aries, and the Sun is the exalted lord of Aries.

As for houses, I mainly Placidus houses but I do use whole sign houses in order to get further information (particularly with some ancient techniques). I first look at the locations of the planets within Placidus houses, and then in whole signs. If a planet is close to the cusp of the next house I count it as being in that next house, especially if it is in the relevant whole sign. For example, suppose Sagittarius is rising, and Jupiter is placed in Leo in the 8th Placidus house, but close to the cusp of the 9th Placidus house. Since Leo is the ninth whole sign from Sagittarius already, I treat Jupiter as being in the 9th. Sometimes I prefer whole sign houses in profections because whole signs are traditionally the basis of profections. For intercepted signs, I first consider the ruler(s) of the house cusp and then those of the intercepted sign as secondary rulers.

I do use derived houses and find them very useful in getting further information from both natal and solar return charts, especially regarding individuals other than the native and their conditions.

Finally, although I give priority to the Ptolemaic aspects, I use minor aspects as well (especially the quincunx). I use 13° orb in aspects between the Sun and the Moon, 10° between a luminary and a planet, 8° for aspects between planets in major aspects. For the minor aspects I use 3° between any of the planets and the luminaries. I use the 5° rule for intermediate house cusps and 8° for the conjunctions and aspects to the angles. For the luminaries, I can extend the orb to 10° for the angles. I consider the closer aspects separately, because I find them to be more event-oriented. I give priority to applying aspects, especially applying aspects of the Moon if there are any.

PLATO

CHAPTER 1: THE AGES OF MAN

THE "AGES OF MAN" TECHNIQUE IS USED FOR DETERMINING LONGER PERIODS WITHIN A LIFE, IN ORDER TO EXPLAIN THE TYPICAL DEVELOPMENTAL PROCESS OVER A HUMAN LIFESPAN. THE SEVEN ANCIENT PLANETARY SPHERES CORRESPOND IN ORDER TO SEVEN AGE PERIODS, FROM CHILDHOOD UNTIL DEATH. AS THE CELESTIAL BODY NEAREST THE EARTH, THE MOON RULES THE FIRST AGE, WHILE SATURN RULES THE LAST PERIOD OF LIFE.

The earliest account of dividing the lifetime into these periods are found in Ptolemy's *Tetrabiblos* IV.10. Ptolemy states that there are seven ages in an archetypal life, each associated with one of the seven traditional planets:

"…it begins with the first age of man and with the first sphere from us, that is, the moon's, and ends with the last of the ages and the outermost of the planetary spheres, which is called that of Saturn. And in truth the accidental qualities of each of the ages are those which are naturally proper to the planet compared with it, and these it will be needful to observe, in order that by this means we may investigate the general questions of the temporal divisions, while we determine partic- ular differences from the special qualities which are discovered in the nativities."

In other words, when assessing the various periods of life with the Ages of Man technique, we begin generally with the natural signification of the time lord; but also very important is its natal place: its sign, house, and as- pects. In addition, these lords should not be evaluated only in isolation; we should consider them as a whole. A single planet cannot rule the life of the native alone, whether it is benefic or malefic. While making assessments about a certain period of life, in addition to the lord of that period we should always consider other planets that are in contact with it.

Below is a table of the ages assigned to each planet:

☽	Ages 0–4	4 years
☿	Ages 4–14	10 years
♀	Ages 14–22	8 years
☉	Ages 22–41	19 years
♂	Ages 41–56	15 years
♃	Ages 56–68	12 years
♄	68–end of life	1+ years

Figure 1: Planetary ages of man

Moon period (ages 0-4)

The period of the Moon is related to the mother. By considering the Moon's position in the zodiac, we can evaluate the psychological and physical characteristics of the mother and how the native is affected by her. This evaluation is valid especially for the first four years of the native. The Moon's sign is treated as a rising sign, and the rest of the signs are arranged as whole-sign houses derived from it.[1] By observing where the planets are located relative to the Moon, and their aspects to her, we may acquire information about the general situation of the mother during this period.

The first chart presented here is my own natal chart, in Placidus houses. Below, it is put into whole signs: we can then imagine that the Moon is her own Ascendant, so that Scorpio is a 1st house representing the mother. Likewise, the 4th house from the Moon (Aquarius) represents the mother's relationship with her family and her housing conditions, the 7th house (Taurus) represents her husband, and the 10th house (Leo) represents her career.

---

[1] **BD**: That is, the Moon's sign is treated as the Ascendant or 1st house for the mother, the next sign as the mother's 2nd, etc.

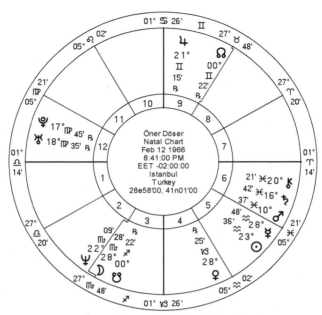

Figure 2: Öner Döşer nativity, Placidus houses

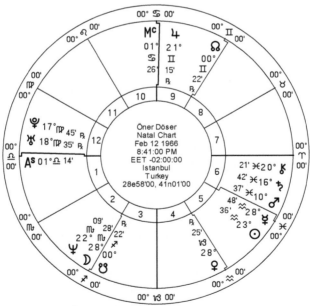

Figure 3: Öner Döşer nativity, whole-sign houses

Ptolemy explains this period in the following way:

> "For up to about the fourth year, following the number which belongs to the quadrennium, the moon takes over the age of infancy and produces the suppleness and lack of fixity in [the native's] body, its quick growth and the moist nature, as a rule, of [his] food, the changeability of [his] condition, and the imperfection and inarticulate state of [his] soul, suitably to her own active qualities."

The sign and house where the Moon is placed, and her aspects, show us what the development of emotional intelligence is like during that period. The Moon is the representative of naked emotions and automatic tendencies, and our unconscious mind (the Moon) develops earlier than our conscious mind (Mercury) does. So, the position of the Moon in the chart shows what we are like psychologically, physically, emotionally, and also mentally in the early years. The Moon's characteristics based on her sign are retained and displayed during ages 0-4. Of course, the effects of the Moon's position are with us throughout our lifetime; but as we grow up, our consciousness develops, and our experiences accumulate, these effects are manifested in a more controlled manner.

The Moon in the signs

Moon in Aries: Being peregrine in this sign, the Moon cannot display her nature easily here: the cold and humid nature of the Moon is incompatible with the hot and dry nature of Aries. The Moon needs peace and security, and an emotional bond, but cannot find these in Aries. The Moon in Aries represents a strong struggle for survival. Her needs are self-directed. The native's reactions will be direct and reckless, and possibly indiscreet.

Moon in Taurus: The Moon is exalted in this sign and also dignified by triplicity (nocturnal) and decan (the 2nd decan). Some ancient astrologers claim that the Moon is more comfortable in Taurus than in Cancer. The Moon here represents the need for physical and financial security, and because she is not in detriment the native will find the security he needs. A native with this placement cannot give up his habits easily. He may be highly conservative and stubborn. On the other hand, he is patient and slow to take action.

Moon in Gemini: The Moon is peregrine in this sign and cannot display her nature easily here. She cannot find the peace and stability she needs in this sign, because Gemini continuously adapts to changing conditions. The Moon here needs to act quickly, so the concentration she needs is lost. This position represents a talkative and adaptable native with a cheerful nature.

Moon in Cancer: Here, the Moon displays her natural characteristics strongly and the native can feel emotionally secure. With this placement, the native also looks for secure conditions for everyone else, and not only for himself. It also shows that the native is talented at expressing his feelings and understanding the feelings of others.

Moon in Leo: The Moon is peregrine in this sign. Since the Moon's nature contrasts with the forward display of the Sun (Leo's lord), she does not feel comfortable in this sign. A native with this placement is instinctively open and direct.

Moon in Virgo: The placement of the irrational Moon in the rational Virgo indicates that the emotions are blocked and the native is restless. The Moon's need for physical security is apparent in the earthy sign of Virgo. A native with this placement is critical and selective, and does not like anything very readily. The native experiences emotional ups and downs.

Moon in Libra: The Moon's desire for emotional security and peace is highly satisfied in Libra because she is positioned in a sign ruled by Venus, whose nature is very similar to the Moon's. The native likes making others happy and being loved by them. He is satisfied when he does something for the good of others, and has a strong sense of justice. He does not discriminate against people and has the ability to be in accord with them.

Moon in Scorpio: The Moon here acts contrary to her nature. The cold and humid nature of the Moon is fine in this sign, but as Scorpio is ruled by Mars, this placement brings explosive emotions and abrasive feelings. Intuitions are very strong, but jealousy and revenge are also characteristic with this placement. The positive side is that the native has a shrewd emotional intelligence and has a good understanding of human nature.

Moon in Sagittarius: The Moon is not comfortable in Sagittarius, which is totally contrary to her nature. The Moon needs stability, but Sagittarius is active and adaptable to changing conditions. Likewise, the Moon is introverted but a native with this placement seems more extroverted and friendly. Consequently, the native does not display a very emotionally sensitive approach to others: on the contrary, he ignores others' feelings and is prone to say anything without considering its results. This is an indication that the native may experience emotional ups and downs.

Moon in Capricorn: The Moon is in detriment here, but on the other hand she is one of its triplicity lords. This placement shows that responsibilities and duties have first priority, while emotions are behind the scenes or are totally ignored. As the Moon does not find love and caring here, the native may have a depressive mood. His rational, cautious, practical, and serious manner suppresses his emotions. The native is anxious in general and afraid of losing control of his sense of order. For him, being approved of by others is crucial.

Moon in Aquarius: The Moon cannot find emotional and physical security here, as the irrational Moon is not comfortable in rational Aquarius. While the Moon craves belonging, Aquarius is related to independence and individualism. The native may believe that he does not need the emotional and physical security he does in fact require.

Moon in Pisces: The cold and humid nature of the Moon are compatible with Pisces, but her sensitivities are deeper here. So, the native is talented in maintaining empathy with others and also has deep intuitions. On the other hand, as the Moon is in a mutable sign, the native will have some difficulties in maintaining emotional stability. The Moon's need to be cared for by others is more apparent in Pisces.

Applications and separations of the Moon

The planets with which the Moon is separating and applying, are important factors which the ancient astrologers cared about. Here are a few examples:[2]

In a diurnal chart, while the waxing Moon is separating from Jupiter and applying to Mars, the native is subject to slavery and the need to beg from others; he is faced with diseases and difficulties and has a violent death. But in a nocturnal chart, while the waxing Moon is separating from Jupiter and applying to Mars, the native's family is harmed at an early age, and he wastes all of his inheritance and falls into poverty. If the Mars is in the 2nd or in the 8th house, then the native suffers a lot and has a severe death.

---

[2] See for example *Mathesis*, IV.3b (Holden edition), IV.10 (critical edition). **BD**: Please note that the extreme language in these paragraphs is typical of some traditional texts: it is designed to outline both best and worst scenarios.

If the Moon in the natal chart is separated from the benefic planets (by aspect or conjunction) and applying to the aspect or conjunction of a malefic planet, the native is subject to slavery after being free: thus the overall status of the native begins at a good point but gets worse in the coming years.

If the Moon separates from Mercury by aspect or conjunction in a diurnal chart, the native falls into a decline, financially weakens, suffers from diseases, and loses touch with the direction of his life. He may face a violent death, or he may be imprisoned and experience some dangers.

Mercury period (ages 4-14)

The Mercury period is a time of mental development, learning, and the first steps into schooling. So, Mercury's position in the natal chart shows the native's learning capacity and his basic education. For this period, Ptolemy says:

> "In the following period of ten years, Mercury, to whom falls the second place and the second age, that of childhood, for the period which is half of the space of twenty years, begins to articulate and fashion the intelligent and logical part of the soul, to implant certain seeds and rudiments of learning, and to bring to light individual peculiarities of character and faculties, awakening the soul at this stage by instruction, tutelage, and the first gymnastic exercises."

According to Schoener,[3] we should look at Mercury for evaluating the intellectual and mental state of the native. Mercury is the planet of wisdom, logic and ingenuity, learning, and understanding. So again, Mercury's position, sign and aspects are important factors in evaluating the native's mental development. Mercury's position gives us information about his education, learning capacity and learning process, and also will tell us how he communicates with others. All of these mental developments take place between the ages of 4 and 14.

---

[3] Schoener, Ch. 7.

According to Abū ʿAlī,[4] if Mercury is in one of the cardinal signs the native will have a quick understanding, be very intelligent, and may be interested in different branches of science and religion. People who have Mercury in mutable signs have an average intellect: they may react and get angry quickly, and may lack responsibility and stability in their ideas and actions. If Mercury is in one of the fixed signs, then natives will be determined and prudent, and will be aware of their responsibilities.

Mercury in Aries: Mercury in this sign has a tendency to be self-confident, assertive, energetic, and blunt. The native with this position is quick in learning and making decisions which are real brave ones. As Aries is a dry sign, he does not accept others' perspectives easily. He is talkative, speaking before thinking, and is full of creative ideas. He may be excessively bold in his speech and may face some troubles because of his impatience.

Mercury in Taurus: Mercury's nature tends toward coldness and dryness, and as a result Mercury feels comfortable in this sign. The native with this position has a practical, constructive, and cautious speaking style accompanied by a slow learning ability. The decisions of the native are stable and long-lasting. This position brings an ability to make practical and prudent decisions, with fixed ideas and decisiveness, and strong concentration.

Mercury in Gemini: Mercury in Gemini brings good communication skills, talkativeness, the ability to persuade others, and find quick solutions. The native has a rational approach towards life: he is always mentally alert and is keen to learn new things. He is curious and may be interested in everything from Divine sciences to unusual fields.

Mercury in Cancer: Mercury is not comfortable in humid Cancer. As Mercury is a rational planet while the lord of Cancer (the Moon) is an irrational one, the native cannot be objective in his thoughts and may tend to have prejudices and prejudgments. He is highly affected by his emotions while making decisions.

Mercury in Leo: Mercury's dry nature is compatible with Leo's dry nature. On the other hand, as Leo is a fixed sign, the native may be stubborn and fixed in his thoughts. A self-confidence and bossiness is felt in his speeches. The native has an authoritarian personality; he is a natural leader who has the ability to affect the course of events.

---

[4] Abū ʿAlī Ch. 5 (in Dykes, *Persian Nativities I*). **BD**: Please note that Abū ʿAlī was not speaking of the ages of man technique here, but about the natal Mercury in general.

Mercury in Virgo: This is a wonderful placement which points out a strong mental capacity and scientific studies. The native is talented at solving problems, he is good at speaking and writing, and he is also a perfectionist with critical thinking.

Mercury in Libra: Mercury displays a diplomatic and reconciliatory approach in this sign. He gives advanced communication and social skills. A native with this position is friendly and talented in perceiving various aspects of a discussion, and in solving the disagreements.

Mercury in Scorpio: Mercury is not comfortable in this sign because Scorpio has a humid and cold nature, which is incompatible with his own. Mercury brings fixed ideas, high concentration, research, and a huge intuitiveness in Scorpio, but he may also bring irrationality and obsession. The native has the ability to sense others intuitively, to decide how to communicate with them, and understand the strengths and weaknesses of others.

Mercury in Sagittarius: Mercury is in detriment in this sign and cannot display his qualities well. On the other hand, as he is in harmony with the dry nature of Sagittarius, he will bring talents in scientific subjects. The native may have quick judgments and prejudices before reaching the final results, and he can also display enthusiastic (if impatient) attitudes.

Mercury in Capricorn: As Mercury's cold and dry nature is similar to Capricorn's nature, he displays its qualities easily. However, as Saturn is the lord of Capricorn, the native may need more time and concentration. The native is slow to solve problems and is in need of being systematic. He looks for logic when communicating. His thoughts may be melancholic and anxious. He is introverted and cannot build intimate relations easily.

Mercury in Aquarius: Mercury in this sign shows a scientific mind which can successfully evaluate abstract concepts. On the other hand, being in a fixed sign, Mercury may bring fixed ideas and stubbornness. Both intuition and logic are well developed. The native has a visionary, unusual point of view; he is liberal and humanist. He has a contemporary perspective: he is interested in new, original, and extraordinary things and discoveries.

Mercury in Pisces: Mercury is in detriment and fall in this sign, and his cold and dry nature is not compatible with the cold and humid nature of Pisces. The native does not have an analytical mind; his mind and motivations may be confused. If Mercury has harsh aspects, or if Jupiter is not well placed in the chart, the native may be disingenuous. Mercury in Pisces is not wholly bad: the point is that standard Mercurial skills do not perform well here. The intuitional sense of Pisces might be more evident in childhood.

Since the Moon and Mercury are most clearly related to the emotional and rational character of the native's earlier years, I have provided brief explanations for them in the signs; for the rest of the planets, I will speak in a more general way.

Venus period (ages 14-22)

The Venus period is related to adolescence, and the position of Venus in the chart particularly shows the native's sexual tendencies. If Venus is detriment, then the native may have some unusual sexual tendencies during these ages. Ptolemy says:

> "Venus, taking in charge the third age, that of youth, for the next eight years, corresponding in number to her own period,[5] begins, as is natural, to inspire, at their maturity, an activity of the seminal passages and to implant an impulse toward the embrace of love. At this time particularly a kind of frenzy enters the soul, incontinence, desire for any chance sexual gratification, burning passion, guile, and the blindness of impetuous lover."

Sun period (ages 21-41)

For this period, Ptolemy explains: "[The Sun] implants in the soul at length the mastery and direction of its actions, desire for substance, glory, and position, and a change from playful, ingenuous error to seriousness, decorum and ambition."

The Sun period is the time when creativity is gained. The native displays himself and becomes known during this time; of course, the level of this recognition is related to the Sun's position. Recognition especially takes place when the Sun is in upper houses like the 10th or 11th, or if the Sun rules these houses and is not in harsh aspects with malefic planets but in good aspects with benefic ones. However, if the Sun's position does not support any of

---

[5] **BD**: That is, the number of her lesser planetary period (8 years).

these conditions, it does not mean that recognition will not be realized: good placement of other planets may also commit recognition.

The house where the Sun is shows us the field that the native will be recognized in, especially during the Sun period itself. For example, if the Sun is in the 5th house (and in contact with the MC or its lord), then the native may be recognized in the subjects of the 5th house such as artistic fields, sports, or in brokering deals and mediating. However, if the Sun is in the 12th house and in detriment, then the native may be exposed to diseases and hidden enemies. As a result, the difficulties of the 12th house will be experienced during the Sun period.

Mars period (ages 41-56)

The Mars period is a time of challenges and conflicts, and the place of Mars in the chart determines the area of struggle. To survive the struggles, Mars should be well placed in the chart. Ptolemy explains:

"[Mars] introduces severity and misery into life, and implants cares and troubles in the soul and in the body, giving it, as it were, same sense and notion of passing its prime and urging it, before it approaches its end, by labor to accomplish something among its undertakings that is worthy of note."

Jupiter period (ages 56-68)

The Jupiter period is the time when the native matures, becomes wise, and learns how to leave things behind. In Ptolemy's words:

"[This period] brings about the renunciation of manual labor, toil, turmoil, and dangerous activity, and in their place brings decorum, foresight, retirement, together with all-embracing deliberation, admonition, and consolation; now especially he brings men to set store by honor, praise, and independence, accompanied by modesty and dignity."

Saturn period (age 68 to end of life)

During the Saturn period, the native gains deep wisdom and experience. However, now his body is restricted due to aging and disease. Ptolemy says:

"Now the movements both of body and of soul are cooled and impeded in their impulses, enjoyments, desires, and speed; for the natural decline supervenes upon life, which has become worn down with age, dispirited, weak, easily offended, and hard to please in all situations, in keeping with the sluggishness of his movements."

Chart distinctions according to the waxing and waning Moon

The waxing or waning phases of the Moon in the natal chart help us to predict when the promises of the chart will take place within the native's lifetime. If the natal Moon is waxing, then they will be realized during the first part of life; whereas if the natal Moon is waning, the commitments will take place in the second part of life. (Of course, this does not mean that the other half of life will be empty.)

Put differently, if the native has a waxing Moon, the difficulties promised by his chart will put pressure on him during the first half of his life, while they will become easier in the second half. The opposite is true for a native with a waning Moon: the difficulties promised will create pressure in the second half of his life. Of course, if benefic features are prominent in his chart, he may have beneficial developments during that time.

According to Hellenistic teachings from Firmicus Maternus,[6] we should focus on the most recent and the next aspect of the Moon. Combined with the rules above, this means that if the next aspect perfected by the Moon is with a benefic planet, the native's life will be easier. Similarly, when it is with a malefic planet, the native's life will get hard.

Assuming that the average human life is 75 years, the second half of the native's life will start at age 37.5. Of course, we may also take one-half of the life according to the longevity determined by the house-master calculation.[7]

---

[6] See throughout *Mathesis* IV.
[7] **BD**: See the Glossary. For some medieval versions of this calculation, see ʿUmar al-Tabarī's in *Persian Nativities II* and the extensive discussion by Bonatti in *Bonatti on Nativities*.

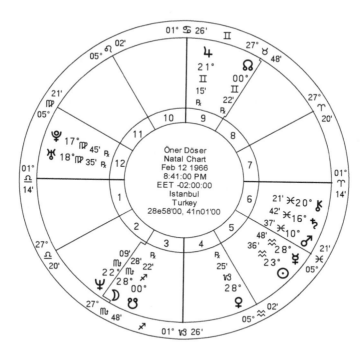

The Moon is waning in my natal chart, which means that the things promised by my chart will be more prominent in the second half of my life. This was the case. The 9th house issues which are promised in my natal chart became prominent in the second half of my life:

Note that the Moon was separating from Venus and applying to Mercury. During the first half of my life, I was working in souvenirs, apparel, and ladies accessories especially. After taking steps in the second half of my life, I began to study astrology. Of course, I had already been interested in astrology and similar subjects, but I began to act on this interest after the age of 36 (especially when I was 37).[8]

We may also use dispositors to determine the timing of events. A planet provides the start for an action in the house it occupies, and the dispositor of that planet represents how the matters of this house will develop. I was not satisfied with my higher education, as my father did not want me to study

---

[8] **BD**: Mercury is a significator of astrology and interpretation, and here rules the ninth by whole signs.

astrology (Saturn squares Jupiter).[9] Of course, he did not prevent me by force but convinced me not to (Jupiter receives Saturn). But by the beginning of the second half of my life, I began to satisfy my wish by studying astrology. As Jupiter was in detriment in my 9th house, I did not feel satisfied enough at the beginning; however, his dispositor is Mercury and I achieved that satisfaction in the following years because Mercury is in Aquarius, in his own triplicity and in the 5th house, he is not blocked by the malefics, and is strong due to being eastern.

Now, my Mercury is combust but is departing from the combust position. This may be explained as: combust Mercury was prominent in the first part of my life, and I was highly dominated by my father (the Sun); however, as I grew older Mercury's departing from combustion began to be effective. At the same time, Mercury is in trine with Jupiter and is the lord of my 9th house (by whole signs). All of these elements indicate that I would be drawn towards 9th house subjects (astrology) and that I would be successful in them.

---

[9] **BD**: The lord of the 4th (Saturn) signifies parents, and especially the father.

CLAUDIUS PTOLEMY

10
20
30
40
50
60
70

CHAPTER 2: DIRECTING BY TRIPLICITIES

DIRECTING BY TRIPLICITIES WAS USED BY ARABIC ASTROLOGERS, WHO DREW ON ANCIENT TEXTS. IT IS USED FOR PREDICTING DEVELOPMENTS RELATED TO A PARTICULAR HOUSE OVER THE NATIVE'S LIFETIME. HERE, A STANDARD HUMAN LIFE IS CONSIDERED AS LASTING 75 YEARS, AND IS DIVIDED INTO THREE EQUAL PARTS, EACH PART BEING RULED BY THE RELEVANT TRIPLICITY LORD. BY INTERPRETING THE TRIPLICITY LORD, ONE BROADLY PREDICTS THE COURSE OF EVENTS SIGNIFIED BY THE HOUSE.[1]

The Method

In this technique, the most critical information is whether the chart is diurnal or nocturnal,[2] because the sect affects the order of the triplicity lords. In diurnal charts, the first third of the native's life is ruled by the diurnal triplicity lord, then the second third by the nocturnal lord, and the last third by the partnering lord. On the other hand, in a nocturnal chart the first third is ruled by the nocturnal triplicity lord, then the diurnal and partnering lords, in order. The partnering triplicity lord always rules the last part of life.

The table below shows the Dorothean triplicity lords, which were used in Hellenistic and Perso-Arabic astrology. You should always keep in mind that there are three lords for each triplicity: the diurnal, nocturnal, and partnering.

Element	Diurnal	Nocturnal	Partner
Fire	☉	♃	♄
Earth	♀	☽	♂
Air	♄	☿	♃
Water	♀	♂	☽

Figure 4: Dorothean triplicity lords

If two of the three lords of a house are well placed, then the native will be successful in the topics of the house. If only one is well placed, our evaluation

---

[1] **BD**: This was the Arabic and medieval Latin method, gotten from the Arabic edition of Dorotheus; but Valens used only the first two triplicity lords (*Anth.* II.2).
[2] **BD**: That is, whether the nativity was by day (with the Sun above the horizon) or night (below the horizon).

will be based on the power of that planet and its position in the zodiac, but the success will be decreased. If all three are badly placed, then success will be even less.

The house each lord happens to be in, shows us which themes will prevail in a given period. For instance, let's assume that the ASC is in one of the airy signs, in a nocturnal chart. So, Mercury will be the first triplicity lord, being the nocturnal triplicity lord of the airy signs. Saturn will be the second triplicity lord, as he is the diurnal triplicity lord of the airy signs. Jupiter will be the third triplicity lord, since he is the partnering triplicity lord of the airy signs. Let's also assume that Mercury is in the 5th house, Saturn is in the 10th, and Jupiter is in the 2nd. This means that in the first period of the native's life, Mercurial themes and those of the 5th house will be prominent. So, Mercury's position (his dignity, aspects, the lord of the house where he is, and his relations with that ruler) will show us to what extent the native will be successful in 1st house matters during this first period of life. We make the same evaluation for the second and third triplicity lords.

Triplicities were frequently used by Arabic astrologers. Indeed, in some cases they paid more attention to the triplicity lords than the sign lord, victor, and exaltation ruler. When choosing one of the triplicity lords, they preferred the one having the strongest placement or which was most compatible with the sect of the chart (which means the diurnal lord for a diurnal chart, and the nocturnal lord for a nocturnal chart). For instance, if Cancer contains the 2nd house in a nocturnal chart, they might prefer Mars, because Mars is the first triplicity lord of watery signs in nocturnal charts, and so it is the ideal indicator.

This method may be used for all of the houses. For instance, to predict the financial position of the native in each third of his lifetime, we should examine the triplicity lords of the 2nd house. These lords will show both the income level of the native and its source.

Let's say that Scorpio contains the cusp of the 2nd house in a nocturnal chart. Mars is the first, Venus is the second, and the Moon is the third triplicity lord of watery signs by night. Now we may predict the financial status of the native for each third of his lifetime. Assuming that the average lifetime is 75 years, each period will take 25 years. (According to Bonatti,[3] each period consists of 30 years, as per Saturn's lesser planetary period. Valens states[4] that the length of each period depends on the lesser planetary period of the triplicity lord in ques-

---

[3] In *Bonatti on Basic Astrology*, p. 68.
[4] *Anth.* II.2.

tion, or the ascensional time of the sign where that lord is. However, Valens does not give any information as to how he made this decision. We will follow the more generic version by dividing life into three equal parts of 25 years apiece.)

Let us consider the MC, which is the cusp of the 10th house for the chart example below. The 10th house represents the professional status, career, and actions of the native, his style of reaching his goals, and the capacity for realizing his fate.

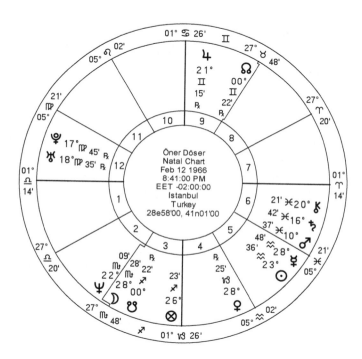

Here the 10th house begins with 1° Cancer. As this is a nocturnal chart, the order of triplicity lords will be Mars, Venus, Moon. The first lord Mars is in Pisces, in conjunction with Saturn. This shows us that the native will have some difficulties in reaching his goals and will not be able to achieve early success, as Mars is both in conjunction with Saturn and in the 6th house. Although Mars is in his own triplicity (Pisces, a watery sign), this chart does not promise important career victories; it brings many challenges.

The second triplicity lord, Venus, is in Capricorn in the 4th, and is in contact with the Moon and the Nodes.[5] Although Venus is in her own triplicity (Capricorn, an earthy sign), since she is retrograde the native experiences difficulties and delays in reaching his goals. On the other hand, Venus is not in detriment and is in a positive aspect with the lord of the 10th house. So although there will be some difficulties, the native has an important advantage for reaching his goals or fate, as Venus is in one of the angular houses, somewhat dignified, has no negative aspect to the malefics, and is in positive aspects with one of the luminaries. We should also keep in mind that Venus is the ASC ruler. During this period, the native (me) was employed by and with his family. I only started to work from my home office after age 36. (Note: Venus is also the second triplicity lord of the MC, indicating work, and is in the 4th house.) Venus, as the lord of my 9th house, is an indicator of my astrological studies, and she is in good aspect to the lord of the 10th (Moon).

The Moon is the third triplicity lord, and is in fall in Scorpio on the cusp of the 3rd house. Although the Moon is not in harsh aspects to the malefics, she is in conjunction with the South Node, which is a negative condition. So, the third period of my lifetime (between 50 and 75) seems to be a negative period. The Moon is in a square with Mercury and the Sun. That period promises Mercurial activities and recognition due to them. The Moon is weak due to her house placement, but on the other hand this house placement shows that one of my goals will be based on writing activities (3rd house). This is also implied by the Moon-Mercury contact.

Times of success and welfare in life

According to Abū Alī,[6] in order to understand when the native will have success, welfare, and property, we need to examine the indicators below:

First, examine the triplicity lords of the Sun (diurnal chart) and those of the Moon (nocturnal chart). If these lords are in angular houses and safe from the effects of the malefic planets, the native is lucky in terms of success and welfare. The closer the first triplicity lord is to the angular houses, the more the chances increase.

---

[5] **BD**: The Nodes, by an out-of-sign trine and sextile.
[6] In his Ch. 7, in *Persian Nativities I* (Dykes 2009).

These triplicity lords tell us about the success, chances, and welfare of the native during each third period of life. If the first lord is in a good position, the native will be lucky and successful in the first third of his life; but if the second and third lords are in detriment, he will be unlucky and unsuccessful and have some troubles during the remaining parts of his life. Or, if the first and second lords are in detriment and the third is in a good place, then the native will have to work hard for a long time and will not be very successful, but he will find success and wealth during the last part of his life.

If all triplicity lords are in cadent houses or in detriment, the native will have to work hard and deal with many difficulties during his life. When the triplicity lords are all located in succeedent houses, it brings hard work with less success and gain. However, if the benefic planets are in angular houses and the malefics are cadent, the native may achieve success and welfare. If the luminaries are also well placed, the native will be rewarded with a high position.

If the lord of the ASC and the Moon are in the angular houses—if they are not affected by the malefic planets and are in aspect to planets in the angular houses, and especially if they are in reception with planets that are in aspect—the native is supposed to have luck, success, and welfare.

If the lord of the ASC is applying to an aspect with the luminaries and the luminaries are dignified (by rulership), or the luminaries are applying to an aspect with the lord of the ASC and the ASC lord is dignified, the native is supposed to have good luck throughout his lifetime.

If the Lot of Fortune and its lord are safe from the damages of the malefic planets, and if eastern[7] planets in the angular houses make an aspect to the ASC, the native is supposed to have never-ending good fortune and will enjoy an important status and reputation. However, if the related indicators (the Lot, its lord, and the eastern planets) are in detriment and in cadent houses, and if they do not have any aspects with the ASC, then the native works hard but obtains less success and earnings.

If the lord of the ASC is in one of the cadent houses but makes an aspect to a planet in one of the angular houses, the native works hard and then attains success and wealth. If the lord is in one of the cadent houses, and if it is debilitated and making an aspect to a dignified planet, the native reaches success and wealth after much hard work.

---

[7] **BD**: This probably means that they are rising before the Sun, not under his rays.

If the triplicity lords are not well placed in a chart, we should examine the Lot of Fortune. If the Lot makes a contact with Jupiter or Venus, the native has the potential to reach splendid conditions in terms of position, power, money, and luck.

We may also look at houses derived from the Lot of Fortune, by treating the Lot as its own 1st house. For instance, Jupiter placed in the 11th house from the Lot of Fortune brings success and a good position.

If the Lot of Fortune is in one of the angular houses and in aspect to malefic planets, the native's success and wealth will be at a medium level.

If both malefic planets are in the 11th house or are with the Lot of Fortune, or if they are with the Sun in a diurnal chart or with the Moon in a nocturnal chart and they are not dignified, the native is faced with the risk of missing out on good opportunities.

If the Moon is separated from a malefic planet in a nocturnal chart, and making a contact with a malefic planet, the native loses his good opportunities.

If the house-master[8] is in one of the cadent houses and makes contact with one of the malefic planets, the native loses his opportunities.

Moreover, if the malefic planets are in the angular houses and the benefics are in the succeedent houses, the native has to work hard at the beginning of his life but reaches good luck at the end of his life.

If the Sun (in a diurnal chart) or the Moon (in a nocturnal chart) separates from the malefic planets and applies to a benefic planet, then the native attains good welfare after a period of hard work.

If the triplicity lords of the Sun (in a diurnal chart) or the Moon (in a nocturnal chart) are in detriment and in contact with dignified planets, it also signifies that the native will obtain good luck after a period of hard work.

According to Māshā'allāh too,[9] we should examine the triplicity lords of the Sun in a diurnal chart and the triplicity lords of the Moon in the nocturnal chart. If these lords are in angular houses and are safe from the harmful effects of the malefic planets, the native will be lucky throughout his life. If they are in cadent houses and harmed by the malefic planets, the native will always be unlucky. But the specific prediction for each period should be made according to its particular lord: for instance, if the triplicity lord is in a cadent house, the native will be poor and will have trouble during this peri-

---

[8] **BD**: See the Glossary.
[9] In his *On Nativities* §6, in *Works of Sahl & Māshā'allāh* (Dykes 2008).

od. If the planets are benefic and in angular houses, if they are in contact with the ASC and not in detriment, then the native's luck is better. At the same time, if the luminaries are not in detriment, this confers greater advantage.

If the Lot of Fortune and its lord are in angular houses, and if they are eastern and in aspect to the ASC, this is an indication of the greatest wealth for the native.

All of this information that we acquire from Abū 'Alī and Māshā'allāh shows us how important the triplicity lords were in Arabic and medieval astrology. Later on, such analyses were rarely used, especially after William Lilly's lifetime.

HERMES TRISMEGISTUS

CHAPTER 3: *FIRDARIA*

THE ARABIC (AND LATER, LATIN) *FIRDARIA* COMES FROM PERSIAN, AND ITSELF SEEMS TO TRANSLATE THE GREEK WORD *PERIODOS*, WHICH MEANS A PERIOD OR CYCLE. *FIRDARIA* IS A PLANETARY PERIOD SYSTEM PRESENTED BY MANY ASTROLOGERS, ESPECIALLY ABŪ MA'SHAR (WHO ALSO DESCRIBED MUNDANE VERSIONS OF IT). IT WAS SIMILAR TO THE *DASHA* SYSTEM IN VEDIC ASTROLOGY, SO THAT THE PLANETS ARE ASSUMED TO ACT AS LORDS OVER SUCCESSIVE PERIODS OF LIFE.

In *firdaria* periods, each planet in turn rules a period of life, which we will call "ruling periods." These ruling periods are also subdivided into seven shorter "sub-periods." As a result, each *firdaria* has a longer-term primary lord and a shorter-term secondary lord. The two lords determine the quality of the period, with the themes of the primary lord being emphasized. When the longer-term and shorter-term lords are in contact in the nativity, the themes of that particular contact are emphasized. The influence of the period is based on the houses the lords are in and the ones that they rule: so, for evaluating the characteristics of a *firdaria* period, we need to investigate the house positions, dignities, and rulerships of both lords.

Because these positions and rulerships can vary so much, the most comprehensive books on the use of *firdaria* included only the general meanings of the planets instead of their mutual relations, places, and rulerships. Examples of such books include those by Abū Ma'shar[1] and Schoener.[2]

---

[1] See *Persian Nativities III* (in Dykes 2010).
[2] See Bibliography.

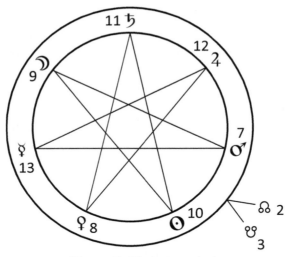

Figure 5: *Firdaria* periods

The order of *firdaria* periods

Firdaria periods follow a simple order, with a slight difference in diurnal and nocturnal charts. In diurnal charts the primary ruling period begins with the Sun, and with the Moon in nocturnal charts. Then the "Chaldean" order is followed, in the order of planets from slowest to the fastest (Saturn, Jupiter, Mars, Sun, Venus, Mercury, Moon). When we reach the end of this order, we start again with Saturn. In addition to the 7 periods ruled by the 7 traditional planets, there are also Nodal periods: 3 years for the North Node and 2 years for the South Node. The sum of these 9 periods makes 75 years. After 75 years, the cycle begins from the luminary which began the series.

There were two different views on where to add the Nodes. Astrologers like Schoener, but also many others, put them at the end of the series, no matter whether the chart was diurnal or nocturnal. But Bonatti (along with others) puts them between Mars and the Sun, a practice we will follow here. The table below shows the series:

	DIURNAL CHARTS			NOCTURNAL CHARTS		
	Lord	Period	Last Age	Lord	Period	Last Age
1	☉	10	10	☽	9	9
2	♀	8	18	♄	11	20
3	☿	13	31	♃	12	32
4	☽	9	40	♂	7	39
5	♄	11	51	☊	3	42
6	♃	12	63	☋	2	44
7	♂	7	70	☉	10	54
8	☊	3	73	♀	8	62
9	☋	2	75	☿	13	75
	TOTAL	75		TOTAL	75	

Figure 6: Bonatti's *firdaria* periods table

As was stated above, major *firdaria* periods are divided into 7 equal sub-periods. The first sub-period is ruled by the same planet which happens to rule the major period, followed by the others in order. For example, the period of the Sun, broken down into sub-periods, is: Sun-Sun, Sun-Venus, Sun-Mercury, Sun-Moon, Sun-Saturn, and so on. The Nodes do not rule or have sub-periods. The lengths of the subperiods are below.

RULING PERIODS	♄	♃	♂	☉	♀	☿	☽
1	♄	♃	♂	☉	♀	☿	☽
2	♃	♂	☉	♀	☿	☽	♄
3	♂	☉	♀	☿	☽	♄	♃
4	☉	♀	☿	☽	♄	♃	♂
5	♀	☿	☽	♄	♃	♂	☉
6	☿	☽	♄	♃	♂	☉	♀
7	☽	♄	♃	♂	☉	♀	☿

(Left axis label: SUB-PERIOD LORDS)

Figure 7: Table of *firdaria* sub-period lords

In the table below, you may see the durations of ruling periods and sub-periods.

	RULING PERIOD	SUB-PERIOD
♄	11 years	1 year, 6 months, 26 days
♃	12 years	1 year, 8 months, 17 days
♂	7 years	1 year, 0 months, 0 days
☉	10 years	1 year, 5 months, 4 days
♀	8 years	1 year, 1 month, 22 days
☿	13 years	1 year, 10 months, 9 days
☽	9 years	1 year, 3 months, 13 days

Figure 8: Length of *firdaria* sub-periods

Practical information on the use of *firdaria*

When interpreting a period, the first step is to determine if the chart is diurnal or nocturnal: the periods begin with the Sun in diurnal charts, but with the Moon in nocturnal charts. Remember that the full cycle is 75 years long, so after that age the cycle goes back to the beginning.

After we determine the primary lord and sub-period lords of the periods, we must focus on their total condition: their places, the houses they rule, their dignities, aspects, and their contacts with their dispositors as well as the positions of the dispositors. But really there are three major points to look at with each lord:

1. Its natal house
2. The natal house(s) it rules
3. The natal house it rules by exaltation

After this, the natal aspects of the major period ruler are important.

When looking at a specific period, it may also be helpful to observe the roles of these planets in previous periods. For example, in a diurnal chart Mercury is the sub-period lord between ages 11 and 12 (when Venus is the primary ruler). If we can understand how Mercury worked during this period, then we may estimate how Mercury will work between ages 18 and 31, when he rules the major period itself. In fact, a diurnal native will be in a Mercury-Venus period from ages 29-31, the contrary of ages 11-12. Venus will be more dominant in the first period (when she is the primary lord), but each planet should act in a similar way in each period.

Remember that the Nodes do not have secondary or sub-period lords. We evaluate the Nodes according to the houses they are in: for instance, if the North Node is in Gemini in the 9th, then the native will be focused on the themes of the 9th house when he experiences the 3-year period of the North Node. The placement of the Nodes' lords will also be helpful.

Examples: Princess Diana

As an example, let's consider Princess Diana's chart by examining the *firdaria* period when she had and accident and passed away. In the table below, you may see the beginning dates of each of her *firdaria*:

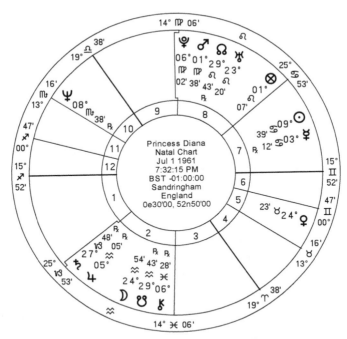

Figure 9: Nativity for Princess Diana

☉	**1 Jul 1961**	☿	**1 Jul 1979**	♄	**1 Jul 2001**	♂	**1 Jul 2024**
☉ ☉	1 Jul 1961	☿ ☿	1 Jul 1979	♄ ♄	1 Jul 2001	♂ ♂	1 Jul 2024
☉ ♀	5 Dec 1962	☿ ☽	10 May 1981	♄ ♃	26 Jan 2003	♂ ☉	1 Jul 2025
☉ ☿	10 May 1964	☿ ♄	18 Mar 1983	♄ ♂	22 Aug 2004	♂ ♀	1 Jul 2026
☉ ☽	13 Oct 1965	☿ ♃	25 Jan 1985	♄ ☉	19 Mar 2006	♂ ☿	2 Jul 2027
☉ ♄	19 Mar 1967	☿ ♂	4 Dec 1986	♄ ♀	14 Oct 2007	♂ ☽	1 Jul 2028
☉ ♃	22 Aug 1968	☿ ☉	13 Oct 1988	♄ ☿	9 May 2009	♂ ♄	1 Jul 2029
☉ ♂	25 Jan 1970	☿ ♀	22 Aug 1990	♄ ☽	5 Dec 2010	♂ ♃	2 Jul 2030
♀	**1 Jul 1971**	☽	**1 Jul 1992**	♃	**1 Jul 2012**	☊	1 Jul 2031
♀ ♀	1 Jul 1971	☽ ☽	1 Jul 1992	♃ ♃	1 Jul 2012	☋	1 Jul 2034
♀ ☿	22 Aug 1972	☽ ♄	13 Oct 1993	♃ ♂	19 Mar 2014		
♀ ☽	13 Oct 1973	☽ ♃	26 Jan 1995	♃ ☉	5 Dec 2015	☉	**1 Jul 2036**
♀ ♄	4 Dec 1974	☽ ♂	10 May 1996	♃ ♀	23 Aug 2017	☉ ☉	1 Jul 2036
♀ ♃	26 Jan 1976	☽ ☉	23 Aug 1997	♃ ☿	10 May 2019	☉ ♀	4 Dec 2037
♀ ♂	18 Mar 1977	☽ ♀	5 Dec 1998	♃ ☽	26 Jan 2021	☉ ☿	11 May 2039
♀ ☉	9 May 1978	☽ ☿	18 Mar 2000	♃ ♄	14 Oct 2022	☉ ☽	13 Oct 2040

Figure 10: *Firdaria* for Princess Diana

Diana had a fatal accident in August 31, 1997. We see that she was in the Moon-Sun period which began on August 22, 1997. Now, let's make a grid to see which houses this period is related to, as well as the natal aspects of the period lords:

MOON	☽□♀ ☽☍♂ ☽☌☋	SUN	☉☌☿ ☉⚹♂
In: 2nd		In: 7th	
Rules: 8th		Rules: 9th	
Exalted: 5th		Exalted: 4th	

Since Leo, ruled by the Sun, is intercepted in the chart, we will use the whole-sign position of Leo: Leo is the ninth sign.

The natal placement of the Moon is not good. First of all, she is in an out-of-sign opposition with Mars, the lord of the 8th—this is a totally negative aspect. Then, the Moon is in conjunction with the South Node, which also causes malefic influences. So, we may conclude that the native will not be at ease during Moon periods in general. She had been in the Moon period since 1992.

When we observe the secondary lord (the Sun), we may say that his aspects are better than the Moon's. Now let's examine the Sun's natal position. The Sun is peregrine in Cancer. His lord (the Moon) is in a difficult position, not being dignified in Aquarius, and as she is both inimical to the nature of Saturn as well as being in aversion[3] to him, she cannot get the support of her ruler. The Sun is in sextile with Mars in the 8th house. Although this is not a malefic aspect, an aspect to a malefic planet in one of the malefic houses is not a good one. Moreover, although Mars is in his own triplicity, because he is conjoined to the North Node, his malefic qualities are increased.

Finally, the Sun is the lord of the 9th house, according to whole-sign houses. The 9th house represents themes like faraway places, foreign countries, and foreign people.

When Diana had her accident, she was in Paris (9th house) with her partner Dodi Fayed (Sun in the 7th). The Sun being placed in the 7th and ruling the 9th represents a relationship with powerful and foreign people. The Sun is also in conjunction with Mercury, the lord of the 7th itself, and Mercury is the

---

[3] See the Glossary.

lord of the 9th in the Placidus system. Undoubtedly, this accident and death is the theme of the Moon-Sun firdaria period, especially because Diana was already experiencing a 12th-house profection. (The profected ASC was in her 12th house, and was about to reach the degree of her natal ASC.) As the natal chart already promises a harsh death,[4] the promise of the natal chart may be realized particularly during profections of the ASC to houses like these.

Again, *firdaria* alone are not sufficient for important predictions. The findings that we get through this technique should be evaluated and supported by profections, solar and lunar returns, and transits, to achieve accurate results.[5]

Let's continue with Princess Diana's chart and examine some important life events in the light of the *firdaria* periods. Here are some important events of her life:

Engagement announced. February 24, 1981: Mercury-Mercury. Mercury is generally related to announcements and news. Mercury is the lord of the 7th house and is also placed there, in conjunction with the Sun. Unsurprisingly, this indicates an announcement of engagement.

Marriage. July 29, 1981: Mercury-Moon. As mentioned above, Mercury signifies 7th-house matters. The Moon is also generally related to the topics of home and family. We may use the table below to understand which areas the Mercury-Moon *firdaria* would affect:

MERCURY	MOON
In: 7th	In: 2nd
Rules: 6th, 7th, 9th	Rules: 8th
Exalted: 9th	Exalted: 5th

---

[4] Note the Moon-Uranus and Moon-Mars oppositions. Since the Moon is the general significator of the body and rules the 8th, and Mars and Uranus are in the 8th, the chart indicates sudden and dangerous accidents threatening life.

[5] Of course we cannot say that this is the only time she could have died, but it is one of the more likely times, especially when we combine several techniques, particularly transits: transiting Uranus has a partile conjunction with natal Jupiter, who is the ruler of the ASC and also the profected lord of the year. Jupiter is also the exaltation ruler of the 8th house of death. Since Uranus is in the natal 8th, he brings the signification of death with him. Transiting Neptune has a partile conjunction with natal Saturn too, which is the "killing planet" in medieval calculations.

When we observe the houses of the Moon and Mercury in the natal chart, we see that the houses of marriage and money are significant. The Mercury (the lord of the 7th) – Sun conjunction already shows us that her marriage would be with a "royal" man. The Moon is in the 2nd house and rules the 8th, showing that the reason behind her marriage would be financial power. The 2nd house supports what we like to do in general, and since the lord of the ASC is also in the 2nd house, it supports the notion that the native's priority in life is to maintain secure financial conditions. When we look at the Moon-South Node conjunction, and Mars opposition to them, we could conclude that the native may not achieve this goal. (We should also keep in mind that Mars is the victor of the 2nd house.) Another reason for this marriage was the raising of children who would preserve the future of the kingdom: the Moon, as the lord of the sub-period, is also the lord of the 5th house and in aspect to Venus in the same house. But as the lord of the house of marriage is combust and peregrine, and the Moon is peregrine and in detriment, the marriage does not bring happiness to the native. The Moon–Venus contact is not enough for happiness, because Venus also squares Mars. Moreover, Mercury (the lord of the house of marriage) and the Moon do not aspect each other.

Divorce. August 28, 1996: Moon-Mars. Let's create a table to see which houses the Moon and Mars affect during this period, along with their aspects:

MOON	☽□♀ ☽☌♂ ☽☌☋	**MARS**	♂☍☽ ♂□♀ ♂☌☊ ♂⚹☉ ♂⚹☿
In: 2nd		In: 8th	
Rules: 8th		Rules: 4th, 11th	
Exalted: 5th		Exalted: 2nd	

The Princess might have had some difficulties beginning in March 1996 when she entered her Moon-Mars period, because these two planets aspect each other harshly; moreover, the Moon is in conjunction with the South Node, and Mars is with the North Node. Bonatti states[6] that the North Node increases the influences of the planet it conjoins with, whereas the South Node decreases its influence. In this chart, as the Moon is waning and also in conjunction with the South Node, she has lost all of her benefic na-

---

[6] See *Bonatti on Basic Astrology*, p. 187.

ture. Moreover, the Mars-North Node conjunction increases his malefic influences. So, we may easily conclude that this period might bring malefic influences. For instance, we might have concluded that Diana might experience a problematic period in financial matters.

Now, please consider the aspects of Mars, as he is the secondary lord of the period. We have already mentioned the Moon-Mars opposition. Mars is also in square with Venus, the lord of the 10th house: this indicates that her marital problems (4th house) would end up in the public eye (10th house). As the Mars-North Node conjunction increased his malefic qualities, the Mars sextile with the Sun and Mercury in the 7th is not a good thing for her marriage. All of those indicators point to a kind of separation. The Mars-Sun sextile here may represent a relationship with a foreigner and powerful male figures, because the Sun is in the 7th house and rules the 9th (by whole signs) and in conjunction with Mercury, the lord of the 7th and 9th houses (Placidus). However, this relationship may not bring much profit.

Accident and death. August 31, 1997: Moon-Sun. We have already discussed this period above. Here, we may state that this accident is also related to the Princess's partner, because the secondary lord (the Sun) is in the 7th house and in contact with the 9th, as mentioned above. This represents the foreigner in the relationship. The Moon, the ruling planet, is in the 8th house from the 7th by derived houses, which tells us of the death of the partner. We have also mentioned the detriment of the Moon.

Times of recognition

If the natal chart promises fame and recognition, we should examine the Sun's *firdaria* to predict the time of recognition, especially if the Sun is the natal planet that promises fame. Similarly, the periods where the Sun is the secondary lord should also be examined (such as Jupiter-Sun, Mercury-Sun, Moon-Sun, etc.). Here, we should examine the periods when the Sun is the secondary lord and the ruling planet is the lord of the 10th. For instance, if Venus is the lord of the 10th house, then the Venus-Sun period is important.

Similarly, periods when the victor or exalted lord of the 10th house is the ruling planet, are also important. For example, if Libra is on the MC, Saturn will be important as the exalted lord and possibly the victor. If Saturn is well-placed in the chart and is not in tough aspects with the luminaries, then hard work and effort may bring fame and recognition during the Saturn-Sun period, especially if there are positive aspects between the Sun and Saturn.

We should also observe the periods when a planet in the natal 10th house is the ruling planet, with the Sun as the secondary ruler. If the planet placed in the natal 10th house is a benefic planet and well-aspected, then the period when this planet and the Sun are the lords may bring recognition. If the lord of the 10th is a benefic planet, the *firdaria* period ruled by this planet may also bring recognition.

If the natal 10th house promises fame and recognition, the recognition may come when the ASC is profected to the 10th house.

If the lord of the 10th is in a good place in the chart and has supportive aspects with benefics, fame and recognition may come within the year that the progressed ASC reaches the house where the lord of the 10th house is placed.

If benefic planets are in the 10th house of the solar return chart, recognition may come within this year, if the natal chart also promises fame and recognition.

Sun and Jupiter transits are short and superficial. So, they should not be considered as valuable as other transits.

We should also consider the planets in terms of their exaltation rulerships.

The Sun's primary directions to the benefics, and especially his direction to the lord of the 10th house, may bring recognition and fame if these planets are dignified.

If the malefics are well placed in the zodiac and are in aspect to the benefics, this may also bring fame and recognition in fields pertaining to their nature: for instance, Saturn may bring recognition in scientific areas, and Mars in military issues.

Finally, planets bring the potential for recognition during their *firdaria* periods, if:

1) They rule the 10th house (by sign, exaltation, or as the victor).
2) They are in aspect to the 10th house or the Sun.
3) They are in the natal 10th or 11th.
4) They are in one of the angular houses, and exalted in the MC.

AL-KINDI

CHAPTER 4: PROFECTIONS

IN PROFECTIONS, THE ASC OR SUN IS ADVANCED TO THE NEXT SIGN ON ONE'S BIRTHDAY EVERY YEAR, BEGINNING WITH AGE 0 (ON THE DATE OF BIRTH). THE THEMES OF THE HOUSES ARRIVED AT, GAIN IMPORTANCE FOR THIS ONE-YEAR PERIOD, AND THE LORD OF THAT SIGN (CALLED THE "LORD OF THE YEAR") HAS A GREAT ROLE TO PLAY IN THE EVENTS THAT WILL OCCUR THROUGHOUT THE YEAR.

The technique of profections

In the technique of profections every year some point is "profected" or "advanced" to the next sign. There are two common points to profect: the natal Sun or the rising sign (the ASC).

The oldest studies on profection were written by Manilius in 15 BC. According to Manilius,[1] each year of the native's life is ruled by a zodiac sign, beginning from the Sun sign. For instance, if the native has a Gemini Sun, he is ruled by Gemini during his first year (age 0-1) and by Cancer in the second year (age 1-2), and so on. Monthly lords are also applied in the same way, but these begin from the Moon sign. Then, the first day of the month is ruled by the sign of the current profection, the second day by the next sign, and so on. Hourly lords also begin in this way.

For the annual profection of the ASC,[2] we may use the table below. For instance, my natal rising sign is Libra (1st house). When I was 4 years old, my profected ASC reached the natal 5th house (Aquarius). When I was 16, 28 and 40 years, the profected ASC likewise returned to my 5th house. On the other hand, when I am 49 years old, my profected ASC will be in my 2nd house, Scorpio. So, for that year it will be as if my natal Scorpio is my 1st house, Sagittarius my 2nd, Capricorn my 3rd, and so on.

---

[1] Manilius III.510ff, described in Hermes 2002, pp. 51-52.
[2] **BD**: Manilius offers this as an alternate scheme, and it was preferred by later authors.

House	Age							
1	0	12	24	36	48	60	72	84
2	1	13	25	37	49	61	73	85
3	2	14	26	38	50	62	74	86
4	3	15	27	39	51	63	75	87
5	4	16	28	40	52	64	76	88
6	5	17	29	41	53	65	77	89
7	6	18	30	42	54	66	78	90
8	7	19	31	43	55	67	79	91
9	8	20	32	44	56	68	80	92
10	9	21	33	45	57	69	81	93
11	10	22	34	46	58	70	82	94
12	11	23	35	47	59	71	83	95

Figure 11: Table of ages and houses for profected Ascendant

Hellenistic astrologers generally used the whole-sign system when erecting the houses of a chart, and we will use this below.

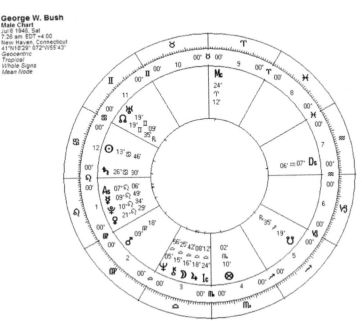

Figure 12: George W. Bush nativity

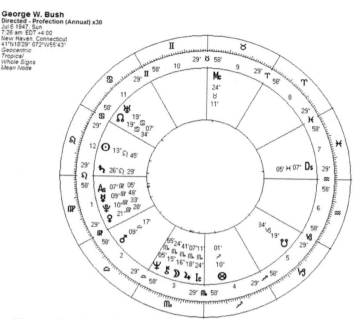

Figure 13: George W. Bush profections for 1947 (age 1)

Above is the 1946 nativity of George W. Bush, former President of the United States: in this chart, he is age 0. In Solar Fire 9 we can erect his profection chart for the next year (1947, age 1) by clicking File > Tran/Prog/Dirn. In the dialogue box, click on "Profection Annual" under Chart Type, and enter in his birthdate for 1947. The resulting chart (above) shows that the planets and ASC have advanced by one sign. To see how these affect the natal chart, we must create a bi-wheel and superimpose the profections onto the nativity (below). In the outer wheel or ring, the Sun and Saturn have profected to the natal 1st house, Venus, Mercury, and the ASC to the 2nd, Mars to the 3rd, the Moon and Jupiter to the 4th, and so on.

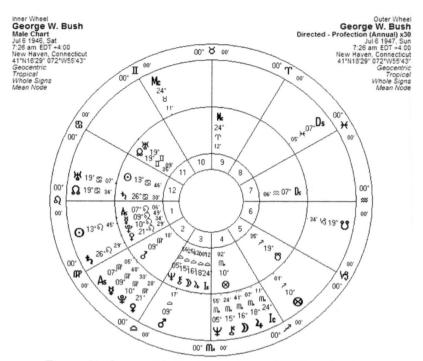

Figure 14: George W. Bush nativity and 1947 profections

Now let's see how to interpret the profections using the method of Dorotheus.[3]

Dorotheus

According to Dorotheus,[4] the ASC of the nativity should be profected so that each year is represented by one sign (as explained above). The lord of the sign which is reached, is called the "lord of the year." There are two important features to analyze:

1) What is the nature and natal placement of the lord of the year?
2) Does the profected ASC reach a sign where benefic planets are placed, or malefics?

---

[3] Much of the following is based on Hermes 2002.
[4] *Carmen* IV.1.

Let's continue studying Bush's chart, profecting the ASC but also the other planets. In 1947 (age 1), the profected ASC reached the 2nd house. We see that the ASC arrived at the house where natal Mars is placed (Virgo). This is not a good indicator according to Dorotheus, because Mars is one of the malefics. We may guess that he had an inflammatory disease or something like that. Mercury, the lord of this profected ASC, is natally in Leo, the 1st house, and by profection the Sun and Saturn have also reached this house. Here, we may conclude that he got the attention of his family (natal Mercury in the 1st house, the profected Sun in the 1st house and also in Leo), but we can suppose he had some health problems or other difficulties (profected Saturn in the 1st house).

Now let's see what other Hellenistic astrologers said about profections:

Ptolemy

In *Tetrabiblos* IV.10, Ptolemy discussed several techniques for determining the time lords at different periods of life, including profections. According to Ptolemy, we may profect all of the following by one sign per year: the ASC, Lot of Fortune, Moon, Sun, and MC. The lord of the month is identified similarly by profecting these from their respective signs that year, at a rate of 1 sign per 28 days. "Daily" profections may be gotten in the same way, by profecting at a rate of 1 sign for about every 2.5 days, from the sign of the month.

Firmicus Maternus

Julius Firmicus Maternus completed his famous book *Mathesis* in about 352 AD. In Book II.28,[5] he speaks of a system which is similar to profections. As above, the first year of life is represented by the natal ASC, the next year by the next sign, and so on. But to identify the lords of shorter periods within a year, we begin from the lord of the year and assign it a number of days, and then assign other days to the rest of the planets in the order in which they are placed: the Sun has 53 days, the Moon 71, Saturn 85, Jupiter 34,[6] Mars 42, Venus 23 and Mercury 57 days. The sum of these days is 365.

---

[5] This is II.27 in the critical edition.
[6] **BD**: Amended from "30" according to Holden's notes in his translation, p. 78 (see Bibliography).

Paulus Alexandrinus

Paulus Alexandrinus wrote an *Introduction to Astrology* in 378 AD. In Chapter 31, he explains how he finds the lords of the year, month, and day. For the years, begin with the ASC as usual, advancing one sign per year. The months are counted from the sign of the current profection, advancing by one 1 sign per month. For daily lords, start with the sign of the month and give it the first day of that month, advancing thereafter by 1 sign per day.

Vettius Valens

According to Valens in his *Anthology* Book IV, when a profected planet reaches a natal planet, they enter into a kind of "give and take" relationship. For instance, if Jupiter is the financial significator in a native's chart and the chart is profected to age 35, Jupiter himself is also profected by that much. If then Jupiter reaches the sign where the natal Mars is placed, Jupiter "hands over" his responsibilities about financial matters to Mars for that year, and Mars "takes on" those duties from Jupiter. Then of course, we should see if Mars is fit to take those responsibilities. First, Mars is evaluated according to his rebellious nature: does Mars's nature bring luck in financial issues? Answer: not usually. Then the position of the natal Mars is evaluated, including the sign he is in, his aspects to other planets, his rulerships and dignities, etc.

In the chart below, you can see this very example. Bush's chart has been profected to age 35, and the profected Jupiter has reached the sign of the natal Mars, in Virgo. Mars is already related to Bush's financial situation, because he is in the 2nd house. Mars is in his own triplicity (Virgo, the earthy triplicity), and is not in detriment. Moreover, Mars is the lord of his natal Lot of Fortune, and is in sextile with it. So, when Bush was 35, we should expect that his earned income rose together with that profection.

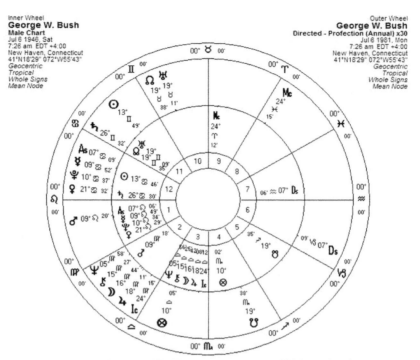

Figure 15: George W. Bush nativity and 1981 profections

Profecting for specific issues

Valens advised[7] using the profection of the Sun, Moon and ASC for "general times" so that we may understand what is happening very generally within the native's life. He also listed some specific issues that different points can be profected for:

- The ASC should be profected for interpreting vital, physical, and mental activities.
- The Sun should be profected for dignity, reputation, the father and other authority figures, since these are themes related to the Sun.
- The Moon: illnesses, injuries and other physical damage to the body.
- The MC: one's occupation and other activities which help earn a living.

---

[7] Valens, *Anth.* IV.11; see also Hermes 2002, pp. 55-56.

- Lot of Fortune: good luck and wealth.
- The DSC: death and critical changes or problems.
- The IC: institutions, secret issues, and death.
- Venus: the spouse, relationships, society, and women.
- Mars: military and similar issues.
- Saturn: separations, illnesses, and inheritance.
- Jupiter: dignity, friends, partnerships, and profits.
- Mercury: servants, gifts, paperwork, the community, and issues related to the physical body.

Example: George W. Bush

Let's examine Bush's chart in light of some of these Hellenistic techniques. In the chart below, you may see the profection chart for the year he won the 2004 election (age 58), superimposed on his natal chart.

The profected Jupiter and Moon have positive effects on the natal 1st house. Mercury and Venus are there natally, and are not in detriment. The fact that natal Venus (the lord of the natal 10th) is in the 1st, shows that career matters will come to the native relatively easily and he will be lucky in that area of life. (Note also that the natal Moon and Jupiter, in the 3rd, are in a sextile with the natal Venus.) In addition, since the profected MC has come to the natal 8th (Pisces), and its lord Jupiter has profected to the ASC, means that both benefics affect him and his career well this year.

The house of the profected ASC is very important. Here, it is in the 11th house (Gemini), which is the house of great luck. The natal North Node is here. Mercury, the lord of the year, is natally in the 1st house, in a strong position: this is a great advantage.[8]

Profected Venus and Mercury have advanced to the natal 11th house and so bring luck to that house (especially Venus). Venus is already the lord of the 10th house. The profected Sun and Saturn are in the natal 10th house. Although Saturn brings pessimism, anxiety, and negativity, the Sun represents a great advantage in elections.

---

[8] **BD**: That is, because Mercury rules the 11th and is in the 1st, it shows good luck coming to Bush: since the profected ASC is now on that natal 11th, it activates that good luck this year.

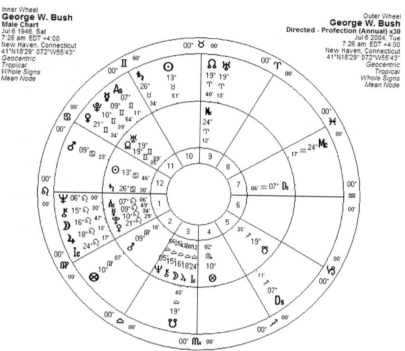

Figure 16: George W. Bush nativity and 2004 profections

Handy rules for profections

According to Martien Hermes,[9] the following profections indicate times when events are more likely to manifest:

- When the profection reaches a sign in an angular house.
- When it reaches a sign whose lord (i.e., the lord of the year) is in an angular house.
- When it reaches the sign in which the lord of the year is (such as in monthly profections).
- When it reaches a sign in which the significator of a particular issue is. For instance, in the matter of finances, see when the profected body or point reaches the sign in which the lord of the 2nd is.
- When it reaches the sign that signifies the topic itself. Thus for financial issues, when it reaches the 2nd house.

---

[9] Hermes 2002, p. 55.

- When it reaches a planet in a particular house, or a planet which powerfully aspects the house.

For marriage in particular, if the profected ASC reaches the 7th house, or if the degree of the solar return ASC is close to the degree of the natal ASC, a marriage is likely to take place in that very year.

According to Robert Zoller,[10] we should also have a look at the time when the profected 7th house reaches the house in which its lord is actually placed. Or, marriage is also possible if the profected ASC or 7th reaches any sign ruled by the lord of the 7th house. For example, if the lord of the 7th is Venus, then profections of the ASC or 7th to Taurus or Libra will also be relevant.

See also when the primary direction of the Moon reaches the significator of marriage.[11]

When will good things happen?

This is most likely when:

- The profected element (whether a point or body) reaches a sign in which a benefic planet is—but this sign and planet should not be involved in difficulties like detriment.
- The profected element reaches a sign ruled by a benefic planet, even if there is no planet in it (again, without their being involved in difficulties).[12]

Of course, the amount of luck that this benefic planet will bring to the native depends on its position within the chart. If the benefic planet is dignified, possibly a wholly good thing will happen; if not, a partially good thing will happen. If this benefic is in a bad position and condition, generally nothing good or bad will happen.

---

[10] Zoller 2003, *DMA* Lesson 21 pp. 19-20, quoting Bonatti's version of 'Umar al-Tabarī (in *Persian Nativities II*).

[11] **BD**: See the Preface for a discussion of victors.

[12] **BD**: In other words, when the lord of the year (or month, etc.) for that profected object is a benefic.

When will bad things happen?

This is most likely when:

- The profected element reaches a sign where a malefic planet is placed.
- The profected element reaches a sign ruled by a malefic planet, even if there is no planet in it.

Again, the amount of misfortune that this malefic planet will bring to the native depends on its position within the chart. If this malefic is not dignified, really bad things will happen; if it is dignified, partially bad things will happen. If the malefic is in a magnificent position, perhaps nothing bad will happen, and on the contrary good things may happen.

Interpretation summary

Based on the information above, let me suggest three principles for approaching profections:

1) The natal house of the profected ASC is the most important. For instance, if the profected ASC is in the natal 11th house, then the themes of the 11th house will be dominant within that specific year.
2) The whole chart may be interpreted in light of the new profected ASC. For instance, if the profected ASC reaches the natal 11th, then the natal 11th will be the 1st house for that year, the natal 8th will be the new 10th house for that year, and so on.
3) The influences of transits should also be evaluated along with the profections, since each profection will bring somewhat different results as compared to 12 years before, when it had also been there.

Example: Öner Döşer, age 37

As I have mentioned before, on June 21, 2003 I rented out my stall at the Grand Bazaar in Istanbul and left my work there. That was the end of 20 years in a merchant profession and the beginning of a career in astrology: so, it was the most critical year of my life. Now, let's analyze this year through

profections. As I was born on February 12, 1966 I was 37 years old beginning on my birthday in June 2003. So, my profected ASC was in my natal 2nd
(see the table of ages and houses above).

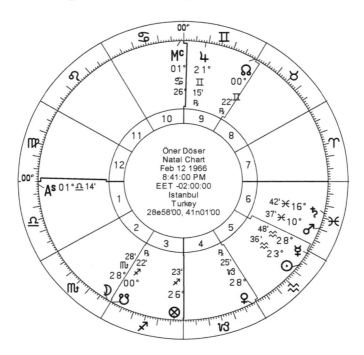

Mars, the lord of the 2nd sign (Scorpio), is the lord of the year, and natally
in conjunction with Saturn. The Moon, the lord of the natal 10th, is within
the natal 2nd. (Remember, when we use whole signs, any planet in that sign,
even within the last degree, is in that house. So, as Scorpio is in my 2nd
whole-sign house, the Moon is also in the natal 2nd, even though by Regiomontanus houses she is in the 3rd.)

The lord of the natal MC being in the 1st house by profection this year,
means that this will be a time for critical decisions about my career. The
Moon signifies indecisiveness and inconsistency. She is in a square with Mercury and the Sun, in a sextile with Venus, and in conjunction with the South
Node. As she makes many aspects to other elements of the chart, this year
should be a busy one. Let's examine these aspects one by one:

The conjunction of the Moon and South Node tells us that in addition to
losses, problems, and work-related constraints, a fated change will be experi-

enced. The South Node is related to the past, and the Moon is also related to the past and family bonds. By quitting my traditional family business at the Bazaar in that year, I also cut off my bonds with the past.

The Moon in sextile with Venus (the lord of the natal ASC) shows that decisions taken now are critical for myself personally, and that I would see positive results despite the difficulties. Venus is in my natal 4th, and I started to work in a home office environment after I quit my work at the Bazaar.

The Moon squaring Mercury and the Sun signifies that themes related to astrology will be important (Mercury ruling Gemini, the 9th) and my social circle will change (the Sun ruling the natal 11th). Within that year, I wrote for an astrology column in a journal (Mercury). My column was half a page, and although it was hard for me to write as a daily routine, it was pleasurable.

The Moon's contact with the Sun also represents a kind of recognition. In 2003, I appeared as a guest on many TV shows, an unexpected development for me. On the other hand, I started giving professional consultations. The Moon, as the exalted lord of the 7th house (one-on-one interactions), is in the sign of the profected ASC.

Mars, as the lord of the year, is in the natal 6th (illnesses, weaknesses, difficulties, working environment and conditions, subordinates, tenants), in conjunction with Saturn. As my working environment and conditions changed this year, the environment of my former employees also changed. I rented out my store to another company and transferred all my workers there. At first they were happy with their new conditions, but were soon discontented, and left that company shortly thereafter.

In terms of health issues, I had to deal with the illnesses of my grandfather and grandmother. As my father was dead, I had to look after them, along with my aunt. They died within 6 days of each other in July 2003. This was a very difficult time. Mars, the lord of my 7th house (the 4th from my 4th, the father of my father), represents my grandfather, and Saturn (the victor of my 1st, the 7th from the 7th or spouse of my grandfather), represents my grandmother. They are conjoined in the 6th house. They had a fire (Mars) in their house, and my grandfather died (Saturn) from exposure to smoke.

Sagittarius falls into the profected 2nd house this year, and Jupiter, the lord of this sign, is natally in Gemini (the 9th): I started to earn money from offering astrology consultations this year.

Capricorn falls into the 3rd house of the profection, and its lord Saturn is in my natal 6th. I started to take medieval astrology courses from Robert

Zoller this year. I had to work hard during this period (Saturn in the 6th). Venus is also placed in the profected 3rd house. The lord of my ASC being placed in the 3rd house shows that education, learning, and writing will be the themes of this year.

We may also interpret the chart by profecting the other houses. For instance, we can examine the profected 10th house (which came to Leo), to evaluate developments in my career and business life. The Sun is in the profected 4th house (Aquarius), and is in trine with Jupiter in my natal 9th house. I started working in a home-office environment, giving astrology consultations, writing a column in a newspaper, giving private lessons, and getting an education in medieval techniques from abroad.

Timing

After drawing the annual profection chart, we may determine the timing of events by making monthly profections. As in the example above, we know that we reach Scorpio, the 2nd house, on my birthday in 2003. So, on February 12, 2003 the profected ASC was in Scorpio. It stayed in Scorpio between February and March 12, and was in Sagittarius between March 12 and April 12, in Capricorn between April 12 and May 12, in Aquarius between May 12 and June 12, and finally it reached Pisces between June 12 and July 12. Those dates were very important for me because the lord of the year (Mars) was in that sign. The most critical events of the year took place in that month.

As I mentioned, a fire broke out in my grandparent's house at that time. My grandfather was hospitalized for a month due to the smoke he was exposed to, and he died on July 17. My grandmother was already sick and was in the hospital; she died in July 11. I really had a difficult time during these dates.

I left the Grand Bazaar on June 21. As I mentioned, my employees started to work with the people to whom had I rented out my store; after a while, they were discontented and left. (The company also had a difficult time and had to empty the store one year later.) Thank God, I found a new tenant in a short period.

I moved to another house on July 3. I rented out my old house and found a new apartment, but then moved again five months later because the apartment was in a very out-of-the-way, inconvenient place for giving consultations. My five months there were full of pessimism even though it was a quite natural place to live in: Mars, the lord of the year, placed in the 6th and in conjunction with Saturn, represents all these developments.

After calculating the monthly profections, we may work on daily profections. Although this technique works perfectly in some cases, I found that it is does not work in others. In daily profections, each sign is equal to 2.5 days. For instance, Scorpio is the profected sign of the year, but also represents the first month (February 12 to March 12), and also the first 2.5 days of that first month (February 12-14 or 15). The daily profections will then be in Scorpio for 2.5 days, then in Sagittarius beginning on February 15, Capricorn on the 17, and so on.

To determine my sign and house for June 21, first I need a monthly profection and a daily one. By monthly profection, I was in Pisces (the 6th) from June 12 to July 12. From Pisces or June 12, I need to count in increments of 2.5 days until I reach Taurus on June 21. So, we reach Taurus on June 17 and Gemini on June 21. Since the month is ruled by Jupiter (who rules Pisces), then because Jupiter is actually in Gemini I might have expected some important events around that time. According to Robert Zoller,[13] when we reach the signs of the lord of the year or the lord of the month, or other signs ruled by them, we may expect important life events at that time.

---

[13] Zoller 2003, *DMA* Lesson 18, pp. 17-18.

IBN ARABI

CHAPTER 5: TRANSITS

THE NATAL CHART IS A PICTURE OF THE PLANETARY POSITIONS IN THE SKY AT THE TIME OF BIRTH. HOWEVER, THE PLANETS ARE NEVER STATIC: THEY CONTINUE TOURING AROUND THE ZODIAC. TRANSITS REFER TO PLANETS' REAL-TIME BEHAVIOR AND THE RELATIONSHIPS THEY HAVE TO THE NATIVITY. THE EVENTS WHICH THEY TRIGGER ARE PREDESTINED IN THE SENSE THAT THEY ARE IN CONFORMITY WITH (OR AT LEAST CANNOT BE CONTRARY TO) WHAT IS PROMISED IN THE NATIVITY.

Transits show us important trends and events in the life of the native. In contrast to other techniques, transits may point out events that have the possibility of occurring within shorter periods of time. A transiting planet will be in a certain sign position for everyone in the world at a given time, but the important point here is the specific relationship between a transit and the *natal* chart.

The speed of the planets is the most important factor in the strength of transits. The slow planets are more effective because they remain in the same area for longer periods: the developments they bring are spread over a longer period of time. The transits of the fast planets act like triggers, indicating when the scenarios indicated by the slow planets will take place.

In their transits, planets may be in contact with a certain degree more than once. After contacting a certain degree, a planet moving directly may later go retrograde and contact the same degree again: consequently, the effect of that transit will be more significant. We may not be able to understand what is going on at the first contact, but the second contact is determinate: we then realize the energy of that planet. The second contact of the slow planets is always more effective.

The effective orb of a transit begins a few degrees before exactness, and strengthens when it reaches the exact degree. Applying transits are more effective than separating transits. The nature of the transiting planet and the nature of the natal planet are also important: the transit of a malefic planet to a benefic natal planet may be troublesome.

☽	27.3 days
☉	1 year
☿	1 year
♀	1 year
♂	22 months
♃	12 years
♄	29.5 years
♅	84 years
♆	165 years
♇	248 years

Figure 17: Approximate transit cycles of the planets

How transits are particularized through the natal chart

As mentioned before, the planets have general characteristics, and transiting planets are in the same zodiacal positions for everyone in the world. But the transiting meanings become specific when interpreted in the context of a particular chart, which already makes its meanings specific through house placements and rulerships. For instance, a person with a natal Jupiter-Sun trine will be lucky in some fields of life. Such a trine is beneficial when the Sun is in Aries and Jupiter in Sagittarius, as compared with a trine between the Sun in Aquarius and Jupiter in Gemini (where they are in detriment). People born with malefic planetary alignments (like a Saturn–Mars square) will experience misfortune in certain fields of life. Such a square is less malefic when Saturn is in Capricorn and Mars in Aries, as compared with the square between Saturn in Cancer and Mars in Libra. What makes these general themes especially specific to individuals, is their position and rulerships in a given chart. So, while those who are born on dates close together have the same planetary patterns, they also have important individual differences, because the planets will be placed in different houses in each individual chart. In transits therefore, while the transit of a planet will have a general meaning because of that planet's nature, it will only have a more narrow, specific meaning when judged in relation to a certain person's chart.

Key issues in transits

Three key elements will guide us in evaluating the transits and interpreting the chart in light of them:

1) The transiting planet.
2) The aspects of the transiting planet.
3) The natal planet or reference point (ASC, MC, Lot of Fortune, etc.) being contacted by the transit.

Let's examine these elements:

The transiting planet

The transiting planet is the first important factor. Each transiting planet projects its general characteristics upon the natal chart. For instance, Saturn transits restrict and bring separation and absence. On the other hand, these transits put things in order and restructure them. Saturn transits create relations with people in authority and themes related to rules. To give another example, Jupiter transits expand and bring prosperity and riches. On the other hand, Jupiter may also bring exaggeration. Jupiter transits bring prestige, luck and opportunities, social support, expansion of the social environment, and the chance to meet new people.

But each transiting planet also carries the characteristics of its placement in the natal chart. For instance, if natal Saturn is in the 6th house, its transiting relation by house placement with any planet or reference point carries the 6th house themes to that house, planet or reference point, in a Saturnian style. The same is true for the houses which Saturn rules in the natal chart. If Saturn rules the 4th and 5th houses in a natal chart, his transiting aspects with any houses, planets, and reference points will bear the themes of those 4th and 5th houses.

If the transiting planet is well placed in terms of house, sign, and aspects, it will bring more powerful results. By contrast, if the transiting planet is badly placed or weak or under stress, positive transits will manifest less benefic results, whereas negative transits will bring more malefic consequences.

The transiting planet may also trigger the progressions of planets and other important reference points like the ASC and MC, according to the secondary progression chart.

Finally, the transiting planet may also trigger the degree of important eclipses. The native may experience either positive or negative events at the exact time of such triggers.

The aspects of the transiting planet

First of all, the aspects of the transiting planet should be analyzed to see if they are positive or negative, since the nature of that aspect is an important indicator for predicting its results. If the transiting planet is in conjunction with another transiting planet, then the nature of that other planet should be taken into consideration.

Conjunctions (0°) affect us personally. We strongly feel the effects of a conjunction on our natal planet. Our chart seems to be defenseless here, because the transiting planet in conjunction with a natal planet wants to be integrated with the chart. It transfers its characteristics to the natal planet without any mediation. The conjunction has the energy of unity, oneness, and similarity, so the energy of the transiting planet is blended with the energy of the natal planet. The native may suffer from a type of imbalance due to that new energy, and must then adapt himself to it. As the conjunction is subjective, the native may not experience the change immediately. However, the change will be realized by others.

Oppositions (180°) manifest the theme of "me and others." In an opposition, some events develop which are contrary to our will, and someone or something else makes us reach a decision. That event develops because of others. We also tend to blame others under the effect of this transit, but we also learn a lot from them. We are faced with events which mirror us. Others seem to dislike or criticize our ideas and actions. Transits which make oppositions to our natal planets create extreme changes, like love suddenly turning into hatred. They bring separation and extremism.

Trines (120°) create a smooth flow of energy and bring quick developments: so, life and events run smoothly, and dreams come true quickly. On the other hand, preventing an existing problem may also be difficult, as everything continues to flow along easily. Trines may bring both rapid victories and rapid failures. For instance, when a benefic planet like Jupiter makes a trine by transit, it can bring an easy death. And if we make an effort to produce a positive outcome, trines will help it. On the other hand, things we want to avoid may also happen before we know it: if transiting Saturn makes a trine with the natal Sun, our responsibilities may increase rapidly: the native has to undertake new responsibilities and be involved in organizations or obligations that are necessary.

Squares (90°) bring events that test us. They create difficulties and obstacles. They push us to make corrections and change. We may be faced with aggravating conditions. We may experience some new themes and events, and feel stuck. We need to develop new methods to deal with these challenges, as this is the only chance to move forward. A change is needed and we have to adapt, so we had better take action to help the change happen!

Sextiles (60°) tell us that we will have chances and opportunities for things we need, but we should make an effort to take advantage of them. So while we generally like the results we get, we have to work for it. If the sextile is between masculine signs (fiery and airy signs), the results may be gotten more rapidly, but we still need to take action. Sextiles show us the gifts of the cosmos but we have to reach and grasp them; the doors are opened, but the result is based on our decision to enter through those doors (or not). In any event, sextiles always support us in experiencing new paths in our lives.

Semi-squares (45°) and **Sesquiquadrates** (135°) teach us patience and endurance because they rarely bring success: since any action may create tension, the best reaction to these aspects is to wait patiently until the dust settles. We should be aware of the obstacles and wait for better times to take action, because it is very difficult to change matters when these aspects are active.

Quincunxes (150°) emphasize realizing problematic areas of life and the need to correct and make replacements in these things: a change is needed whether we are ready or not. This aspect symbolizes a lack of coordination and organization; uncertainty and indecision prevails. It is also possible to experience events which make us leave something behind. For instance, a quincunx between transiting Saturn and the natal Sun may trigger us to give up our responsibilities, to leave a position which we had once made a big effort to get, and to retire from it. Or, a spouse may refuse his responsibilities and leave home. The most challenging feature of this aspect is that we may have difficulty in understanding what we are required to do: so, we may experience anger and stress. The stress in these relationships stems from a lack of understanding and being unaware of the problem. Some astrologers claim that this aspect is related to diseases and death; I personally do not support this idea, but I do agree that it brings major stress.

Semi-sextiles (30°) give minor support. Bernadette Brady says that semi-sextiles are a function of timing: they can be effective if one is in the right place at the right time.[1] Otherwise, this aspect is not that active.

There is a kind of hierarchy between all of these aspects, such that the smallest harmonic aspect gives the greatest effect. (We should also refer to this fact when several aspects are active at the same time.) In order of strength from the most powerful to the weakest: conjunction, opposition, trine, square, sextile, semi-square, and then the other minor aspects.

1st **Harmonic Aspect**	$360° \div 1 = 360° (= 0°)$	Conjunction
2nd **Harmonic Aspect**	$360° \div 2 = 180°$	Opposition
3rd **Harmonic Aspect**	$360° \div 3 = 120°$	Trine
4th **Harmonic Aspect**	$360° \div 4 = 90°$	Square
5th **Harmonic Aspect**	$360° \div 6 = 60°$	Sextile
6th **Harmonic Aspect**	$360° \div 8 = 45°$	Semi-square

Figure 18: Aspects as harmonics

As I mentioned, the transits of slow-moving planets are more effective than the transits of fast-moving ones. When more than one aspect is active, we need to refer to this harmonic criterion to assess which one is stronger.

The sign of the transiting planet is also important: transits bring rapid results in cardinal signs, medium-speed results in mutable signs, and slow but long-lasting results in fixed signs. Likewise, look at the house in which the planet is transiting. Transits bring most effective results in angular houses, middling results in succeedent houses, and weak results in cadent houses.

The natal planet or reference point being contacted by the transit

As compared with contacts to collective natal planets, transits to personal planets have more prominent results in the native's life and the physical world. For instance, transiting aspects to the natal Moon are more effective

---

[1] Brady 1999, p. 28.

in the native's life than the same aspects to natal Uranus. Aspects to the ASC and MC are also important.

Another key factor is the harmony between the natures of the transiting planet and the planet contacted by it. For example, a transiting Neptune–natal Mercury conjunction may bring pressure on the native, whereas a transiting Neptune–natal Venus aspect will be soft, since Neptune and Venus are friendly to each other and their natures are in harmony.

If the natal planet being contacted by the transit is well placed in terms of house, sign and aspects, that planet may overcome the difficulties of hard transiting aspects. However, if a natal planet in hard aspects by transit is in a weak position (in terms of house, sign and aspect), the native may not cope with that transit and be harmed.

If a natal planet is in aspect to several transits at the same time, different results will be manifested.

The aspect between a transiting planet and the lord of the ASC is an important one which affects the native physically, emotionally, and mentally.

Transits to the Lot of Fortune and Nodes are also important. When transits make a negative aspect to the Lot of Fortune, the native may lack good fortune and money. If the aspect is positive, the native meets opportunities which bring him luck and earnings. When transits make an effect upon the North Node, we need to be conscious so as to grasp the lessons and opportunities which will help our development. When they make an effect upon the South Node, problems from the past may come to the surface. *Déjà vu* experiences may be explained by the South Node.

Transits in traditional astrology

Transits are widely used for prediction in contemporary astrology. But nowadays, astrologers are beginning to use the techniques of traditional astrology as well. Robert Zoller, Robert Hand, and Bernadette Brady are some of the astrologers who use both traditional techniques and the modern ones.

Unlike modern astrology, traditional astrology prefers transits as the last method when making predictions. Even then, certain transits are prioritized. One important kind of transit is the time when planets return to their natal positions. Transits are also generally used for their ingresses into signs, especially when using Whole Sign houses: in the Whole Sign system, the ingress of a transiting planet into a sign is simultaneously its ingress into a house.

The most important transits are those that pass through the angular houses. The nature of the transiting planet is more significantly seen at the axis of the angular houses, since the axes are the keys of the chart: they represent primary themes of life.

Each planet in the zodiac signifies its own characteristics by natal placement and rulership (including what it rules by exaltation) during its transit. The nature of the planet is the first important factor in making an interpretation. The transits of the malefic planets are not the same as those of benefic planets.

Transits of malefic planets

The hard aspects of malefic planets' transits bring harmful results. If the transit is in cadent houses, the results should be worse. If the transit is in benefic houses, benefic results are prevented, and the native may experience misfortune under that influence. If the transiting malefic planets are badly placed in the zodiac, they display their malefic influences more powerfully. If the transiting planet is malefic and in hard aspects to the Sun, Moon, or the lords of the ASC and MC, the results will be malefic, especially when they are badly placed in the zodiac. The squares and oppositions of the greater malefic Saturn always create difficulties when badly placed in the zodiac. The trines and the sextiles of Saturn create good results when Saturn is in a good place in the zodiac, but they may create bad results if Saturn is in detriment.

The transit of a malefic planet from the axes generally brings negative events. The quality of that negative event is based on the nature of the transiting planet. For instance, Saturn transits from the axes represent the need to reshape life mandatorily, an increase of discipline and responsibilities, and the need to be more serious than before. These are not easy periods. Saturn transits in the 7th house bring problems, separations, divorces, and endings in existing relations. His hard aspects may clear out all of the unsuitable relationships for our future. There may be other endings, too. We may need to take on responsibilities with respect to our partner. The spouse may experience some health problems. Some legal problems may also bring troubles during that period.

On the other hand, Mars transits in the 7th house do not bring such deep and permanent effects. The energy is directed towards relationships, marriages, and partnerships during this transit. We may also engage in new ventures. At any rate, such a period would be full of tension in terms of relationships: hostility, disputes, and fights will prevail.

Of course, Mars and Saturn can bring difficulties in the cadent houses as well, especially in the houses of their "joys" (such as Mars in the 6th and Saturn in the 12th). In these houses, they can bring problems more easily according to their own nature: Mars brings health problems and fever in the 6th, Saturn can bring hidden enemies and isolation while in the 12th house.

We should also examine the chart to see if the malefics are in harmony with the nature of the sign on which the house cusp falls. If the malefics transit from the cusp of a house in an incompatible sign, their effects will be harmful. However, if they ingress to a sign which is compatible with their nature, they may display their positive effects.

Transits of benefic planets

The ancient astrologers state that positive aspects by benefic planets tend to bring positive results, and their hard aspects tend to bring less negative results. The positive aspects of the transiting benefic planets from malefic houses (such as the 6th or 12th) are also positive because they tend to mitigate the difficulties. However, their hard aspects from the malefic houses will bring misfortune and difficulties. If the transiting benefic planet is in detriment, its positive aspects bring very small benefits, while their hard aspects will cause more harm.

When a benefic planet transits from the angular houses, positive events are likely and these events are indicated by the nature of that planet. For instance, Jupiter transits from the 7th house may bring opportunities pertaining to partnerships. This transit is ideal for marriage and other committed partnerships. A spouse or partner with good financial prospects is likely. We may be supported by others, be optimistic in close relationships, successful in consulting businesses, and get help and advice from others. We may have a consultation with a doctor, lawyer, or financial expert, and enjoy positive results in legal cases. But Venus transits from the 7th house do not bring such grand results as compared with the Jupiter transit. Venus is more about peacemaking and signals that bilateral relations will prevail. This is a good time to make business agreements and start new partnerships. It is also ideal for marriage. Legal cases are also positively affected by this transit. During it, we may have the chance to make peace with those we have quarreled with or even with our enemies.

When benefic planets are in detriment, they cannot provide their goods in the fields in which they transit; they cannot bring effects as good as they are expected to be.

Whether benefic or malefic, transits in the succeedent houses are also important. Saturn transiting in the 2nd house may negatively affect the native's financial situation. Jupiter's transit in the same house may affect the finances of the native positively, if the other financial indicators indicate the same. Mars transiting in the 5th house may negatively affect relations with children and may indicate some Martian events like fever, microbial infections, accidents, etc. Venus transiting in the 5th house brings romantic and positive effects in love relations and also for one's relationship to children.

Eclipses, New Moons, and Full Moons

Eclipses are more effective when they contact the natal planets, the ASC, or MC. Any transiting planet which reaches the degree of the eclipse activates the effects of that eclipse. It is also important in which house new and full moons appear, and their contacts with the natal planets.

Retrograde motion of the planets

The retrograde motion of a planet is its motion "backwards" in the zodiac, contrary to its usual motion. If we observe the sky every night, we see that the planets normally move forward in the zodiac, each following another. This normal motion from west to east in the zodiac is called "direct motion," which is a counter-clockwise motion.[2] But sometimes the planets slow down, stop, and seem to move backwards in the zodiac, in a clockwise direction: this is called "retrograde motion." When the planet stops and seems as if it is not moving, we call it "stationary." The retrograde planet then slows down again, stops, and begins to move direct again in the order

---

[2] **BD:** That is, in the northern hemisphere.

of signs. (Of course these direct and retrograde motions are from our geo-centric view; in fact, no planet goes backwards astronomically.) The Sun and Moon are always in direct motion, they never retrograde.

Retrograde motion means that the planets will not be able to display their natures easily. For instance, with Mercury retrograde we may have problems in areas of communication. We may have problems in any new venture, or some articles of an agreement we are about to sign must be changed unex-pectedly. We may be faced with problems related to documents or we may suffer from a lack of information. Another manifestation of Mercury retro-grade is that we may come across people or events from the past: this may be related to our job or relationships. Events related to the retrograde Mercury begin to manifest themselves just before the retrograde motion begins.

Each planet (apart from the Sun and Moon) retrogrades for different pe-riods:

☿	24 days
♀	42 days
♂	80 days
♃	120 days
♄	140 days
♅	150 days
♆	157 days
♇	157 days

Figure 19: Standard retrogradation periods

The effect of transits may be weak or distorted if the transiting planet is in retrograde movement. This effect may be more significant if the natal planet being contacted by transit, was also retrograde. Nevertheless, when a transit makes several aspects with natal planets, it causes significant changes in the native's life.

Pluto transits

Pluto is the slowest planet. One circuit around the zodiac takes 248 years, and he spends approximately 21 years in each sign. He retrogrades for 5 months. Pluto represents transformation: he destroys and rebuilds. He shows us that we should first destroy old structures in order to build new ones; it is a time for restructuring, and brings permanent changes. Pluto also represents transformative groups, collective events, organized crimes, and occult and secret groups. As he makes us focus and deepen with respect to a specific subject, we cannot take a superficial approach. He represents fated events which are out of our control. Pluto's transits in the angular houses represent the main transformational periods.

Pluto transits in natal houses

Pluto in the 1st: The most significant feature of this position is that it restructures the personality: the native wants to display his power, with a will to change and control others, to manifest his hidden features, and to show his challenging nature. The native does not bow down: on the contrary, he may fight for his rights. If the transit is close to the ASC degree, health problems may be forced upon the native. If the transit does not make any hard aspects with the natal planets, he will be stronger than ever.

Pluto in the 2nd: This placement may bring a restructuring process, important changes or challenges in financial matters, a desire for earning more and gaining power, selfishness, and greed. The native may have a strong desire to have power in financial matters, managing his possessions strongly or using the power of money more effectively. If Pluto in the 2nd house has a hard aspect to the lord of the 2nd or 8th houses, the native may lose money due to speculations and taking risks. Contrariwise, if he has positive aspects with these planets in addition to the personal planets (the Sun in a diurnal chart and the Moon in a nocturnal one), the native may be financially in a strong position. When there are several aspects to natal planets, the native's perspective on his possessions will transform radically.

Pluto in the 3rd: The neighborhood of the native may change during this transit. Relations with siblings or close relatives may transform. Hard aspects may bring power struggles in these relationships. The native may desire to be more active and display his power with respect to close friends and siblings. Other manifestations of this transit are focusing on mental subjects, challenges in matters related to education, interest in various teachings (like astrology, yoga, etc.) and transformations in intellectual areas. If the transit makes aspects with the lords of the 3rd and 9th houses or with the personal planets, the native judges his ideas, restructures them, and tries to impose them on others. The native may find himself in some intellectual power struggles. Travels may also create radical changes in the native's life.

Pluto in the 4th: This transit causes radical changes in the family and home-related matters. The native reshapes the infrastructure of his life and plans future trends. He may be deeply affected by some people in his private life, and such people may create some personal and inner radical changes for him. Some endings and new beginnings may be seen. The native may move to another house. If Pluto in the 4th makes hard aspects with the lords of the 4th and the 8th houses or with the Sun or Moon, some difficulties like power struggles, endings, and deaths may be experienced.

Pluto in the 5th: This transit brings fated events related to children, important changes in relationships with children, changes and crises related to sexuality and love, and desires in love. If Pluto makes hard aspects to the Moon, the Sun, and the lord of the ASC, the native probably experiences transformations regarding love and sexuality. If he is in hard aspect to the lord of the 5th house, problems related to children will be inevitable. During this transit, relationships with children are redefined and restructured. A child may leave home during this transit. Speculations may also attract the native's attention.

Pluto in the 6th: If this transit makes hard aspects with the Moon, the Sun, and the lord of the ASC, or with the lord of the 6th house, the native's health may be under stress; he may have neural and psychological problems or may need to change his eating habits and lifestyle. The native may make some changes in his daily routine. He may serve and help others more than before. He may have radical changes in his business life. Daily work needs to be adjusted. The native may experience some power struggles with his coworkers and subordinates. If the native has pets, they may require intense caretaking.

Pluto in the 7th: During Pluto's transits in this angular house, change and transformation in relationships is inevitable. The native needs to redefine his relationships, may deepen them and also experience some power struggles, especially if Pluto is in aspect to the Sun, the Moon, the lord of the ASC, or the lord of the 7th house, and Venus. If these are hard aspects, then the native may feel tension and troubles in his relationships. Divorce may be one of the outcomes. Some legal cases may also be on the agenda. If Pluto is in positive aspects with natal planets, the native may gain power with the help of his relationships. Powerful people he meets may pull him upwards. This transit may also show that the native's partner is in need of restructuring his or her life; he may also fight for what he desires.

Pluto in the 8th: During this transit, the native may face themes such as other people's money, death, and inheritance. The native experiences major and inevitable transformations, and some challenges related to the partner's money (if Pluto is in transit with the lords of the 2nd and 8th), credits, and debts. The native's expenses increase and he may not know how to deal with them. If Pluto makes positive contacts with natal planets during this transit, the native may get financial support from others.

Pluto in the 9th: The positive part of this transit is that it brings a deeper understanding of mundane matters and depth in spiritual and religious matters. The native may have radical changes in his beliefs, his life-perspective, and his ideas. He may meet with new, charismatic, and effective people who have the power to change his perspective. If Pluto makes hard aspects with important planets and the lords of the 3rd and the 9th houses, the native may experience some crisis related to education, travels, and legal matters. The native may need to work abroad or study there, and as a result he may face some challenges. The native may go deeper into astrology or similar subjects.

Pluto in the 10th: This is a very powerful transit. The native may find himself facing more challenges than before. He may need to make radical changes in order to realize his destiny. If Pluto makes hard aspects with the important planets (especially the Sun and lord of the MC), the native may experience big challenges, and important changes and problems with people in authority related to his goals and profession. This transit proves that the native is about to display his power in order to realize himself. He may be in the public light more than before, may dominantly show his power, and gain charisma and efficacy. If his chart supports it, he may misuse his status for more power: in a case of taking such risk with hard aspects, the native may be disgraced.

Pluto in the 11th: This is an important time for expectations. The native may experience changes in his expectations, social groups, and friends. If Pluto has hard aspects with the most important planets or with the lord of the 11th, the native may witness the death of his friends or some problems or intrigues among them. He may have Plutonian (effective, charismatic, and doing anything to succeed) people around him. If there is already a tendency for it in the chart, the native may fight for social ideals, display his power within big groups, meet with some influential people, and participate in some secret and occult groups. If Pluto makes positive aspects with the natal planets, the native may be raised up by some influential friends. He may earn more.

Pluto in the 12th: The native looks for power within himself during this transit. He may isolate and meditate. He may get prepared for transformation. If Pluto makes hard aspects with the important planets or with the lord of the 12th, some serious illnesses and psychological imbalances may be experienced. Some losses and challenges of life, uncontrolled events, relations with secret people, and some changes that cannot be realized, may put the native's mental health out of balance. Some secret enmities may occur. The native may develop an interest in metaphysics.

Aspects of transiting Pluto

Conjunctions: Pluto conjunctions bring high concentration. The subjects we are concentrating on may undergo great and intentional changes. On the positive side, Pluto brings decisiveness and charisma. This power should not be misused, because it is so powerful as to be even beyond the ego. This power may be either constructive or destructive. It awakens and activates. The native may display obsessive behaviors. If the native has never been able to show his power, this transit may set him in motion. As it brings great strength in facing challenges, the native may find the chance to achieve the impossible; he is not limited anymore. This transit may bring incredible strength and determination. The native has to discover his inner strength with the help of this transit's awakening effects. The native feels the power of rebirth in his life. On the other hand, he may take everything very seriously and be deeply affected by events. He may also feel desire for things he did not realize before.

Squares and oppositions: Outer influences are active with these aspects of Pluto. In square aspects, events develop more rapidly, while oppositions extend them over a period of time. The effects are provoking, challenging, and push one into power struggles. These aspects may bring pressure, violence, and threats. Murders, holocausts, and massacres are all related to Pluto. Transformation is inevitable with squares and oppositions of Pluto. Oppositions may bring some secrets to the surface. The native may not feel comfortable without a transformation, and resisting change would be harsher.

Sextiles and trines: The support of influential people brings positive results to the native. The native may feel that he has to be the best, and has a
deep desire for that. He may find himself fated to be on the path that helps
him reach his goals in life. Pluto also offers collective support with his positive aspects, which bring decisiveness, vigor, charisma, discipline, a strong
will, and the ability to take the initiative. The effects of Pluto these aspects
are based on our capacity to handle them.

Transiting Pluto's aspects to natal planets

Pluto–Sun: The personality may undergo a huge change. A desire for
change, an ambition for success, powerful concentration, using one's energy
for the sake of one's aims, displaying leadership, outspokenness, courage,
strength, hard work, taking the initiative and not letting problems stop him,
compulsiveness, avoiding shallowness, changes in life perception, and egoism
may be the key words for this aspect. If the native had not yet used his Solar
initiative before this transit, it will provoke him to. Positive aspects bring
support from authority figures, an ability to display charisma and power, approval from others, ease in making changes, success in organizations (the
sextile requires some effort while the trine easily brings success, even in a
passive mode), physical health, energy and vitality, entrepreneurship, outspokenness and courage—so that the native may be successful even in
impossible situations and may strongly influence others. The hard aspects
may suppress and impinge upon others. The native may tend to manipulate
events, use force, suppress some threats and provoke others. With the opposition, power struggles may be seen; the native may misuse power and abuse
people. The native may also experience problems with men and father figures. He may desire to be dominant in his relationships and always want to
be right. With squares, the cruel and domineering side of the personality may
negatively affect one's health. Resisting change may be more destructive.

Pluto–Moon: This union is not that good even at the conjunction (and is
hard, as compared to the Pluto-Sun conjunction), because severe Pluto
smashes the graceful Moon. With Pluto-Moon contacts, emotional suppression and emotional situations that threaten the native's mental state may be
experienced. These aspects may cause pressure on the family. The native may
be focused on his mother, spouse, or on women in general, and may have
some changes related to the home and family life. The habits of the native

may change as a result of this transit. On the positive side, his emotions may deepen. He may be constructive in his relationships with women and his family; he may value humanity, he may have a strong sense of belonging, and he may need to make some changes related to the home during this transit. If the Pluto-Moon aspects are hard ones, then the native may experience some destruction related to, and even the death of, the mother or the spouse. Some past events may come to the surface and may be bothersome. With the Pluto-Moon opposition, the native may have problems and emotional tension with female figures. The native may be fighting, but he is also hurt internally. He may be possessive, jealous, and skeptical in his relationships. Pluto-Moon squares may bring health problems, and the native may have difficulties and the need to change his routine and attitudes. If the Moon is in mutable signs, the change may be easier. Conditions may challenge the native's weaknesses. Under the influence of this transit, the native cannot feel emotionally and physically secure.

Pluto–Mercury: Pluto's aspects with Mercury, the planet of communication, may develop communication skills. Their conjunction may empower mental concentration: the native may easily focus his mind on any subject. This aspect is a good condition for research and other mental processes. The native feels open to learning new things. Ideas may be restructured and old ideas may be transformed. Mental capacity increases. The native may focus on any subject and achieve expertise in a specific field. Positive aspects bring writing and speaking talents. The native may think in a reforming and innovative way; he may break his mental walls and transform. If these two are in hard aspect, the native may be skeptical, obsessive, unkind, and insistent, and may speak accordingly. The capacity for perception may increase, but the native may be fanatical and obsessive. The native should preserve flexibility and keep pace with the transformation. Challenging aspects may make the native suppress the ideas of others: the native may want to impose his ideas, threaten, and criticize others. Such hard transits may be frustrating.

Pluto–Venus: This transit brings a restructuring in private relations and perceptions about them. With the conjunction, the native wants to draw himself into a totally different arena. He may deepen and transform his relationships, his desires may increase, and this transit may bring an insistence on a specific person. With Pluto-Venus conjunctions, squares, or oppositions, we cannot expect a smooth flow in relations. In Pluto-Venus conjunctions, the native may need a deep relationship instead of a smooth, more superficial one. He may sometimes feel some pressure and need to express his feelings. He may also use pressure on others. On the negative side, the native may misuse that power (especially in his relationships), manipulate events, push others, and experience power struggles and intrigues. A new approach in relationships is inevitable in any case. Desires may cause trouble. For instance, the native may like someone else even though he is married, and this may cause big problems for his marriage. On the other hand, a new relationship under this influence is not a permanent one. The couple may have problems due to jealousy and over-possessiveness. As Venus represents things that we like, eating habits may also undergo a compelled change during this transit. Positive aspects of these two planets may help the native display his charisma, make financial arrangements easily, get support from others, and establish good relations with influential people. During the conjunction, trine, and sextile, important relationships or friendships may be started. As Venus represents creative artistic talents, these talents may be actively expressed during strong Pluto transits. This is more significant with the hard aspects: for instance, the native who experiences dramatic changes in his love life may channel his emotions into the arts and create wonderful and radical artworks.

Pluto–Mars: As Pluto is the higher octave of Mars, when Pluto transits make aspects with him, Martial characteristics are more significant. Hard aspects may emphasize accidents, violence, and fights. These aspects may cause risks to life. The conjunction brings high concentration, and the energy manifested is so high that it should be channeled somehow. The native may be more courageous and confident. This transit pushes the native to act. It triggers rivalry instincts and increases the desire to assert one's leadership. Its negative use gives an aggressiveness and foolhardiness which may cause some troubles for the native. He may act cruelly to gain power. Hard aspects like the square and opposition may bring the risk of violence, accidents, and death. The risk of over-exaggerating is very high. The native may want to achieve the impossible. The positive aspects increase the native's capacity for action, leading him to succeed easily in the hardest things. He may have the chance for progress. Due to his increased courage and energy, he achieves success, and more so than before this increase in his working power and endurance. He has the potential to achieve victory in physical activities. The native may push for making changes, as this is the right time to do so.

Pluto–Jupiter: This transit enlarges one's power and pushes one to use it in the social arena. It may also exaggerate one's power. When Pluto and Jupiter conjoin, the native has the opportunity to achieve great success and meet with influential people who are well educated and reputable, perhaps from religious areas that are known by masses of people. The native has to fight to reach success, but the chance of winning the battle is rather high. On the other hand, the native may have some changes and restructuring in his moral values, beliefs, and life-perspective. He may tend to deal with metaphysics and issues of personal development. The positive aspects between these two planets may bring the chance for increased power, richness, and a wide social network. The native may attain victory with the support of charismatic and powerful people. During this transit and aspect, the native may easily find solutions to his legal disputes. His ethical, moral, and religious values may positively change. If transiting Pluto makes a hard aspect to Jupiter, then the native may experience some mistakes, moral corruptions, lack of confidence, and may misuse these experiences or waste such opportunities. If the natal chart supports it, the risk of exaggeration, arrogance, and fanaticism may be triggered. The native may have difficulties in legal issues and may lose money. He may have some destructive and radical changes in his religious beliefs.

Pluto–Saturn: The conjunction, squares, and opposition of these two stressful planets may bring stressful results. These aspects show that the native experiences some important tests. First of all, the native now has to make structural changes. His fears and worries have to be transformed and even cleaned out. These aspects trigger those changes, but it will take time to see the results of the transit: the native needs to be patient. On a positive note, these aspects increase the native's strength and may help him get rid of all forms of suppression and free him from all impositions. The native may easily be successful in the areas that require deep research. The conjunction and hard aspects of these two may create pressure on his business life. The things he assumes to be concrete and guaranteed may be destroyed. Managing conditions and preserving the status quo may be difficult. The native has to be realistic and clean out the things that he no longer needs. Instead of resisting changes, the native should be able to flow with them and make necessary revisions when needed—otherwise he may have more difficulties. Positive aspects between these planets help the native make these changes easily and permanently. The native will be stronger in business and his working energy will increase. Adapting to changes and eliminating unnecessary things will be easy. The native may get advice from old and wise people. He may get support from executives and achieve long-term victories.

Neptune transits

Neptune's tour in the zodiac takes 165 years; he visits each sign for approximately 14 years. His average speed is 2°–5° degrees per year. Neptune's effects are complicated, and he is confusing and difficult to define. He deceives people so they may believe that even impossible things may happen. He brings confusion, dissatisfaction, disintegration, and escapism. When we need permanent results, Neptune transits do not help; they may even prevent them. Neptune ignores logic and increases emotionality. These transits make us go beyond materialism and make us idealistic and open to the collective mind, directing us to serve collective benefits. Neptune transits increase the imagination and creativity in line with the native's own talents and capacity.

Neptune transits in natal houses

Neptune in the 1st: The native may not express himself in a significant way. He is not clear about what he really wants, and exhibits that directly. He may display some mysterious and weird attitudes. He may have a tendency towards mysticism and spiritualism, while his intuitions increase. The native feels idealistic, whole, and full of love. His creativity and imagination peaks during this transit. If transiting Neptune makes hard aspects with the Sun, Moon, and lord of the ASC, the native may become divorced from reality. Positive aspects bring inspiration and a rich imagination.

Neptune in the 2nd: The native may experience some changes in his financial resources, and may begin to show a different approach towards financial matters. He may like to spend his money in accordance with his ideals and some spiritual themes, or he may realize that money does not matter. The native may give up his possessions and money. If transiting Neptune makes hard aspects with the lords of the 2nd and 8th houses, the native may be deceived in matters of money. His financial sources may be imbalanced. If Neptune makes positive aspects with the lords of these houses or with the other important indicators of the chart, the native may earn money with the help of his intuitions, imagination, and inspiration, or through spiritual subjects or the arts.

Neptune in the 3rd: This transit means that the native is about go beyond his ego with respect to his relatives, and mercy and love will be emphasized. If transiting Neptune makes hard aspects with the natal planets, and especially with the lord of the 3rd or Mercury, he may suffer from some misunderstandings and problems in contractual issues. His close relatives may experience some deceptions, delusions, and uncertainties. The native may also experience some turmoil and uncertainties in his mental world; he may separate from reality. During this transit, the native should be careful about contracts and documents. If transiting Neptune is in positive aspects with the Sun, Moon, lord of the ASC, Mercury, and the lords of the 3rd and 9th, the native's creativity may increase and he may produce new ideas.

Neptune in the 4th: In a positive sense, emotional themes, solidarity, compassion, and devotion within the family may increase. This is more significant when Neptune is in positive aspects with the Sun, the Moon, the lord of the ASC, and the lord of the 4th. On the negative side, some separations and disappointments within the family may be seen. As the inner world of the native is so confused, he may have problems in organizing his life and making decisions about the future. For instance, the native may want to move to another place, but he may not finalize the decision about it. Neptune's hard aspects with the Sun, Moon, lord of the ASC, and the lord of the 4th may cause such influences. Such stressful aspects may also bring some losses within the family. Neptune's hard aspect to the lord of the 8th brings similar results.

Neptune in the 5th: This transit emphasizes themes related to children, relationships, and love. If transiting Neptune makes hard aspects with the Sun, Moon, lord of the DSC, Venus, or the lord of the 5th, the native may experience sensitivity in his romantic relations, emotional turbulence, disappointments, and deceptions in love. He may have some problems with children and the health of his own children. Hard aspects may bring creativity in artistic fields but also addiction in pleasure-giving substances. Indecisiveness and uncertainty in love matters may be seen. The native may not be sure if he wants to have children or not. He may be dissatisfied by life's pleasures. If Neptune makes positive aspects, then positive results will be achieved. The native may find what he truly needs in love and may have spiritual satisfaction in his relations with his children.

Neptune in the 6th: If this transit makes hard aspects with the Sun, Moon, lord of the ASC, or the lords of the 6th or 12th, then the native may suffer from illnesses and weaknesses. The native may suffer from diseases whose reasons are unknown, or may be at risk due to alcohol addiction. He may be dissatisfied in his daily routine and may be open to deception. However, if the aspects with natal planets are positive, then the native may feel satisfied by his daily work environment and he may want to offer service for the well-being of others. The native may tend to get involved in spiritual themes. He may actively use his imagination, intuition, and creativity in his business life. He may have pets. On the other hand, the negative aspects of Neptune transits may bring some losses and grief related to pets.

Neptune in the 7th: This transit emphasizes partnerships. If transiting Neptune makes hard aspects with the natal Sun, Moon, lord of the 7th, or Venus, the native may experience disillusionment, disappointment, and wrong decisions in his relationships. He does not act with his ego but tends to sacrifice himself. He may idealize the other person, depart from reality, and make the wrong decisions. If Neptune makes hard aspects with Mercury or the lord of the 7th, the native may have difficulties about agreements, partnerships, legal cases, and similar areas of life. The opposite is true if Neptune makes positive aspects with those indicators. If Neptune makes positive aspects with the lord of the 7th, Venus, or the Moon, the native may have happy and harmonious love relations. Through positive aspects with Mercury and the lord of the 7th, the native may relate to the right people with the help of his instincts. He may also sacrifice himself in his relationships.

Neptune in the 8th: This transit emphasizes joint incomes and expenses, credits and debts, death and inheritances, and occult or mystical issues. If Neptune makes hard aspects with the natal Sun, Moon, or the lords of the 2nd and 8th, the native may suffer from some monetary losses, mistakes, or being misled. If transiting Neptune is in a hard aspect to natal Mercury, the native may experience some misunderstandings or deceptions with regard to inheritance and debts. This transit is not a proper period for making monetary agreements. During a Neptune transit from the 8th house, if in hard aspects with the Sun, Moon, and lord of the 8th, the native's parents or close relatives may die. Hard aspects with the lord of the ASC may point to the native's own risk of death. The opposite is true if Neptune makes positive aspects with these indicators. The native may get support from others in common endeavors and in matters of credit and debt. He may obtain income through his intuitions and power of imagination. This is a good period for esoteric and metaphysical interests. The native may be curious about the secrets of life during this transit, more so than ever.

Neptune in the 9th: This transit emphasizes religious themes, scientific researches, teachings that contain a life perspective, travels and educational matters, and relations with foreigners. The native may experience transcendent states of consciousness and may have a tendency towards spiritual realms he has never experienced before; he may have some consultations in these subjects or have a wider imagination and an increase in dreams. He may travel overseas. If the aspects of transiting Neptune to natal planets (especially the lords of the 3rd and 9th houses and Mercury) are hard ones, the native may become confused; he may lose his direction and his life-perspective. He may have some losses and difficulties in travel and educational fields. If transiting Neptune is in hard aspect to natal Jupiter or the lord of the 9th, the native may experience difficulties and disintegration in religious areas. On the other hand, if transiting Neptune is in good aspects with the natal planets and the cusps of the above-mentioned houses, the native may expand his perspective, find his balance in spiritual themes, and find the truth by foreseeing the trends of the future. He may also get good results from educational and travel issues.

Neptune in the 10th: Neptune's transit from the MC means that Neptunian events will be more prominent in the native's life. The native may experience uncertainty and indecisiveness in his aims. He should work in a devoted way and go beyond his ego in order to reach his goals. The native may work to serve the Divine plan; he may be happy by helping others. If transiting Neptune in this house is in hard aspects with natal planets or the lord of the 10th house, the native may have some problems, deceptions, and separations on the career front; he may be involved in some scandals. The native may experience some disappointments related to people in authority and top management. On the other hand, if transiting Neptune is in good aspects with natal planets and the lords of the 1st and the 10th, the native may make the right decisions with the help of his intuitions and get support and love from important people. The native may be successful in works which require artistic and creative talents, imaginative power, and design skills.

Neptune in the 11th: This transit emphasizes relations with friends and social groups. The native may have Neptunian (creative, intuitive, devoted, and spiritual) acquaintances and may get involved in Neptunian (spiritual) groups. This is a period for pursuing idealistic aims, but one should not drift away from reality. If transiting Neptune is in hard aspects with natal planets, especially with the Sun, the lord of the MC, the lord of the ASC, and the lord of the 11th, the native is exposed to disappointments relating to his friends and social environment. If transiting Neptune is in hard aspect to the natal Mercury, the native may be misled by those in his social circle; the natal chart should be observed in this regard. If transiting Neptune is in good aspects with the above-mentioned indicators, the native is well supported by those in his social circle. He may have the opportunity to help others. Devotion and love take first place in the native's approach to his friends.

Neptune in the 12th: This transit emphasizes isolation, retreat from daily life, meditation and prayers, behind-the-scenes events, secret enemies, and situations which are out of one's control. Neptune is prone to spiritual activities and meditation, so during this transit the native may be interested in such things. This is a good time for discovering inner wisdom, but the native may be totally removed from daily life. He may leave reality and the responsibilities of daily life behind. If transiting Neptune in this house is in hard aspects with the natal Sun, Mercury, Saturn, the lord of the MC, or the lord of the ASC, the native may be stuck in his imagination, his mind may be scattered and he may have difficulties in determining his direction, he may ignore his responsibilities and he may lose control. He may be vulnerable to behind-the-scenes games and secret hostility. If transiting Neptune is in hard aspects with the natal Moon, Venus, or lord of the DSC, the native may experience disappointments and deceptions in his romantic relations.

Aspects of transiting Neptune

Conjunctions: It may take some time to understand Neptune's role in the conjunction. It may bring softness, pacification, disintegration, intuition, telepathic skills, and a tendency for spirituality. The native may have Neptunian friends who change the course of his life. The effect may change according to the planet in conjunction. Neptune feels comfortable with the benefic Moon and Venus: a conjunction with those planets may bring romanticism, empathy, and devotion. But Neptune's nature does not match those of the Sun and Mercury, as these planets represent logic and the will: such a conjunction may bring disintegration in the use of logic and will power. Conjunctions with planets like the Sun and Mars bring a pacifying effect and a sense of devotion to life and its challenges. A conjunction with Mars may decrease energy and tension, while also causing difficulties in taking action. Neptune's idealistic nature fits well with Jupiter, bringing peace and spirituality. The conjunction with Saturn brings the disintegration of one's standard patterns; the native may have difficulty in being disciplined.

Squares and oppositions: They bring fancifulness, disappointments, idealizing others, deception and disillusion, exaggeration or ignorance of ideals, the inability to realize projects, and a lack of enthusiasm. Misunderstandings, disintegrations, and sharing faulty information may be seen. However, creativity comes to a peak. Materialistic and logical people may need to head towards spirituality and intuitions. The Neptunian people around the native may blame him for being a materialistic type and may direct him to spirituality. The native may have difficulties in maintaining a balance between materialism and spiritualism, logic and intuition.

Sextiles and trines: The native may easily manifest his spirituality and devotion. He does not have difficulty in maintaining a balance between materialism and spiritualism, logic and intuition. He does not feel pressure to tend towards Divine themes, as such themes are already taking place around the native. The native works idealistically for the well-being of others, his artistic talents and creativity are high, and he may find the meaning of life by going beyond the material.

Transiting Neptune's aspects to natal planets

Neptune–Sun: The Sun represents the ego and people in authority. The nature of the Sun does not match the nature of Neptune. So, the opposition, square or conjunction (or other minor and hard aspects) of the Sun and Neptune may create some problems in the native's manifestation of his ego. This transit may decrease confidence in powerful people or male figures (the boss, father, husband, etc.) in the native's life. At the conjunction of these two planets, the native may be drawn to spiritual themes. He may think of others who are in need and may be sensitive to events around himself. If the aspects between the Sun and other natal planets support it, the native may be full of inspiration and he may be intuitive. If the aspects between the Sun and natal planets are hard ones, this stress may bring psychological problems and dissatisfaction. The native may lose track of his goals and run away from life. He may have some health problems. He may have difficulties in adapting to the real world because of his spiritual experiences. The conjunction and other harmonious aspects between these two may help spiritual experiences. The native may use his intuitions correctly; he may have mercy towards others and enjoy helping them. He may be interested in Divine and religious themes, and he may want to understand life's deepest meaning. His imagination and creative powers increase and he may be recognized in artistic fields if his natal chart promises that as well. This transit overcomes materialism.

Neptune–Moon: The Moon represents the emotional direction of our lives. She is related to our basic instincts and needs. Transiting Neptune's aspects with the natal Moon make the native more emotional and emphatic towards others, and he is focused on his own emotional needs and desires (this is more significant with the conjunction). He feels a great desire to integrate with others at an emotional level. But the native may become too sensitive and be emotionally scattered. He may have psychological problems like depression and dissatisfaction, although this would be more significant if the Moon has tough aspects with the natal planets. He may have some emotional problems related to the family and women (especially the mother and wife). The hard aspects between transiting Neptune and the natal Moon may point out disappointments in relationships with women, the mother and the wife (in a male chart) and some health problems. As the Moon is related to bodily health, the native may show sensitivity related to the stomach and breasts. Psychological imbalances, pessimism, stress, allergic reactions, oversensitivity, misunderstandings, and deceptions for emotional reasons may be experienced. Positive aspects between transiting Neptune and the natal Moon bring empathy, creativity, inspiration, sensitive and devoted relationships with women, ideals, mercy, and a need to help others.

Neptune–Mercury: The aspects of Neptune (the planet of imagination and intuitiveness) and Mercury (the planet of mind, logic, and rationality) are not easy. This is more significant if Mercury is in one of the rational signs in the natal chart. The conjunction may scatter one's ideas, so this is not a good time for making important decisions. Due to mental turmoil, the native may not express himself clearly. He may make bad decisions if the aspects between transiting Neptune and natal Mercury are hard. He may be alienated from daily reality. Signing contracts is not recommended during Neptune's hard transits with Mercury. The native should be careful in buying and selling and other commercial activities. But the conjunction and other harmonious aspects between these two may bring a tendency towards spiritual and metaphysical themes. The native may well express his imagination and inspiration. He may display idealistic thoughts, creativity, intuition, and romanticism. A balance of the rational and irrational is maintained. This is an ideal time for learning spiritual subjects and teaching them to others.

Neptune–Venus: Neptune's nature is similar to Venus's, so their aspects are not problematic. They bring inspiration and creativity in artistic fields. Emotional and romantic effects are more significant with the conjunction. The native likes to integrate with others, and works for the welfare of humanity. In private relations, he always thinks of the other and devotes himself to the other. He is faced with the risk of over-idealizing his partner, which is more significant if Neptune makes tense aspects with Venus, and the native may be disappointed or deceived in the end. Platonic romances (and suffering as a result) are difficult features of this transit. He may have high expectations in love and relationships, act as though blindfolded, and he may be subject to slander and scandals if it is also promised by the natal chart. Positive aspects between these two bring balanced and harmonious relations. During this transit, emotions may be expressed easily and the two parties are devoted to each other.

Neptune–Mars: These aspects are pacifying rather than active, operative ones. They may decrease the effort that is needed for taking action. Dealing with these aspects may be a little bit hard when the native needs to act, react, and be decisive and strong. Physical energy may be low; the native may even be lazy. The conjunction, square, and opposition of transiting Neptune and natal Mars may weaken the immune system and cause some allergic reactions. The native may be prone to accidents due to carelessness and inattentiveness. He may not have self-confidence, or be dissatisfied and full of fears and worries. He may have difficulties in following through on decisions and directing himself. He may suffer some deceptions, disillusionment, and misunderstandings related to his work and other ventures. With negative aspects, the native should stay away from risky ventures. On the other hand, positive aspects may draw the energy and effort of the native toward spiritual and metaphysical themes and religions. The native may be able to balance his own ego drives in his ventures. This is not the time to be brave, but this transit may display the native's idealism and help him show effort in this field.

Neptune–Jupiter: As Neptune and Jupiter are the joint lords of Pisces, these are easy aspects. The conjunction triggers the idealism of Jupiter, his imaginative power, and the desire for expansion. The native may be interested in mystical, spiritual, religious, and Divine themes. Negative aspects may bring extremism, dreamy and idealistic tendencies, and fanaticism; the native may be liable to be abusive. He may drift away from reality. His goodness and generosity may be abused by others. He may suffer some deceptions and abuses with respect to financial matters, so this is a risky period for investments. The native may experience disappointments as a result of his high expectations. He may have problems, disappointments, and mistakes in educational matters. Positive aspects bring development on the spiritual level and positive results in educational and legal matters. Optimism as well as positive results from idealistic ventures and educational and legal matters are likely. Positive aspects also bring generosity, both physically and spiritually.

Neptune–Saturn: This transit melts down the native's habitual patterns, principles, and barriers. Since Neptune and Saturn have opposite natures, it is hard to deal with their square and opposition. The conjunction is a rather easy aspect: the native may easily loosen his rigid principles and he does so willingly. The conditions which expose him to fears and anxieties begin to dissolve with the help of this conjunction. Of course, this may rock his foundations and make him escape from reality. This is especially valid when Neptune makes hard aspects to natal Saturn. Negative aspects may cause anxiety and fear without any reason. The native may be subject to dissolution in financial and business matters; he may be prone to scandals. The native may not preserve his existing conditions and status. The foundations that he has set after many years' effort may be broken and scattered. His career life may be stagnant. Negative aspects may also trigger depression, fears, and paranoia. Positive aspects help the native use material things in a positive way. The native may manifest the things he dreams of. During this period he may become interested in philosophical and spiritual themes; he may apply discipline to these things and bring them to reality.

Uranus transits

Uranus's tour in the zodiac takes 84 years; he spends approximately 7 years in each sign, and retrogrades for 5 months. His average speed is 2' per day. Uranus transits bring unexpected, shocking, extraordinary, and accelerated results. We are suddenly faced with highly positive or negative events. These transits may change the rigid and *de facto* rules of society. They destabilize and help us refresh and renew life by getting rid of areas we are bored of. If we want to follow the status quo, we fall into trouble. They awaken and stimulate the mind, bringing limitless evolution. They vitalize and accelerate one's energy level. Due to its electric quality, this transit may bring unease and nervousness, but we may have an easy transit if we are flexible enough. This transit helps us be open to new and different things. A need for freedom prevails.

Uranus transits in natal houses

Uranus in the 1st: Uranus's transit in this house may bring sudden and unexpected decisions, changes, and innovations in the native's life. He may express himself in a different style and may individualize himself. This is the time for demolishing old patterns and for renovation. He may need to be free; he may be more interested in changes and new things. He may become bored of his old habits. He may make some changes in his physical appearance, attitudes, and style of speech. He may feel more active and dynamic. He may perceive the world differently than before; he may display some original, unexpected, and rebellious attitudes towards life. He may react in a nervous way. His increasing need for freedom may force him to end old relationships. Others may not adapt to the changes the native is experiencing. This is especially valid when transiting Uranus conjoins, squares, or opposes the lord of the 7th house or Venus. This transit may also bring sudden changes in health matters: the native may be prone to accidents and clumsiness. This is more significant when Uranus makes tough aspects with the lord of natal ASC, the Moon, Sun, or lord of the 6th.

Uranus in the 2nd: This transit emphasizes sudden and unexpected developments in financial conditions and all of the native's values. His income level may have ups and downs, leading to difficulty in maintaining a fixed income: this is more significant if Uranus makes tough aspects with the lords of the 2nd and 8th and the Lot of Fortune, as the native may experience unexpected financial losses. On the other hand, if transiting Uranus makes positive aspects with the above-mentioned indicators, the native may gain some surprise earnings. The things he already has may increase in value. The native's perception about money may change during Uranus's transit in this house. The native may discover new ways of earning money. He may start earning money from alternative scientific areas, new discoveries, and astrology.

Uranus in the 3rd: Uranus's transit in this house emphasizes sudden and unexpected developments related to siblings and close relatives, together with extraordinary events. The native may change his social circle. He may be somewhat different in his communication style and his approach to events. This is a time when the native comes to be open to mental changes and learning new things. He may continue his education in different subjects: this is more significant when transiting Uranus aspects the lords of the 3rd or 9th, or Mercury. During this period, the native may produce creative ideas, inventions, and discoveries. Positive aspects bring surprises and opportunities related to areas like education, publishing, travels, and siblings. Negative aspects bring unwanted surprises and unexpected changes in these areas. When transiting Uranus makes hard aspects with the natal planets (especially Mars), the native may suffer some accidents during his travels.

Uranus in the 4th: Uranus's transit in this house emphasizes sudden and unexpected developments concerning the family and household matters. During Uranus's transit in this most private place of the chart, the native cannot remain still: he may move to another place in an unexpected way or he may decorate his house. This is more significant when Uranus makes hard aspects with the lord of the 4th house, the ASC or the lord of the ASC, or the Moon or Sun. This transit may bring separations and uneasiness within the family. The native may have difficulties in settling down and may compulsively move to another house. With positive aspects, the native makes these changes willingly, but with negative aspects the native or his family may not feel secure and at peace where they are. Events from the native's past may come out in surprising ways. He may also experience some changes related to his future goals, which will also be reflected in his career (10th house). The native may meet these sudden and rapid changes easily, if transiting Uranus makes positive aspects with the natal planets.

Uranus in the 5th: This transit may bring exciting effects in the love life and relationships. During this period it is hard to stabilize relationships, as surprises and rapid developments and unexpected beginnings and endings are possible. The native is in need of excitement in his love life. He may have relationships with weird and strange people. The native may experience some separations and unwanted surprises in his relationships, and extraordinary sexual experiences if Uranus makes negative aspects with the lords of the 5th and 7th houses and Venus. As the 5th also rules children, the native may also experience some changes related to the health of his children and some radical changes in his relationships with them. Speculation in finances may bring losses. Positive aspects bring nice surprises related to children, sudden and joyous love experiences, and freedom is emphasized. This is a good period for dealing with different hobbies. Creativity is triggered. The native may express himself in a different way. He may also take up some freelance jobs.

Uranus in the 6th: This transit indicates that the native may get rid of his daily routine due to sudden events. The native may now experience some changes in his working life, his relationship with coworkers and the working environment, and his very position. The native may experience some troubles and unwanted changes in the organization of his daily work if transiting Uranus makes tough aspects with the lords of the 6th and the ASC. If the chart supports it, he may also experience some unexpected health problems. Sudden nervous attacks and ups and downs in blood pressure may be seen. The native may have some changes in his work methods and in his approaches to work; he may also show interest in other fields. He may experience sudden and nice developments, promotions, and changes in position if transiting Uranus makes positive aspects with the lord of the 6th, the MC, the Sun, or the lord of the 11th. He may also decide unexpectedly to have a pet.

Uranus in the 7th: Uranus's transit in this house emphasizes sudden and unexpected developments in relationships. This transit may sometimes be challenging for one-on-one relations. The need for freedom is observed during this transit. The native cannot accept another's dominance. Sudden marriages and sudden divorces are possible, and relationships are never stable during this period. The native may behave weirdly and unreliably. He may also like extraordinary people. The native's existing relationship may not work as well, as it has been monotonous and boring for a while; it may come to an end if the parties do not make an effort to rescue their relationship. Rebellious attitudes may harm the relationship, especially if Uranus makes tough aspects with the lords of the ASC and DSC, and with Venus. Such tough aspects may also signify sudden changes related to the spouse or partner. Positive aspects may bring sudden relationships, partnerships, and business collaborations. The monotony of the relationship may be overcome and excitement may be had. The native's partner may experience rapid and positive developments.

Uranus in the 8th: This may bring crisis and dramatic changes. Fated events stem from the characteristics of this house. The 8th is related to death in both traditional and modern astrology. Moreover, this house is also related to the occult and metaphysics. During Uranus's transit therefore, these themes may unexpectedly prevail in the native's life. The native may witness sudden deaths and unexpected developments related to inheritances and payments, especially if transiting Uranus makes hard aspects with the lord of the 8th. If Uranus makes hard aspects with the lords of the 4th and 10th or the Sun and Moon, the native's parents may die or witness some vital dangers, or undergo some surgical operations. The hard aspects with the lord of the ASC and the Sun and Moon mean that the native may be exposed to some critical situations. If Uranus makes hard aspects with the lords of the 2nd and the 8th and the Lot of Fortune, the native may experience sudden financial losses and crisis. He may also have some problems related to other people's money. For example, his spouse or partner may have some unexpected financial problems. Credits, debts, taxes, and insurance may cause some financial turbulence and losses. On the other hand, positive aspects may bring rapid and sudden gains through money owed, payments, inheritances, and other financial sources. The native may earn money from partnerships.

Uranus in the 9th: This transit brings a potential for awareness and enlightenment. The native's perspective may expand and his personal development may pick up speed. During this period the native is open to new ideas, travels, meeting with foreign people, internet-based businesses, and scientific and technological opportunities. He may attend or offer courses and seminars on astrology and alternative branches of science, he may reach out into wider circles, he may travel and collaborate with foreigners. This is more significant if transiting Uranus makes positive aspects with the lords of the 3rd and 9th, Mercury, Jupiter, or the Sun. The native may generate original ideas and expand them. If Uranus makes negative aspects to natal planets, especially the lords of the ASC and MC, Mercury, Jupiter, and the Sun, the native may experience turbulence related to his beliefs. The native may not find his current ideas reasonable and as a result he may experience some problems related to the values he believes in. He may also have problems in his travels and relationship to what is foreign. He may experience immorality and lawlessness with immoral people.

Uranus in the 10th: Uranus's transit in the MC may bring radical changes in the native's life and job. These may be fated events which help him acquire a new direction in his life. The native may enjoy jobs he did not before, and try techniques which have never been tested. He may experience some changes in top management and sudden job opportunities during this transit. If the transit makes tough aspects with the lord of the MC, the Sun, or the career indicator, the native may experience some compulsory and challenging developments which annoy him. He may be fired, he may lose a top position, and he may experience sudden problems with his superiors and authorities, or sudden resignations. If Uranus makes positive aspects with the above-mentioned indicators, the changes may be easier and quicker. The native may be recognized by the public, with positive aspects causing a positive image but negative aspects affecting him negatively. Even if Uranus does not make any aspects with natal planets, his public image may change. The native may become interested in unusual subjects like astrology and metaphysics, and also with humanitarian themes. During this transit, the native may find the courage for new ventures and make changes in his life, he may feel rebellious against his former conditions and find it hard to accept others' authority. He likes taking the initiative and puts his individuality at the forefront.

Uranus in the 11th: During this transit the native may experience important changes in his social circle. He may be involved in different groups (such as groups which study astrology or metaphysics) and he may know some people who influence his whole life. He gives priority to those with whom he shares his ideals, and may change his relationship with those who do not share the same vision; he may not like his old friends and old social circle. His long-term relationships may come to an end, as his ideals and expectations have already changed. If transiting Uranus makes hard aspects with the lords of the ASC or MC, the Sun, Mercury, or the lord of the 11th, the changes may be tough ones which occur involuntarily. Some difficulties and disagreements may be experienced. If Uranus makes hard aspects with the lord of the 2nd and planets in it, the native may some problems with his friends due to money matters. The 11th is related to income that stems from ventures (i.e., the 10th), so Uranus's transits here may bring important changes and ups and downs. If transiting Uranus makes positive aspects with the above-mentioned indicators, the native's social life will change in a smooth way. He may benefit from these sudden ventures and developments in his social life. His status in social life may rise rapidly.

Uranus in the 12th: During this transit the influences of Uranus are not very obvious. It may trigger the subconscious and some hidden enemies may arise; this is more significant if transiting Uranus is conjoining with the lord of the 12th or natal planets in it. Unexpected actions by hidden enemies may bring troubles. This may be triggered by hard aspects with the lord of the ASC. The 12th is related to uncontrolled events, so some sudden and unexpected events may be out of the native's control. Some events related to hospitals, prisons, and other places of confinement may occur. The subconscious of the native may come to the surface during this transit. The native may express his fears and anxieties as well as his undiscovered talents. He may feel nervous if he cannot express his tension (indeed, he may create tension around him). He may also harm himself or, on the contrary, may get rid of some bad habits: for example, he may quit smoking suddenly. The native may also get involved in some secret groups or begin some metaphysical studies during this transit.

Aspects of transiting Uranus

Conjunctions: The conjunctions of transiting Uranus bring changing, awakening, and shocking influences. The reforming quality of this planet is fully manifested. When transiting Uranus conjoins with Mercury, the Sun, the ASC or its lord, these influences effect personal attitudes. A conjunction with the Moon and Venus brings changes in emotions and relationships, Mercury in ideas and self-expression, Mars in actions and ventures, Jupiter in ethical perspectives and beliefs, and Saturn in existing structures, principles, and fears.

Squares and oppositions: Hard aspects bring sudden and unexpected separations, and change is inevitable; outer factors bring and force it. With the opposition, the change stems from others. The sudden and explosive influences of Uranus may bring stress if with sensitive planets like the Moon and Venus: the native may experience explosive emotions. Unexpected shifts of direction in relationships, and a need for freedom which leads to random relationships, may be triggered. The native may be rebellious and unreliable in his relationships. Some hidden facts may be revealed. Accidents may occur if Uranus makes a square or opposition with Mars or the lord of the 8th. The square and opposition with Mercury, the lord of the ASC, and the lord of the MC may bring reforming actions. Preserving existing conditions and stability is hard with the squares and oppositions of Uranus. It would be better for the native to remain patient.

Sextiles and trines: Adapting to changes and reforms is easy with the harmonious aspects of Uranus. The changes are spontaneous and easy without any interruption or pressure from the outer world. The native may act quickly and obtain good results. Creative energies prevail. These aspects are vitalizing. Sextiles and trines with the lords of the ASC and MC and planets in the 1st or 10th houses bring rapid and unexpected achievements.

Transiting Uranus's aspects to natal planets

Uranus–Sun: These aspects may bring important changes and developments in the personality according to the Sun's position and aspects in the nativity. One's individuality is significant during this transit: the native needs freedom to a great extent. When transiting Uranus conjoins the Sun, the native may become interested in subjects like metaphysics, astrology, and technological themes he was not interested in before. He may also experience some unexpected and extraordinary situations related to male figures like the father or husband or authority figures. This is one of the most important periods of the native's life. He may now express his personality in a different style. He may attain some awareness and enlightenment. However, negative aspects may bring a personality crisis. He may act impatiently and nervously. The changes are involuntary and from outside, which force the native to change. The native may experience some stress with people in authority; he may suddenly quit his job or change his goals rapidly. He feels the need to rebel against existing conditions; he is impatient and intolerant. He may have some unexpected health problems. Positive aspects may bring easy changes, with events running smoothly and rapidly. The native may make changes spontaneously and voluntarily. He may express his freedom and individuality clearly. He may get the support of authority figures and powerful or well-known people. The native may gain rapid recognition and find success.

Uranus–Moon: The aspects between difficult Uranus and the emotional Moon may bring instability, uneasiness, and tension. Their conjunction may bring emotional ups and downs, unexpected emotional outbursts, and involuntary attitudes. The native may experience some unexpected problems related to family issues, especially with his mother or wife. Negative aspects may bring more stress in these issues. For example, the native may be separated from his spouse or family (or other separations). He may display his emotions in an aggressive and impatient way. Since the Moon is related to the body, some health problems may cause troubles. The native should review and change his eating habits and lifestyle: the stomach is sensitive with aspects to the Moon. Positive aspects bring rapid and positive changes in the family and housing matters. He may be motivated, as he has attained freedom. The energy of change may be adapted easily to daily life. This period is also beneficial for relationships with women (under positive aspects).

Uranus–Mercury: Uranus's aspects with his lower octave Mercury trigger mental changes and enlightenment. They bring vision and farsightedness. This is an ideal period for mental stimulus, new ideas, and education in different subjects. The native may gain new perspectives. He may be open to discoveries, inventions, and creativity. The native may tend to make rapid decisions, but he should avoid hastiness. The risk in taking such decisions is higher with negative aspects. During this period, the native may utter harsh words and be hurtful. As Mercury represents the nerves, hard aspects with Mercury may bring nervousness, and health problems related to nervous issues. Mental difficulties are also likely, as intellectual activities also prevail during this period. Some changes may be experienced in the themes of communication, agreements, and commitments. It is hard to find stability. With positive aspects, the native may easily express his original ideas without getting too many critical reactions: others easily accept and approve of his opinions. He may easily find solutions to his problems. Positive aspects bring success in mental activities, mathematics, scientific issues, and astrology.

Uranus–Venus: During these aspects, relationships become more active. The native's perspective about them may change, as well as their course. The conjunction may bring an excitement about change. This is a time for love at first sight, excitement in love, and surprises. A shy person may overcome his shyness and may behave in an adventurous way when starting new experiences. Negative aspects may bring random and extraordinary relations, and a superficial approach in them. If the native is unbalanced in his desire for freedom, he may experience some separations and unexpected, nasty situations. If his relationship has been boring, he may look for new love. However, we cannot claim that this is the time for permanent relationships and that the future of the relationship will be a fine one. The native may have relations with some unreliable, weird, and unsuitable people. Positive aspects may bring easy changes and excitement for the native's relationships. The native may have surprising and attractive relationships. Any Uranus-Venus aspects trigger creativity in artistic fields. The tough aspects are more significant in bringing creativity, since the native's creative talents may increase when he experiences relationship imbalances. Conjunctions or tough aspects may bring some health problems related to the bodily parts which are ruled by Venus. Balance disorders or problems related to the reproductive system (especially the ovaries and diabetes) may be triggered.

Uranus–Mars: This is a stressful aspect. Triggering unexpected problems, Uranus may activate the reactive nature of Mars. The conjunction brings high energy and effort, and its results may be either destructive or constructive. Such high voltage energy may cause accidents, fights, separations, and rebellious actions. Outbursts of anger may be experienced. With the square and opposition, the energy may be manifested more harshly. The native may be fearless in any action. On the other hand, trying to suppress this energy may bring worse results. The native may consume all his energy. But positive aspects bring about a balanced use of it: the native may (and should) express himself in athletic activities and similar things. He may be bold in any ventures and get good results. Insofar as he is reasonable in his reactions, he may get good results in any activities where he may defend or even compete with others. He may display his high tempo while being accompanied by an idealistic spirit. The native may display his leadership characteristics. He may affect other people and push them into action.

Uranus–Jupiter: This transit brings positive influences in terms of personal and spiritual development. The native is open to new philosophies and worldviews. This transit supports the changes that the native wants to make, bringing adventures and new experiences. The native wants to reach faraway places and masses of people. With the conjunction, the native may seize opportunities rapidly and benefit from them. However, the opportunities may be lost as fast as they come. Developments are realized quickly; the native is faced with sudden and unexpected events. The native may experience life-changing moments due to surprise educational opportunities, travels abroad, and relations with foreigners. With positive aspects, the native seizes these opportunities easily. Group studies and innovative projects may be on the agenda. With negative aspects, finding luck and opportunities is not that easy, so the native must make some effort. He may experience sudden and unexpected losses. He may question his beliefs and life perspectives. His beliefs may undergo a radical change. He may have problems related to education, publishing, relations with foreigners, and financial issues. He may incur some damages by acting without thinking. This period is not suitable for any speculative activities. The native should watch his steps during this period, as he is prone to some unethical attitudes. He may have some legal problems. Due to his exaggerated need for freedom and expansion, the native may experience ruptures in his normal way of life.

Uranus–Saturn aspects: This is a tough transit. The reforming nature of Uranus challenges Saturn's nature, which tends to preserve the status quo. With the conjunction, the energy of change is around the corner: the native has the chance to experience the change and determine a direction for it. This is a good time for changing old patterns and principles and replacing them with new ones. The unusual and awakening influence of Uranus manifests itself upon Saturn in a very significant way. As a result, the native may experience some changes in his perception of reality and in his life perspective. With positive aspects, the native has the chance to make these changes in a controlled and planned way. He may integrate these changes into his life easily. He may make all necessary changes in his professional and social life easily and without any constraints. He may have the support of authority figures as well. However, with negative aspects, getting this support is highly difficult. Making the necessary changes is also hard, and under the influence of negative aspects the changes themselves are all involuntary: outer factors and events force the native to make them. All existing structures of the native are shaken. He may have financial problems and problems related to real estate. Since Uranus brings a desire for freedom and Saturn represents the conditions that he cannot easily change, hard aspects may lead to health problems like depression.

Saturn transits

Saturn's tour takes 29-30 years, and he stays in each sign for approximately 2.5 years. He retrogrades for 5 months. Saturn transits are important periods of life, indeed the most critical ones, as they determine the course of our lives. Saturn represents rules and structures that are generally accepted. He is related to responsibilities, limitations, and discipline. He shows us the realities of life and our limits within existing conditions. Saturn manifests our responsibilities and life lessons that we should learn, as related to the themes of the house he is in. The tests are fated ones. We remember that we need to fight for the things that we need to get from life. If we do not make an effort, Saturn brings us more troubles and challenges. Saturn transits in the axes of the chart (the 1st, 4th, 7th and 10th) tell us that reviewing and reshaping our lives is compulsory: we need to take more responsibility and be more disciplined. Saturn transits are not easy periods, and the house where Saturn transits indicates both great tension in that area of life and that the native should take responsibilities related to that house. Saturn shows and teaches us the lessons we should learn from that particular field of life.

Saturn transits in natal houses

Saturn in the 1st: When Saturn passes through the ASC and starts his transit in the 1st, old patterns lose their validity. Now it is time for a new cycle when important decisions should be made. During this period the native has to make healthy and realistic decisions, as he is about to redefine himself and reshape his life. He now questions his priorities. He has to focus on himself. He now faces a realistic challenge in life. He has to take more responsibilities, but it may take some time. If Saturn makes positive aspects with the natal planets, then all these changes take place easily. The native may feel physically exhausted and bored during this period. He may lose weight. This is more significant if transiting Saturn is in conjunction or aspect to the lord of the ASC, the lord of the 6th, the Moon, and the Sun. Tough aspects bring health problems.

Saturn in the 2nd: This transit emphasizes that the native should take responsibility for financial issues and other values that he has, and he should be careful with them. It is time for saving and healthy investment, not fantasy projects. The native looks for financial security and support. The native may think that he works a lot, but earns less. He may have some financial problems because of his future plans. He may look for new ways of earning money. He may need to consult some financial experts about financial matters and investments. He has to avoid unnecessary spending and should be more controlled. It is hard to reach economic independence. But the native does not suffer due to financial problems too much if transiting Saturn is in positive aspects with the natal planets, and especially with the lords of the 2nd and 8th. On the other hand, if transiting Saturn is in tough aspects with these planets or the Moon, Sun, or lord of the ASC, the problems in financial matters are more significant. If Saturn is in positive aspects and not retrograde, the native may make investments which are healthy and permanent.

Saturn in the 3rd: This transit emphasizes the need to take on responsibilities related to siblings, close social circles, education, informational and communication themes, and travels. It shows that the native will be focused on mental and educational issues, taking exams, writing, and reading. He may be involved in deep researches: for example, he may work on a thesis. He may also have some problems with those activities: for instance, he may need to work hard in order to complete his researches. He may be pessimistic and anxious. He is now in a period when he is learning how to communicate his ideas. He may have some communication problems. If transiting Saturn is in positive aspects with natal planets, the native may achieve success by being realistic and taking on responsibilities. However, he may have problems with these issues under Saturn's negative aspects. He may have problems with his siblings and relatives. Misunderstandings may bring problems and separations. A sibling may leave home during this transit. Agreements and contracts may pose other problems.

Saturn in the 4th: This indicates that the native may now take some responsibilities related to family and housing themes. This is a time for forming new foundations for the future. During Saturn's transit here, the native may experience challenges concerning his life, career, and future. If transiting Saturn is in tough aspects with natal planets, and especially with the lord of the ASC or MC, or the Sun, the native may hit bottom. But after this period Saturn begins to rise up towards the MC: therefore when Saturn is here, the native should set healthy foundations, should take the right steps, and make correct beginnings for the future. As a result, this is an important transit. During this period, the native's career may be in danger. The native may have some difficulties due to issues related to his family and home. This is more significant when transiting Saturn is in tough aspects with the lords of the ASC or MC, or the Sun itself. Tough aspects with the lord of the 4th, the Sun, or the Moon may bring stress related to parents or the native's family. The native may also move to another house or city.

Saturn in the 5th: This transit emphasizes that the native may now take responsibilities related to children, love and sexuality, and hobbies and stage arts. The native may have to take on responsibilities related to children, even if he had not thought about having a baby before. If the native already has a child, his responsibilities may increase and he may need to take solid and consistent steps. He may have problems related to his children's health. This is especially significant if transiting Saturn is in tough aspects with the lords of the 5th or ASC. If transiting Saturn is in tough aspects with the lords of the ASC or DSC, the lord of the 5th, or Venus, he may have problems related to love and sexuality. He may have an affair with an elderly or mature person represented by Saturn. This is a problematic transit in terms of one's love life. The native may also focus on hobbies and athletic activities, taking on responsibilities or work in these fields. Some restrictions may be experienced if transiting Saturn makes tough aspects with the lord of the 5th or with Mars. There are two alternatives related to having fun: first, he may be isolated from all fun activities; second, he may be so fond of fun that he damages his health. The native is not lucky in stock market activities nor in lotteries.

Saturn in the 6th: During Saturn transits in the house which is related to daily routine, co-workers, subordinates, illnesses, pets, responsibilities and duties, paternal relatives, and talents gained through working, the native needs to reorganize his daily life. He needs to take care of his health and diet. Transiting Saturn's tough aspects with the lords of the 6th or 12th, the Moon, or the Sun may bring health problems. The native has to be more organized during this period, as he must work hard and deal with details. Working that busily may be dangerous for his health. During this period his working conditions may be more difficult than before and his responsibilities may increase. He may not enjoy enough support and performance from his co-workers and subordinates. Some may quit working. He may have some disagreements and challenging conditions at work. His responsibilities may become boring. This is especially significant when transiting Saturn is in tough aspects with the lords of the ASC, MC or 6th. If transiting Saturn makes positive aspects with natal planets, the native may display skill in dealing with the problems. He may easily organize his daily routine.

Saturn in the 7th: This transit brings an important test for one-on-one relationships like marriage, partnerships, and agreements: since Saturn brings responsibilities to the sign it is in, so this transit influences relationships. The native should be realistic and patient with his partners, helping them because their conditions may be difficult, and being ready to talk about their responsibilities. Having trust in the partner is important. The native may also experience separations (especially in useless relationships), and this is easy if transiting Saturn makes positive aspects with natal planets, especially the ASC and DSC, and also with Venus. With hard aspects, the influences come from outer conditions and the native feels obliged to solve the problems somehow. It is time to review close relationships like marriage and partnerships. The native may be criticized or opposed by his competitors. This is a time for learning through relationships. If the native has some problems in his marriage, he should consult a marriage counselor. If the native is married while Saturn transits in the 7th house, his marriage may be a stable and long-lasting one: this is possible if it is in a sign where Saturn feels stronger. Saturn's tough aspects with natal planets also bring the possibility of having legal problems and problems related to his representatives. This is not a proper time for initiating legal cases.

Saturn in the 8th: This transit indicates that the native experiences testing and takes on more responsibilities related to financial issues, inheritances, difficulties, surgical operations, joint earnings and resources, taxes, and expenditures and credits. The native should maintain a balance between his revenue and expenses. He may have difficulties in making payments. He should review all his investments and expenditures and make some revisions according to them. He may experience difficulties and delays related to joint resources and payments and credits. The partner of the native may also have some difficulties in his financial outlook. He may plan to quit his job but should also consider making sure he gets his compensation. Applying for mortgages, others' credit, or asking to borrow money is not recommended; this is more significant when transiting Saturn is in in tough aspects with the lords of the 2nd or 8th, the Sun, Moon, and Lot of Fortune. He may have some difficulties related to inheritance. If transiting Saturn makes tough aspects with the lords of the 6th or 12th, the lord of the 8th, the lord of the ASC, the Sun, or the Moon, the native may experience some danger to life.

Saturn in the 9th: This transit indicates that the native will undergo tests, will gain responsibilities, and will stabilize issues related to foreign affairs, travels, relations with foreigners, academic pursuits, publishing, and legal, religious, and spiritual issues. The native may be interested in new subjects that he did not feel an attraction to before. He may attend trainings and make efforts to maintain his progress. He may reevaluate his life perspective in a realistic way. He may value this period, as he will be disciplined in terms of educational issues. If the native is working in a foreign trade industry, he may need to work harder and be more cautious. Saturn represents the deepest secrets of knowledge, wisdom, science, and philosophy, so during this transit the native may be focused on scientific, religious, and spiritual themes, and may have more knowledge in those areas. This is more significant when transiting Saturn makes positive aspects with the lords of the ASC or 9th, the Sun, Mercury, and Jupiter. If Saturn is in tough aspects with these indicators, then the native has some difficulties while traveling.

Saturn in the 10th: This transit means that the native will be tested in relation to profession, communication with the world, future goals, his status in society, managerial skills, and his relations with people in authority. This transit also shows that the native has to work harder and use all of his strength to be successful. If he has already set powerful foundations in the past, he may now see the results; otherwise, he may be dissatisfied with this period. If transiting Saturn is in tough aspects with the lords of the ASC or MC, the Sun, or the planet which is the indicator of his profession, the native may have to change jobs or he may be unsuccessful. In any case, it is a time to be determined and patient in the area of the native's work: the success will probably come when Saturn leaves the house. The native may be steered towards subjects unfamiliar to him, which may cause anxiety. It is also the time to focus on work instead of the joyful areas of life. Because of this need to concentrate on work, the native may feel lonely and push his loved ones into the background. He is now only focused on his profession, responsibilities and obligations, and his need to obtain social approval. The native should be cautious when transiting Saturn is in tough aspects with natal planets, as his social prestige and career may be affected negatively. He may be disgraced due to attitudes which are disapproved of.

Saturn in the 11th: This transit indicates that the native will be tested and take responsibilities in relation to his social circle and friends, organizations, group activities, hopes, and income coming from his profession. He may take on responsibilities in some team activities and organizations. He may play a role in clubs and charities, and display devotion to them. If transiting Saturn is in positive aspects with the lords of the ASC, MC, 11th, or with the Sun, the native may easily overcome his responsibilities and be successful. On the other hand, tough aspects prevent success and the native may struggle a lot. On a personal level, he may have difficulties in making new friends and may be separated from friends due to differences of opinion. He may experience some restrictions, health problems, and even death in relation to his friends. The native may see some of his friends separating from him. Under the influence of tough aspects, the native may have difficulties in preserving his social status. Others may question his leadership qualities. He may experience restrictions related to long-term investments, and his income from his actions may decrease. Positive aspects planets bring better results.

Saturn in the 12th : This transit shows that the native is preparing for a new cycle, as this is a house of preparation (a cadent house) before taking initiative (the 1st, an angular house). Saturn transiting in the area where old and dissatisfying energy must be left behind, displays his nature significantly. Bad habits may be gotten rid of, with some other problems coming to the surface. The native may feel tense. However, this is also a period of purification. Since the 12th is related to uncontrollable factors, anxieties, secret enemies and illnesses, these topics will be pertinent. His tough aspects may be problematic. It is easy to be purified of fears and anxieties if transiting Saturn is in positive aspects with the lords of the ASC or 12th, the Sun, Moon, and natal Saturn. As the 12th house is related to secret enemies, the native may see some behind-the-scenes actions against him. He has to be careful, especially if transiting Saturn is in tough aspects with the natal indicators. In any case, it is not the time to force existing conditions. Instead of being outgoing and active, the native should stay in and turn inwards; he should consider reviewing his own dynamics. This is an ideal time for meditations, as it may bring wisdom.

Aspects of transiting Saturn

Conjunctions: Saturn's conjunctions bring responsibilities. Now is a time to be aware of and shoulder our responsibilities, since there is nowhere to run from them. Being realistic and deliberate is necessary for making sound steps forward. This aspect brings depression, frustration, and restriction. The native may feel these effects physically: for instance, he may lose weight, feel exhausted and bored, or have some health problems. (Depression is a common health problem caused by Saturn's conjunctions.) On the other hand, by taking healthy steps and being persistent, the native may bring his projects into manifestation.

Squares and oppositions: Saturn's nature is similar to that of the opposition. Since the opposition brings distance, criticism, and hard reality (which are also themes of Saturn), the oppositions of transiting Saturn will bring similar results and reveal his influences to a maximal degree. The squares are also difficult aspects: the native's responsibilities may increase, he may have problems in getting the approval of the VIPs in his life, or may be restricted and criticized. Health problems, melancholy, and depression are also influences of Saturn's tough aspects.

Sextiles and trines: With the positive aspects, the native may be productive and manifest himself. However, even though these are positive aspects, since Saturn is involved the native has to work hard and make an effort to maintain progress and achieve success. Saturn's aspects do not bring success easily. The native has to pay the price of success, but the result is permanent and firm. The positive aspects of Saturn bring support from authority figures. The native may overcome his responsibilities in an easier way, accepting them and doing whatever is needed—so the risk of being criticized is lower.

Transiting Saturn's aspects to natal planets

Saturn–Sun: As both Saturn and the Sun are related to authority, all Saturn-Sun aspects emphasize the native's relations with authority figures and the degree of his own authority. The conjunction of transiting Saturn with the natal Sun indicates that responsibilities are knocking at the door, and there is no escape. The native may enjoy permanent results if he embraces the necessary responsibilities, but this may not be easy since Saturn does not like easy achievements. The native has to work hard and pay the price. The Saturn–Sun conjunction teaches life lessons and brings patience and maturity. It is better to accept responsibilities willingly. These responsibilities may bring issues to the surface which are related to goals or male figures like the father, husband, or boss. The native may be busy in his business life. He may have new ventures. He needs to work a lot in an organized way in order to be successful during this period. Saturn demands self-discipline and a sense of mission. Being realistic and cautious is crucial. The native may also be isolated and feel lonely, which is more likely if the Sun is in the 12th or rules that house. Negative aspects between the transiting Saturn and natal Sun slow down progress: authority figures may hinder the native instead of giving support, the native may face heavy criticism, and he risks losing prestige. The native may feel exhausted because of the responsibilities, but should be patient. Tough aspects may also bring health problems, including those related to the native's father or husband or other male figures. If the aspects between transiting Saturn and the natal Sun are positive ones, the native may find success more easily. However, he again needs to be organized and work hard. He may get the support of male authority figures and experience a rise in his professional status.

Saturn–Moon: Saturn has a tough nature and represents being at a distance, so he does not blend well with the Moon, who is empathetic and emphasizes emotional security and a need for belonging. With the Saturn–Moon conjunction, emotions are suppressed. The native may feel emotionally reserved. He may not find the sympathy he needs. He may have some responsibilities related to women such as the mother or wife. He may have to restrict himself with respect to his eating habits, as he needs to take responsibility for his body. This is a tough transit in terms of health issues: the native is open to depression, especially if the aspects are negative, and he may have problems related to the stomach, lungs, breasts or chest, and hormones. He may also need to face harsh realities and responsibilities. He may have problems related to female figures in his life, and the home and family front may also require responsibility. For example, the native may have to move his house or change the arrangement of certain things at home. If the aspects are positive, then the native may easily overcome the problems which stem from these responsibilities. However, he will not be emotionally free. This is a time for maintaining an objective and realistic approach towards events. This aspect is good for making arrangements at home, buying or selling a house, and reorganizing family relations. The native may make some arrangements related to wining and dining, family matters, marriage, and other themes related to this house.

Saturn–Mercury: Saturn's discipline activates Mercury's themes of systematic thinking and concentration. This influence is highly significant when these two planets are conjoined. As the native may focus his mind, he may turn to learning new things and get involved in mental activities without feeling scattered. This transit supports being decisive and logical. The native may find success with the help of his planning skills, but may also be pessimistic and anxious; he may have a narrow perspective. He may have problems in communication and anxiety about being misunderstood, especially when the aspects are difficult. With the difficult aspects, he may not express himself easily, and his freedom of speech may be prevented. He may have problems related to the nervous system, speech and hearing, and mental issues. He may have difficulties in proving his ideas. He may experience delays and restrictions in contractual agreements and any other thing which requires a signature. He may experience communication problems and misunderstandings. He may be hidebound and prejudiced. He may have difficulties in dealing with the realities of life, and being realistic and materialistic may make the native feel depressed. However, positive aspects between these two planets help the native express himself and prove his ideas easily. He does not have difficulties in being focused, and may flow along easily with the realities of life. This transit may be a suitable time for forming plans and organizations, for signing agreements, and making long-term decisions.

Saturn–Venus: This is one of the hardest aspects. The conjunction and other aspects of the restricting and distanced Saturn with the joyful and intimate Venus, always bring seriousness and distance in one's relations. This is a time to be serious and realistic in relationships, and the native takes responsibility for them. On the positive side, this aspect may bring fated, stable, and permanent relationships like marriage. The native becomes more controlled and steady in them even if he did not succeed before. On the negative side, this period may bring restrictions and depression in relationships. The native may prefer creating delays within the relationship and isolating himself. He may restrict himself in matters of wining and dining. A relationship may break up when these two planets are in tough aspects; in general, problems and separations may come to the surface. The native may realize that his relationship is not the one he expected: he feels dissatisfied, anxious, and frightened about it. He may feel dissatisfied about his whole life and may not spend time on the pleasures of life. He may have problems in all of his cooperative ventures as well as aesthetic issues like decoration. When these two planets have positive aspects, the native may easily maintain trust and the continuation of his relationships; he may have a realistic approach to the necessary responsibilities, and know and get what he expects from a relationship. This period brings maturity through relationships as well as interactions with elderly or mature people. Getting positive results from common projects is more likely.

Saturn–Mars: Both of these planets represent stress and challenges, so their aspects bring difficult, problematic, and challenging situations. Saturn's restrictive nature is not compatible with the activating nature of Mars. When they conjoin, the native wants to take action but cannot. Taking quick action is not easy and requires patience: this is the time to act slowly and cautiously. The native experiences challenges and needs endurance; success is achieved through hard work and effort. The native's health may be badly affected as his energy level decreases. He may feel exhausted, restricted, and stressed. He may lose his motivation. When the aspects between these two planets are tough, the native has to make put forth too much effort in overcoming problems. He may also face competition in his professional life. He may have some problems and conflict with male figures, experience some dangerous situations, undergo surgical operations and experience some losses. The suppressed energy may bring harsh results when the energy is unleashed. Fatigue, loss of energy and motivation, health problems related to the body's defense mechanism, or muscle diseases, are likely. When the aspects are the positive ones, the native has a chance to balance this energy. He may use correct timing to undertake actions. He has a chance to make progress patiently, make the necessary interventions and take an effective amount of risk. The native may find success if he makes an effort and is well organized.

Saturn–Jupiter: Saturn's restrictive and narrowing nature is not compatible with the expanding and freedom-seeking nature of Jupiter. So, Saturn-Jupiter aspects are difficult aspects even though they have the potential for being used positively. For example, the conjunction brings the chance for balanced, planned, and organized development. This period requires patience, but the consequences of the aspect help the native develop a sound view of life. The native may acquire wisdom and maturity, and his optimism is limited. The native needs to be cautious: instead of being a dreamer, he needs to be involved in realistic projects. He may achieve tangible success, but may not quite attain the expansion and development he hopes for: some limitation still exists. He may experience restrictions or at least delays regarding educational issues as well as finances. When the aspects are tough, the native's development and freedom in his growth are restricted. He may not be able to use his resources easily in achieving success. He may also have difficulties in balancing his beliefs and values. The positive side of these tough aspects is that they prevent exaggeration and unbalanced growth: Saturn's transit moderates Jupiter's extremes. When the aspects are positive, planned and organized growth is possible. Projects get more tangible and planned growth is maintained. The native may win the support of influential people. As compared to the tough aspects, positive aspects may bring some good opportunities in professional life, finances, and education. This transit may also help the native's spiritual development.

Jupiter transits

Jupiter's tour in the zodiac takes 12 years. He stays in each sign for about 1 year, and emphasizes the themes of the house he transits during that year. He retrogrades for approximately 4 months. Jupiter brings enlargement, development, and richness together with peace, protection, and collaboration. He is the most benefic planet. We are open to opportunities in the areas signified by the house in which Jupiter transits, and try to develop ourselves in that field. This development may be on spiritual, physical, mental, or material levels, as well as in relationships and health matters. Jupiter opens our path, whereas Saturn restricts us. Jupiter is also related to education: he brings knowledge and wisdom and the desire for learning and researching. The native may improve himself in philosophical, religious, and spiritual fields. The ancient astrologers associate Jupiter with finances, so his positive aspects may bring good news about finances. Transiting Jupiter brings self-confidence. Opportunities fall into the native's lap. Jupiter's transits are also socially expanding, bringing solidarity; Jupiter is also related to moral and legal issues. As the native may be over-glad and over-confident, he may experience the negativity of this transit: risks incurred due to exaggeration.

Jupiter transits in natal houses

Jupiter in the 1st: This transit is an indicator of a lucky period. The native now realizes his wishes, comes closer to the things he wants to achieve, has the opportunity to manage conditions as he likes, and his self-confidence increases. The native wins others' trust, gets support from his closest circles, attracts the resources of others, and uses them in an advantageous way. When transiting Jupiter makes positive aspects with the lords of the ASC, MC, 11th, 8th, or with the Sun, the native may benefit easily from these advantages. The native is optimistic about the results of his ventures and his success. However, he should well define the limits of this optimism: he may meet with many opportunities and trample all of them because of over-optimism and confidence. This is especially possible when transiting Jupiter makes tough aspects with the lord of the ASC, with the Sun or Mercury, or the lord of the MC. Jupiter brings advantages related to new interests, travels, and education. This is a beneficial transit for learning new things and having new experiences. If Jupiter is well placed in the natal chart and transiting

Jupiter makes positive aspects with the natal planets, the native may make a start in a new business or other new ventures. This is also a positive period in terms of personal and spiritual development, or moral and religious themes; it expands the native's horizons. However, this transit may also bring physical expansion, which means that the native may gain too much weight. Being fond of luxury and spending too much money are the risks of this transit.

Jupiter in the 2nd: Traditionally, this transit represents earning money and getting rich. During Jupiter's year here the native may have an increase in his earnings, and his talents for earning and managing money are developed. He may discover new ways of increasing his income, and new investment methods. He may receive new commercial and business proposals. During this transit, the native feels satisfied about his possessions: he earns a satisfying income and gains financial independence. His possessions may gain more value. If transiting Jupiter makes positive aspects or a conjunction with the lord of the natal 2nd or 8th, the native has chances and opportunities in financial matters. As his income increases, he feels more confident and brave, but he may tend to take risks and make exaggerated moves in his ventures; this is more significant when Jupiter makes tough aspects with the above-mentioned indicators. The native should decide what he really wants and approach that field in order to earn his income, rather than being scattered across different fields. Exaggerated expenses and arrogance are the problematic influences of this transit. If Jupiter is in positive aspects with the lord of the DSC or 8th, the native may benefit from the advice of experienced people or experts in finances. He may get support and advice from his trusted fellows. This transit is the best time for investments.

Jupiter in the 3rd: This transit shows that the native will experience important developments and opportunities in fields related to siblings, relations within his close circle, mental activities, communication, short distance travels, education, and writing and reading skills. The native's life perspective expands and his prejudices decrease. He makes plans for the future. He may reach out to masses of people through his ideas, especially when transiting Jupiter makes positive aspects or a conjunction with the lord of the 3rd or 9th, Mercury, and the Sun. He may gain optimism in his views on life and may transmit those optimistic thoughts to others. He may have some opportunities to express his ideas: for instance, he may give lectures, be present in the social media, or write and publish books. He may also have the chance to develop his mental skills. He may engage in research, collect materials, and enrich his projects. He may be interested in Divine wisdom, spirituality, and philosophy. He may be skilled in commercial agreements and use this experience in his career. He is open to his closest circles during this transit, getting financial and moral support and benefits from them. Jupiter brings modesty and peace to each house he enters, so this transit helps the native make peace with his close friends and relatives, and offers him the chance to see his relatives who live far away. Not only the native but also his siblings benefit from this transit. The native may travel more and seize some opportunities while travelling. This is a suitable time for having important meetings and making agreements.

Jupiter in the 4th: The native may get chances and opportunities related to family and housing issues. For example, the native may buy a house or other real estate, or move to another location; this is more likely if transiting Jupiter is in positive aspects or a conjunction with the lords of the ASC, 4th, or 7th, or with any natal planets placed in the 4th. This transit has positive influences on family relations as well as expansion within the family and increased opportunities within it. The native may get support from his family, and family members are generous to each other. Peace and security at home is maintained. If transiting Jupiter is in positive aspects with the lord of the 4th or ASC, or with the Moon, this is a beautiful period in terms of maintaining inner peace and peace within family relationships.

Jupiter in the 5th: During the year of this transit, the native may experience positive developments related to children, romance, creative ideas, artistic talents, joyful activities, and vacations. This period is a positive one if the native wants to have baby. If he already has children, then he may see positive developments concerning them. He may make investments for his children, especially when transiting Jupiter is in a positive aspect with the lords of the 5th or 10th. This transit may increase the native's creativity. He may express himself in a strong and holistic manner or in artistic works, and he may make a better profit. He may spend more time on his hobbies and athletic activities. He may also experience positive developments in his love life: love and sexuality may offer more pleasure. He may experience romantic relations with people from different cultures and with experienced people, or his existing relationships may become more exciting. He may also be more social and attend many social events and parties, especially when transiting Jupiter is in a conjunction or aspect with the lords of the ASC, 5th, or 11th. However, the native may be exposed to risk because of an exaggerated sense of fun. Speculative fields like stock market transactions may also be risky, especially when transiting Jupiter is in tough aspects with the lords of the 2nd, 5th, or 8th, or with Mars.

Jupiter in the 6th: During the year of this transit, the native may experience positive developments regarding his health, business relations and conditions, and receive the support of his coworkers and subordinates. He may have opportunities related to his working conditions. He may develop his working skills and conditions, especially when transiting Jupiter makes positive aspects with the lord of the ASC, 10th, or 6th, or with the Sun. The native feels happy at the office during this transit. He may be as successful as his responsibilities are powerful, and overcome them to the same extent. However, these are not great successes because the 6th house is one of the cadent houses: Jupiter brings success in the 10th house more so than in the 6th. As the 6th house represents the native's subordinates, their promotion and successes are more likely, especially when transiting Jupiter makes positive aspects or a conjunction with the lord of the 6th or 3rd (which is the 10th house from the 6th). The native may get maximal performance from his subordinates and benefit from their skills. As the 6th house is the house of illness and diseases, Jupiter's transit through this house brings healing. If the native is in a period of healing during this transit, he may recover quickly, especially when transiting Jupiter makes positive aspects with the lord of the ASC or 6th, with the Moon, or with the health indicator in the chart. Jupiter's transit in the 6th is also beneficial for quitting bad habits. The native should reorganize his daily routine and spend time in athletic activities.

Jupiter in the 7th: The native has opportunities related to 7th house issues, as the house of partnerships is energized: this is an ideal transit for marriage and business partnerships. If the natal chart promises it, the native may have a partner or spouse with good financial prospects. He may meet with important and prestigious people, in both their private and professional lives. Since Jupiter represents foreigners, the native may marry or form a business partnership with a foreigner. The 7th house is the place where we are seen by others, so during Jupiter's transit here the native's success is easily noted. He may receive social support and be respected by others. He may be successful in a consulting business. He may get positive advice from experts such as doctors, lawyers, financial consultants, or astrologers. People from different cultures and backgrounds may expand the native's horizon. Legal problems may be solved during this transit. Jupiter transits do not bring any negative influence in this house, but empty promises and high expectations may bring risks, especially during tough aspects of the lord of the ASC or 7th with the transiting Jupiter.

Jupiter in the 8th: This transit is related to joint resources, death and inheritances, and metaphysics. This house represents financial themes which are out of the native's own control, benefiting from others' opportunities, or facing losses due to the losses of others. This transit shows that people in the native's life (like his partner or spouse) will experience an expansion in cash flow. This is especially possible when transiting Jupiter makes positive aspects with the lords of the ASC, DSC, 2nd, or 8th. The 8th house is also the house of dangers. So, transiting Jupiter in this house protects the native against danger as Jupiter is the greater benefic: for instance, if the native has to undergo a surgical operation, Jupiter's transit in the 8th house helps and protects him. This house is also related to credits, debts, and payments, so Jupiter's transit here may help with those payments. The native may see support from others. He may also recover what is owed to him during this transit. Insurance payments, child support, and alimony are also themes of this house: the native has positive developments in these fields and overcomes all problems. As the 8th house represents joint resources, the native may utilize money that is owned in common. If transiting Jupiter makes tough aspects with natal planets like the lords of the ASC, 2nd, or 8th, then expenses may be exaggerated and the native may suffer due to his debts and credit payments. However, if Jupiter does not make positive aspects with natal planets, then this would be a good time in terms of gaining credits or debts.

Jupiter in the 9th: During this transit, the native may experience positive developments in issues related to long-distance travel, foreigners, education, publishing and broadcasting, and religious beliefs and philosophies. Travels—whether for business or pleasure—may bring luck and opportunities, and should be joyous. These travels especially expand the native's horizons when transiting Jupiter makes positive aspects with the lords of the ASC, 9th, or 3rd, or with the Sun, Jupiter or Mercury. The native may travel for religious purposes. The 9th house also represents activities with foreigners, tourism, international issues, and foreign trade: so, his transit here indicates advantages and profit in these fields, especially when transiting Jupiter makes positive aspects with the lords of the MC, 2nd, 8th, and 11th. Jupiter's nature represents wisdom and knowledge and increases the desire for learning and researching, so the native has the possibility of development in philosophical, religious, and spiritual fields. This transit is also beneficial for giving lectures. Educational issues may bring success, and foreign education is likely. All of these things are more significant when transiting Jupiter is in a conjunction or positive aspect with the lords of the ASC, 3rd, or 9th, or with Mercury. If transiting Jupiter makes tough aspects with the above-mentioned indicators, the native may have difficulties in the associated fields. He may foolishly waste all of his opportunities.

Jupiter in the 10th: At this time the native may experience positive developments in issues related to his business life and career, goals, and communication with the outer world and other powerful people. He may express his actions better and display them to the public. This transit may bring an increase in social status, reputation, and prestige. The native's talents, as related to his job and his ability to manage people, may develop. He may get some awards or prizes. This is an ideal time for taking new steps in one's career. When transiting Jupiter makes positive aspects with the MC or the lord of the 11th house, with the lord of the ASC or with the Sun or the professional indicator, the native may have high goals. He may get the support of authority figures or have interesting opportunities related to his career. He may benefit from his career education or get some training which helps him make career progress. As Jupiter rules travel, he may travel for business purposes. He may make agreements with foreigners or bring his career into the international arena. The projects which he did not care about in the past may be back on the agenda. Jupiter's tough aspects with the above-mentioned indicators may challenge him. He may take on too much risk and get involved in hard-to-achieve ventures.

Jupiter in the 11th: Here the native may see positive developments in group activities and social life. Jupiter is the natural lord of the 11th house, and as the 11th house is the house of great luck, Jupiter is a planet of great luck, too. The native may seize on many opportunities during this transit. As the 11th house is also the house of hopes and wishes, the native's hopes and ideals about the future increase. He now sees the results of his past ventures. He may benefit from his social relations and meet with people who help his career progress. He may get the support of his friends and get advice from those whom he respects. He may be involved in social events and charitable activities, and this transit is ideal for starting such organizations. His professional earnings may increase. All these positive influences are more significant when transiting Jupiter makes positive aspects with the lords of the ASC, MC, 11th, 7th, and with the Sun. Jupiter's tough aspects with these indicators brings the risk of arrogance and exaggeration.

Jupiter in the 12th: During this transit the native may experience some positive or negative developments concerning the themes of that house. Jupiter's influence here is not as significant as in the other houses because this is the most hidden part of the chart. The native may learn a lot about himself; he may discover his hidden talents. This is a kind of preparation period for the future. He may now discover his inner wisdom and his creativity; he may establish his future goals and prepare himself for those. This is a time for inner peace. The native may heal psychologically due to Jupiter's presence in this house. The partner's health problems may also be solved. The native may quit his addictions and solve his own problems, or even work for the good of others. He may help people who are in need, but in a disguised manner. He may also get help from others. As the 12th house is related to hidden enemies, when transiting Jupiter makes tough aspects with the natal ASC or the lords of the MC or 12th, or with Mars or Saturn, hidden hostilities and behind-the-scenes actions may be triggered.

Aspects of transiting Jupiter

Conjunctions: Jupiter's conjunctions generally bring positive results. Jupiter expands, develops, and liberates the qualities of the planet he conjoins with. For instance, if Jupiter is in conjunction with Mercury, the native's vision expands, and he learns independent thinking and optimism. Of course, this over-confidence may incur high costs as the native tends to get involved in numerous ventures. As his conjunctions bring prosperity and richness, this prosperity may be felt on the emotional, mental, or physical level.

Squares and oppositions: Jupiter's negative aspects do not bring too much harm, as Jupiter is a benefic planet and we always expect goodness from Jupiter. So his tough aspects do not bring restrictions and limitations, but rather a kind of expansion and prosperity: therefore, concepts like deformation, degeneration, and wastefulness are more accurate here.

Sextiles and trines: Jupiter's positive aspects, especially the trine, help conditions develop smoothly. These aspects are also of Jupiter's own nature, so the trine may double his influence. The native's efforts and projects get easier and expand. The influences of Jupiter may be felt via rapid development and in positive and early results. Enrichment, independence, enlight-enment, and spiritual themes are influenced by Jupiter's positive aspects.

Transiting Jupiter's aspects to natal planets

Jupiter–Sun: The natures of the Sun and Jupiter are similar: both of them are related to self-confidence, hope, honesty, and generosity. Consequently, aspects between transiting Jupiter and the natal Sun are generally positive. Their conjunction brings an important opportunity in terms of personal de-velopment. The native shows physical and spiritual progress. His optimism and self-confidence increase, but his ego may also increase (which is prob-lematic). This transit may also bring fame and recognition, especially when the conjunction takes place in one of the angular houses (the 1st, 10th, 7th, and 4th). The native gets the support of authority figures, his charisma and power increase, and his relations with his father get better. The native may easily achieve success and reputation. The native may be famous if his natal chart also promises it. He may reach an important point in his career. Others accept his leadership and approve his decisions without any imposition. This transit is also good for health. When Jupiter and the Sun are in tough aspects, the native may have difficulties in getting approval or he exaggerates every-thing. He may have power struggles with his father or with those who treat him like a father, and with other male authority figures. However, if he can find the right balance, he may find success—he may even achieve sudden popularity. The important point here is that the native should avoid inflating his ego and arrogance, and should not foolishly throw away his advantages.

Jupiter–Moon: The natures of the Moon and Jupiter have some similari-ties; both of them are caring and growing. When transiting Jupiter makes a conjunction with the natal Moon, the native feels a need for caring and being cared for; his need for belonging increases. He may need to build a family. He may be more emotional than ever, and may even exaggerate his emo-tions, but will be skilled at expressing them. He may have emotional reactions to events which he did not react to before. He feels optimistic and spiritually strong. He may have good relations with female figures, especially his mother and wife. He may have positive developments in health, family, and personal emotional issues. This transit is suitable for pregnancy in female charts. This transit is suitable for marriage, moving to another house and buying or selling real estate. When the aspects are tough ones, the native's emotions may be exaggerated, bringing outbursts in inappropriate places and times. The native may experience unbalanced relations with female figures such as the mother or wife. He may suddenly have to move to another house, which creates emotional imbalance. However, Jupiter's tough aspects do not bring negative consequences.

Jupiter–Mercury: The natures of Jupiter and Mercury are contrary to each other: Jupiter represents believing whereas Mercury represents questioning and logic. The conjunction between transiting Jupiter and natal Mercury may bring mental development. The native starts being more optimistic, and instead of questioning life he starts to have optimistic expectations and trusts in life's conditions. People who are talented in writing and speaking benefit from this transit. The native may develop his language skills and handicrafts. His self-confidence increases and his perspective enlarges. This is an enlightening transit. When the aspects are positive, the native's perspective shows an easy progress: his worries and anxieties decrease and even disappear for a while, he feels hopeful about the future, and he liberalizes. This is also a suitable transit for travel, education, publishing, and broadcasting. The native may easily convince others. This is a good period for making important agreements, speeches, and discussions. When the aspects are tough, the native may be scattered because of the range of his extensive ideas. He may be mentally exhausted due to being involved in too many subjects. He may be offered a choice between different options and have difficulties in making a decision. He may be confused by different ideas and question everything. He may speak in an exaggerated manner, jump from one subject to another, and lack concentration. The extensive flow of information strains the native's nerves: he should take care with his words when the aspects of these planets are tough ones.

Jupiter–Venus: Jupiter and Venus are benefic planets. All aspects between these two planets bring generally positive results, with there being an increase in love, emotions, romantic opportunities and relationships, and creativity. The transiting Jupiter-natal Venus conjunction brings a positive atmosphere and attractiveness for the native. He may achieve success through his sympathy, attractiveness, and good relations with others. He may be fond of life's pleasures; he likes to have a luxurious and high-quality life. He may also display some laziness. He has opportunities in love and relationships. This is also an ideal transit for marriage and business partnerships. When the aspects are positive, the energy in love and relationships flows easily. Such a period is the best time for marriages and business partnerships. The native may also have surgery for aesthetic reasons and engage in other efforts related to personal care and beauty. He has good relations with everyone, and as a result he is accepted everywhere. This transit also brings positive influences in artistic issues, as creativity flows smoothly. When the aspects between Jupiter and Venus are tough ones, then the native may indulge in eating and drinking, incur high expenses for clothing, and exaggerate the pleasures of life; being too lavish is likely. The native may also wear out his luck in love and relationships. Exaggerated social relations and activities may also affect his health. He may gain weight. However, if he can maintain some balance, then he does not necessarily experience these negative influences.

Jupiter–Mars: Jupiter and Mars have both similar and opposite natures. Their similarities are adventurousness, innovation, courage, and exaggeration. However, while Jupiter naturally tends towards belief, Mars has a problem in believing due to his rebellious nature. Jupiter is ethical and faithful, Mars has a tendency to be anomalous. Transiting Jupiter-natal Mars aspects challenge existing conditions. Their conjunction triggers courage and the need for discovery. The native's energy and power increases and the body's defense mechanism works well. This is a good transit for athletic activities, especially for building muscles and physical growth. Similar influences are seen when these planets have positive aspects: the native may initiate new ventures, show his leadership and courage, and see rapid and important results in his works. They also brings positive influences in matters related to health. The native displays a balanced courage. However, tough aspects bring risks: he may display exaggerated courage and try to force conditions, getting into trouble, losing himself in fights and competition; as a result he may stray from his main goals. The same is true for athletic activities: for instance, he may overdevelop his muscles or take risks in extreme sports. He may act in a fanatical manner in religious, moral, and Divine themes. He may take great risks in financial matters. Of course, all of these things should be evaluated according to the Mars' position in the natal chart.

Jupiter–Saturn: Jupiter and Saturn have opposite natures: Jupiter represents expansion, while Saturn represents restriction; Jupiter is related to optimism, Saturn to pessimism. When transiting Jupiter aspects natal Saturn, the native tries to overcome pessimism, restrictions, and anxiety. He may also try to overcome financial difficulties. He may take healthy and stable steps towards the future. This is more significant in matters related to his career. Taking sound steps will be easier if the natal Saturn is well aspected by the other planets. If they make tough aspects to natal Saturn, overcoming and changing existing patterns will be more difficult and take more time. When the aspects are positive, the native may easily overcome challenges, easily maintaining freedom and expansion in otherwise restricted areas of life. Positive aspects between transiting Jupiter and natal Saturn also bring positive influences in financial issues and the career life. The beliefs of the native will fit into place, and positive expectations are likely in fields like education, travel, and legal matters. When the aspects are tough, all these developments are hard to achieve so the native must challenge existing conditions. Things do not flow easily. The native has to experience some hard experiences before attaining the desired vision. He may not feel at ease in financial matters. Melancholy, depression, fears, and anxiety may increase. The native has to spend much effort in balancing all of these.

Mars transits

Mars's transit in the zodiac takes 22 months, and he spends approximately 2 months in each sign. Once in nearly every two years, Mars retrogrades for 80 days. This planet has the potential to trigger and activate. It represents how we use our energy and how we take action, as well as our survival capacity, physical endurance, muscle force, and the defense system of our body. Mars gives us the physical power we need. When this energy is too active during a transit, we are prone to accidents and quarrels. On the other hand, as he also rules the body's defense mechanism, under the influence of tough aspects the resistance of the body to illness may collapse and we may be open to infectious diseases. Mars is also related to high fevers. The house where Mars transits, shows us in which area of life we should devote our energy and effort, as well as the threats we face. If Mars transits in one of the angular houses (the 1st, 4th, 7th and 10th) it does not bring as tough an influence as Saturn does, because Mars does not stay in those houses for as long as Saturn does.

Mars transits in natal houses

Mars in the 1st: This transit triggers the drive for taking action, manifesting the personality, and making new attempts at things. The native feels active, dynamic, and energetic. He is also impatient due to this high-voltage energy, so he may be open to accidents and injuries. He has very high self-confidence. He likes taking the initiative and gaining independence. He may have a dominating attitude for getting approval for his demands, and force existing conditions to go his way. He may also be rude if the natal chart supports that idea. He may be aggressive. The negative side of this transit is the risk of highly bold decisions which are taken inconsiderately. Another negative feature of this transit is that the native may ignore others due to his inflated ego.

Mars in the 2nd: Due to this transit, Mars's energy is directed towards financial matters. The native is motivated to earn money, and is courageous and aggressive in financial ventures. However, he may need to fight to maintain the financial security and income that he deserves. He may experience some fluctuations in his regular income. Mars also makes him spend more money during this transit; his expenses may increase. The native may experience some losses due to hasty decisions if transiting Mars is in tough aspects with the lords of the ASC, 2nd, or 8th houses, the Lot of Fortune, or the planet which is the financial indicator of the chart. If transiting Mars is in positive aspects with those indicators, then the native may make new attempts and take financial risks successfully.

Mars in the 3rd: During this transit, the native's relationships within his close circle are on the agenda. Due to Mars's nature, the native may experience some aggression in those relations. This is more significant if transiting Mars is in tough aspects with the lords of the natal 3rd or 9th houses, the lords of the natal ASC or DSC, or the natal Mars, Sun, Moon, or Mercury. Transiting Mars provokes the desire to have the freedom to act as he likes. The native may become interested in many subjects, as he wants to learn new things. He may need to make rapid decisions due to accelerated events in his close circle. He may want to express his ideas powerfully, and prefers a quarrelsome style in doing so. He may have discussions with others who do not share his opinions. The native may also be exposed to accidents in traffic and on his travels. This is more significant when transiting Mars is in tough aspects with natal planets. Under the influence of positive aspects, the native may have an active attitude in education, travels, and in the relationships within his close circle. This transit also represents efforts undertaken for siblings and the close relatives.

Mars in the 4th: This house rules the home and family while Mars represents anger, debates and competition. So, this transit may cause stress, debates, problems and even separations within the family. This is the time to be more tolerant in family relations. As Mars triggers the problems, any difficulty may turn into a big problem. This is more significant when transiting Mars is in tough aspect to the lord of the 4th, the Sun, or the Moon. This transit is also related to security at home. As Mars is related to thieves in traditional astrology, during this transit necessary security precautions should be taken in order to avoid home accidents. The native should be extremely careful if transiting Mars is in tough aspects with the lord of the ASC, the lord of IC, the Sun, the Moon, and Mars in natal chart. When transiting Mars is in positive aspects with the natal planets, the native may take steps in important projects for the future. He may move to another house or be involved in renovation or restoration projects.

Mars in the 5th: During this transit the native prefers to be involved in love and romance, matters related to children, artistic talents, sports, and speculative and risky ventures. He may be especially involved in athletic activities during Mars's transit here. If transiting Mars is in positive aspects with the natal planets, the native may use his energy in an athletic way in order to be stronger and balance his energy. His creativity is triggered and he likes acting with a motivational attitude. Love and sexuality are also emphasized. The native should watch out for his children's health, guard against accidents, and should not take bold risks if transiting Mars is in tough aspects with the lord of the 5th or natal planets in it. This is not a good time for new ventures relating to children. The 5th house is related to fun and entertainment, so the native may enjoy attending parties and having fun during this transit; of course he needs to maintain balance and should not go overboard in his fun. If transiting Mars is in tough aspects with the lords of the 2nd or 8th or with the Lot of Fortune, the native should avoid taking risks and any speculative actions in lotteries and stock markets.

Mars in the 6th: This transit is related to daily routine and activities, and one's whole energy and effort is used for them. In this period, the tempo is high with too much work to do. Mars brings aggression into the house he is in, so making quick decisions may bring negative results for the native. If transiting Mars is in tough aspects with the lords of the 6th or 10th, the Sun, and the indicator of the occupation, the native experiences some turbulence surrounding his working life. He may have some problems related to his coworkers and subordinates, and there may be some exaggerated and aggressive competition. Due to there being too many projects needing to be completed, the native may feel aggressive: he may not be patient towards coworkers, and be so pushy that the problems get bigger and bigger. The native should exercise both physically and spiritually to avoid projecting his nervous problems onto others; weightlifting allows the increasing energy to be used well. The native should be careful about his health in general. This is more significant if transiting Mars is in tough aspects with the lords of the 6th or 12th, or the Sun or Moon. The native may be successful in his ventures and get the support of his coworkers and subordinates if transiting Mars is in positive aspects with the lords of the 6th and 10th, the lord of the ASC, and the Sun.

Mars in the 7th: Here, all energy and effort is focused on one-to-one relationships like marriage and partnerships. Aggression, competition, and battles in relationships may be triggered if transiting Mars is in tough aspects with the lords of the ASC or 7th, the Moon, or Venus. The native may make risky decisions concerning relationships, and separations may take place since freedom in relationships is preferred to pretending to be content. Balancing the energy is possible and easier when transiting Mars is in positive aspects with the above-mentioned indicators. During this period, relationships are energetic and active but exhausting. The native should avoid quick and careless actions in his relationships, otherwise he may make enemies. During this transit, the native attracts aggressive, energetic, and active people. With a positive perspective, such people may be the ones who motivate and encourage the native.

Mars in the 8th: At this transit the native may experience actions related to common values and shared resources. Traditionally, the 8th house is related to death, so inheritances and legacies are also the themes of this transit, and Mars may bring them into the native's life at this time. However, this does not necessarily mean the death of the native, just that the theme of death is significant. For instance, the native may witness death in his circle or he may be interested in death and the beyond, metaphysics, and the occult. The 8th house is also related to spending and payments, as is Mars: so, during Mars's transit in the 8th, the native's spending may increase and he may need to make more payments. He may also have some problems related to common resources. This is more significant if transiting Mars is in tough aspects with the lords of the 2nd or 8th, the Lot of Fortune, the Sun, or the Moon. The native may have difficulties in the recovery of debts or he may have to struggle on this issue. He should be careful in relation to taxes, credits, expenditures, and payments. On the other hand, the 8th house is also related to fears, difficulties, suffering, dangers, and medical operations. All of these themes also share the same nature as Mars. Since Mars is a malefic planet, the native should be careful with dangers and disagreements. If the native has to undergo surgery when transiting Mars is in tough aspects with natal planets (the lords of the 8th, 6th, or 12th, the lord of the ASC, and the Sun or the Moon), it is better to postpone the operation until Mars gets out of the 8th house.

Mars in the 9th: This house is related to travels, relations with foreigners, foreign trade, education, publishing and broadcasting, and legal issues. Mars brings the power to fight and take bold actions related to these matters. The native may review his outward goals and decide what to do in this period. He may use his energy in these fields and find the courage to act. While Mars transits through the 9th house (which represents the life views of the native), he may have the power and energy to achieve more success—if Mars is in positive aspects with the natal Sun, Mercury, and Mars. This is a time to act patiently and boldly. However, he should not be too argumentative and impatient; he should balance his need for success and make the best of this high performance. During this transit, if Mars is in tough aspects with the lords of the 3rd or the 9th, the lords of the ASC or of the 8th, he may be at risk for accidents, thefts, diseases, and fights. He may also have some provocative situations relating to religious subjects. The native may be domineering in manifesting his beliefs and views on life. Students may take important exams or find themselves in challenging situations relating to educational themes during this transit.

Mars in the 10th: This transit indicates that the native should fight for his ideals and future goals. The native is highly courageous and his energy is at a peak. He may achieve success due to his decisiveness and motivation. This is more significant when transiting Mars makes positive aspects with the lords of the ASC or MC, and the Sun. These aspects bring more boldness to the native. If the native uses this energy correctly and really focuses on his goals, his chances for success are greater. The native enjoys displaying his authority in his professional life. However, he should keep in mind that Mars is related to impatience and aggression: if transiting Mars is in tough aspects with the natal planets, then the native may experience exaggerated competition, heated discussions, and quarrels with authority figures. He may see unwanted results due to his rapid actions and bold ventures. So, the native should be very careful during this transit, taking care of his reputation and position, acting carefully, and balancing his ambitions.

Mars in the 11th: This transit increases the need for freedom in the social arena. The native likes to act in groups under the influence of this transit. Of course, people should balance their egos, as Mars's aggressive energy is in charge; otherwise, he may experience aggression with his friends and relations within his social circle. He may undergo separations because of a diversity of views. The native may attract Martial people, and individualism and rebellious attitudes may be seen in team activities. This is more significant when transiting Mars is in tough aspects with the lords of the ASC or 11th. On the other hand, Mars's positive aspects with natal planets bring idealistic efforts. The native may display his leadership skills more strongly in the social arena. He may also motivate others. The 11th house also rules the money acquired from one's profession, so positive aspects of this transit may help the native take bold steps in that area.

Mars in the 12th: During this transit the native may experience a decrease of energy and feel exhausted. Mars rules the immune system, so when he is in a weak position the immune system also becomes weak: as a result, the native should be careful about viral infections. He may not channel his stress, incurring some diseases due to keeping all the stress inside. The 12th house is also related to hidden enemies, so if transiting Mars is in tough aspects with the lords of the ASC or 12th, or with the Sun, the native may be exposed to hostility. As the native has a weak image, his hidden enemies will benefit from his situation. Illnesses, hospitals, and other retreats may be emphasized. The native may have some losses due to factors which are out of his control. When this energy is used in a positive way, the native may turn inwards, find his inner wisdom, and listen to his intuition in future decisions. This transit is suitable for activities like yoga and meditation: ones which help the native find his own power within.

Sun transits

The Sun tours around the zodiac in 1 year and moves about 1° per day. He spends almost exactly 30 days in each sign and does not retrograde. Solar transits are highly important in predictive astrology: while the Sun transits in any sign, we should be focused on the themes of that sign and manifest ourselves in relation to those themes.

The Sun signifies health and vitality. He represents people in authority and those who have power. So, we meet with authority figures related to the house in which the Sun transits.

Sun transits in natal houses

Sun in the 1st: The Sun's transit from the degree of the ASC is a recharging and refreshing period for a new cycle. The native may feel that his physical vitality is increasing. This transit is good for any ventures. These are days when the native's self-confidence increases and he may manifest his authority strongly and express himself in a better way. His potential and ability for using his talents, managing situations and attracting others' attention, are higher. The main risk of this transit may be exaggerated self-confidence and arrogance. The native may be egocentric, as he is focused on personal issues during this transit. He may be dominant over others. So, the native should well manage his ego.

Sun in the 2nd: During this transit, financial matters are on the agenda. This transit helps the native's ability to manage his budget. The native may earn money with the help and support of male figures (father, husband, boss, etc.) in addition to his own skills and conscious will. He should trust in his own budget and the income which he earns through his skills. His income may increase during this transit, as does his self-confidence. He also becomes more generous. He may have short-term profits when the transiting Sun makes positive aspects with the lord of the ASC, 2nd, or 8th, or with the Lot of Fortune. On the other hand, tough aspects may increase spending.

Sun in the 3rd: These are suitable days for learning different things. The native expresses his ideas through writing or talking. He is confident about these issues. However he should avoid being closed to others' views, being inflexible, and giving priority to his own ideas and ignoring others. He may act this way when the transiting Sun makes tough aspects with natal planets.

For instance, tough aspects with the lord of the ASC or Mercury may trigger such attitudes. During days when the transiting Sun is in positive aspects with natal planets, the native may attend to important meetings and make agreements. He may be recognized in his close circle and use this transit for advertising and marketing purposes. Relations with siblings are also important during this transit; the native has influence over his siblings. He may also have important roles in the lives of his relatives, neighbors, and others in his close circle.

Sun in the 4th: The family, family life, and the home get priority during this transit. He may experience important developments related to his parents. His family may need him. He may help in solving family problems. During this transit, relationships within the family get stronger. The native may prove that he is "the boss" at home. If the transiting Sun is in tough aspects with natal planets, the native wants to be dominant at home and some power struggles may be seen. When transiting Sun is in positive aspects with the lord of the MC, the natal Sun, or Jupiter, the native may host important and prestigious guests at home. He may move his house, especially when the transiting Sun is in positive aspects with the lord of the ASC, 4th, or 7th. This is a nice period for restructuring the home and family life. Past events may come to the surface and be solved during this period. Such developments may be experienced when the transiting Sun is opposed to the transiting Moon (i.e., the Full Moon).

Sun in the 5th: Events related to children, love, fun, hobbies, and sports are activated during this transit. This is an ideal transit for making new beginnings regarding children. When the transiting Sun makes aspects with the lord of the ASC or 5th, or with the Moon or Venus, the native may easily deal with these issues. This house is also related to how the native displays himself and his talents, especially in artistic and creative fields. For instance, when the Sun enters the 5th house of an artist, he may express his talents better than before, especially when the transiting Sun is in aspect with the lord of the MC. It is also a positive transit for displaying athletic talents. The native may spend more time on the joys of life and fun activities. He may be involved in social activities. Flirting and one's sexual life may gain importance. This is a nice transit for short travels and activities which are not routine. The Sun's transit in this house represents a period to spend time on oneself.

Sun in the 6th: When the Sun transits this house, daily routine and responsibilities gain more importance and have priority. The native should take responsibility and deal with problems and duties more than before. He may need to solve problems which were ignored before. The native may need to work for others because this house is where we do things for other people. Even if the native is the boss of his own business, others may dictate to him what things to do. He may need to take care of other people's duties and this may damage his health. He may not be able to deal with his own needs because of the burden of his responsibilities. He should work patiently during this period. On the other hand, he may be unhappy if he deals with work he does not like. Nevertheless, working for others and helping them will make him feel "official" and as though he is doing his duty. As this house is related to coworkers and subordinates, the native may have problems with those people especially when the transiting Sun is in tough aspects with the natal lords of the ASC, MC, or 6th, or with the natal Sun. On the other hand, the native should be careful about his health. He should be disciplined and manage his diet, especially when the transiting Sun is in conjunction with natal planets in the 6th and in opposition to natal planets in the 12th.

Sun in the 7th: Relationships gain importance when the Sun begins his transit in the 7th. The native may meet famous and special people who are centers of attention: they may support the native or not, according to the positive or negative aspects of the transiting Sun with natal planets. If he is in positive aspects with them, the native gets the advantage of acting along with others. He may make important business agreements. The native should develop a strategy in his one-on-one relations, should be conscious, and be open to sharing. During this transit, he may suddenly need to support others who have importance in his life and deal with their needs. He is never left alone during this transit; he cannot deal with his personal issues. It is the time for interaction with others, helping them or getting their help and support. He may consult experienced people in terms of business partnerships. The native may move to another house during this transit.

Sun in the 8th: During this transit, earnings held in common, the income of the spouse or the partner or issues like debts and credits, taxes, mortgages, and other payments get priority. The native may be dependent on others or wait for things coming from others. Traditionally, the 8th house is related to death and inheritance issues, so these themes may be on the agenda: the native may experience dangerous and risky situations, operations, and deaths.

As the 8th is one of the financial houses, the native should be careful about all types of payments like taxes and credit card payments. If the transiting Sun makes tough aspects with the lords of the 2nd or 8th, or with the lord of the ASC, the native should be extremely careful about these issues. The 8th is also related to metaphysics and issues beyond death, so the native may have an interest in those subjects and make some investigations into them.

Sun in the 9th: During this transit, travels, foreign trade, education, and religious and Divine subjects have priority. Travels with the aim of learning new things are beneficial. The native may expand his business to international markets. He should think big and try new challenges. The native may enjoy the philosophical dimensions of life. He may be focused on extraordinary themes. This is a positive transit for writing a book and publishing it, for learning new things and expanding one's horizons, and for mental activities like giving seminars. The native may publicize himself, or some important, charismatic, and powerful people from different cultures or foreign countries may play an important role in his life. This is a beautiful transit for traveling, getting out of one's routine, and for being interested in different subjects.

Sun in the 10th: As soon as the Sun enters this house, issues like business, career, social status, and recognition have priority. This is a time for attracting others' attention, for attaining success, and achieving progress. He may see the after-effects of past achievements. The native may get compliments and admiration. He may manifest talents, find success, and even reap the rewards. He may get a promotion and reach a strong position. When the transiting Sun is in positive aspects with the lords of the natal ASC or MC, the native may enjoy positive developments in his goals. The native should observe himself because at this time everything is clear and can be seen easily. If the transiting Sun is in tough aspects with natal planets, the native should be careful: this transit has an influence on the future. This is a good period for reviewing one's life and goals.

Sun in the 11th: This transit brings increased activity in one's social life. The native is surrounded by powerful and effective people, as this is a supportive transit. The native should take advantage of his beneficial social relations, including people he meets during this transit. This is not a time to spend alone: the native should be involved in social organizations as often as he can. He may get unexpected support for his future plans. He may display leadership skills within social groups and be accepted easily by their members. He may benefit from team efforts. The importance of friends and socializing gain importance, especially if the transiting Sun is in positive aspects with the lords of the ASC, MC, or 11th. This transit may be used for advancing in big and important organizations.

Sun in the 12th: This transit is suitable for evaluating the year and getting prepared for new things. The Sun's transit illuminates this normally obscure house, so certain issues which were not realized before may come to the surface. The native may have some secret enemies. He should not permit past events to influence his life negatively. He may be successful at working alone. The 12th represents losses and sad conditions, so the native's fears and worries may increase during this period. The Sun in the 12th means that it is too early to take action. Before starting on new initiatives, the native must first strengthen his existing conditions. He should not make urgent decisions in the hopes of avoiding losses. He should be careful about his health. This is an ideal transit for meditation and other similar practices.

Venus transits

Venus completes her tour around zodiac in approximately 1 year, and spends nearly 1 month in each sign. Her average daily speed is a little more than 1°. She retrogrades for 6 weeks, every 18 months.

Venus brings short-term advantages to the house she visits. She brings social events, joy, popularity, and love relations. In general, Venus is related to appreciation and admiration. Relationships flow smoothly where Venus transits. She also represents mediation and contractual issues, and marriage is also related to Venus in part because it is a contractual relation. Socially, Venus represents peaceful methods and approaches and cooperation. She is also related to creativity, especially in music and painting. Venus represents the love of luxury. Cosmetics, clothing, and precious jewelry are also related to Venus. Venus transits are effective when we shop for ourselves or accept beautiful presents from other people.

Venus transits in natal houses

Venus in the 1st: In this transit, Venus easily manifests her charm and sympathy. Due to her conciliatory attitudes and good relations, the native may attract attention and manage conditions in the way he wants. This is a good time for spa treatments and making radical changes in one's appearance and clothing style. These changes are easily recognized by others. The native also enjoys expressing himself and socializing during this transit. This is an ideal transit for having a good time with friends, having fun, and even traveling. The native may also act as a mediator between people who cannot get along easily.

Venus in the 2nd: This one-month transit has positive influences on financial matters, and is also suitable for shopping and investments. The native may have profits from artistic and creative fields and Venusian objects like souvenirs, clothing, and jewelry. This is especially significant if transiting Venus is in contact with beneficial planets in the natal 2nd or if she makes positive aspects with the lords of the 2nd or 8th, or with the Lot of Fortune. This is a suitable time for spending money on clothing, wining and dining, jewelry, artistic objects, home decoration, and fun.

Venus in the 3rd: This transit aids sociability and harmony within one's close circle. The native may communicate positively. Since the native may maintain peace and balance during this transit, he may also act as a mediator between people around him. He may express his ideas through written or verbal communication. He may be successful in the fields of advertising, marketing, sales, journalism, and the internet. This is a good period for making important meetings and agreements, traveling, education, and for using one's communicative skills. This is significant when transiting Venus makes positive aspects with the lords of the ASC or 3rd, and with Mercury.

Venus in the 4th: This one-month transit brings positive influences related to the home and family, and the native feels secure and peaceful when he is there or with them. As Venus represents peace, it brings positive influences for family relationships. This is an ideal time for solving any family problems and maintaining cooperation. The native does not look for fun in the social environment but prefers to spend time with the family. He may organize parties at home. He may feel well-balanced spiritually, but is not very active physically: he may spend most of his time lazily at home. He may make decorative changes to his home, move to another house, make repairs and renovations, rearrange his garden, or buy new furniture. This is significant when transiting Venus makes positive aspects with the lords of the ASC or 4th, and with the Moon.

Venus in the 5th: This transit brings positive influences in terms of love and relationships, as Venus represents the issues of the 5th house. Venus rejoices in the 5th house, so this transit may bring very positive results. The native's sexual life may become more joyous. He may think of having a baby, especially when transiting Venus makes aspects with the lords of the ASC or 5th, Venus, and the Moon. He may also get some good news related to his children (if he has any). As this house is related to creative activities and artistic talents, the native may display his abilities. He may spend time on his hobbies and enjoy doing that. This transit is also an ideal time for short travels, socializing, and having fun with friends.

Venus in the 6th: The native may benefit from his subordinates during this transit, or achieve success at work through the help of good relations with coworkers. The native may negotiate peace in office conflicts. If the native has just changed jobs, he may adapt quickly during this period. He may be quite popular among his colleagues due to his peaceful attitudes. He may enjoy working for others and helping them. Health is also under some protection when Venus is in this house, but the native should still be careful and avoid junk food. He may tend to be lazy during this period, so should not ignore exercising. This period is also ideal for caring for pets.

Venus in the 7th: The native may experience positive developments in one-on-one relations. He may have the chance to change any negativity he has experienced in these issues. This is an ideal transit for marriage, and the best placement for Venus in terms of any relationships. It is also good for building up partnerships and making business agreements. Transiting Venus may display her natural qualities easily in this house. However, the native may be over-agreeable and may act according to the other party's wishes. This transit may also increase one's chances in legal issues and brings positive influences to negotiations. This is significant when transiting Venus makes positive aspects with the lords of the ASC or 7th, the Sun, and Mercury.

Venus in the 8th: This transit represents a period when others' expectations may be satisfied. The native may have the chance to recover debts and engage in negotiation. As the 8th house also represents the financial condition of the partner, that financial situation may improve. Stocks and bonds owned by the native may gain value. Issues like inheritance also show progress. The native may get both financial and moral support. This is a good period for partnership issues. If the natal chart promises it at that time through some other technique, the native may have to undergo operations related to the organs that are ruled by Venus like the genitals, ovaries, and kidneys. This is possible when transiting Venus is in tough aspects with the lords of the natal ASC or 8th, Venus, or Mars.

Venus in the 9th: This is a positive period for foreign travels, relations with foreigners, and education issues. The native enjoys spending time with people from other cultures and learning new things. He may now lose some of his former standards and bring new changes to his life. He may meet with new, interesting, and possibly foreign people; such people and events may bring a positive perspective towards life. He may be interested in themes which relax him, and enjoy life fully. He may find the love he seeks in faraway places. He may also receive benefit from distant places. This is more possible when transiting Venus makes positive aspects with the lord of the natal 7th or Venus. (In male charts, we may include positive aspects with the Moon, and in female charts positive aspects with the Sun.) He may have opportunities in new ventures with foreigners. This is significant when transiting Venus is in positive aspects with the lords of the MC or 9th.

Venus in the 10th: This transit is beneficial for the native's career and profession, his prestige, future goals, and his relations with people who are in a managerial position. As the native may now get along with people related to his profession, this may aid his professional success. This is also a favorable period for maintaining positive relations with VIPs. The native may get benefit and support from his managers. He may also become interested in artistic issues. If he is already involved in an artistic field, this transit helps him in a positive way. His creativity and talents are recognized by the public. This transit is also good for public relations. The native may experience a rise in his status and achieve success if transiting Venus makes positive aspects with the lord of the MC or with the Sun. He may also benefit from strong female figures.

Venus in the 11th: During this period, the native's hopes and wishes increase. This is an ideal transit for group activities and spending time with friends. The native may attend organizational meetings, other activities, parties, and meet with new people. The native may have support for his goals if transiting Venus is in positive aspects with the lords of the ASC or 11th, or with the Sun. He may get the support of female figures in social groups. This is significant when transiting Venus makes positive aspects with the natal Venus or Moon. Positive aspects with the natal Sun or Jupiter may bring prestige and expand the native's social circle. This transit also brings positive developments in terms of business ventures and financial gains. If the native is not involved in any professional life, then he may have joyous times with his friends and acquaintances. This transit brings positive effects for charitable giving and clubs. The native may be surrounded by artistic and talented people.

Venus in the 12th: Venus represents relationships, but brings isolation in the 12th house. The native may withdraw from both romantic and social relations during this transit. Love relationships may bring temporary difficulties, misunderstandings, losses, and events behind closed doors. Venus's transit in the 12th may also bring platonic love. The native may have difficulties in expressing his emotions. On the other hand, this transit is also related to finding happiness while being alone. The native may be happy while being reserved, and may prefer being alone. If transiting Venus is in positive aspects or in conjunction with the lord of the 12th, the native may benefit from this transit. This is also one of the best transits for meditation.

Mercury transits

Mercury goes around the zodiac in 1 year, spending between 15 days and 2 months in each sign. His average speed is 1.5° per day, and he retrogrades three times per year, about 20-24 days each time.

Mercury is related to communication, contracts, written documents, agreements, promises, buying and selling, negotiations, and education. Making agreements and negotiations is possible during Mercury transits. Mercury shows how we relate and communicate with the outer world, and is related to one's daily routine. The house where Mercury transits show us where we are focused mentally and in which fields we communicate. Short distance travels are also ruled by Mercury. But Mercury inherits the characteristics of the planet he aspects, so that his tough aspects bring negative influences. Our words and attitudes may be sharp. With his positive aspects, we may be successful in both written and oral expressions. We may express ourselves clearly.

Mercury transits in natal houses

Mercury in the 1st: This period shows us that the native may now express himself better, use his persuasive skills, and attract attention through his words and ideas. If the native is smart enough, he may tip the scales in his favor through persuasion. He may be successful if he acts with the help of logic instead of emotions. During this transit, the native uses his intellect actively and communication issues move ahead rapidly. Mercury transits are suitable periods for making important speeches and written agreements. The native might favor these Mercury transits for important meetings. If transiting Mercury is positive aspects with the lords of the ASC or MC, the Sun, or Mercury, the native may use his communication skills and persuasive talents for business goals.

Mercury in the 2nd: The native may use his resources correctly, manage his money well, and increase his earning capacity during this transit. He may find practical solutions. Of course, he has to organize his financial matters and he should be smart in his spending. He ought to review his income and see if his income covers his lifestyle needs. He may consult some experts about financial issues and investments. He may receive proposals in commercial issues and business ventures. The native may earn money through his success in commercial matters and communication skills such as reading, writing, and teaching.

Mercury in the 3rd: During this transit the native may have the chance to develop his mental and communication skills. He has an advantage in transmitting his ideas to others through speaking and writing. This is also a suitable period for scheduling important meetings and agreements. The native may have good relations with others if he is open and flexible towards their views and maintains good communication with them. This is one of the best transits for attending to education, teaching, learning foreign languages, learning handicrafts and new communication skills, traveling, and writing. The native may express his opinions effectively, especially if transiting Mercury makes positive aspects with the lords of the ASC, 3rd or 9th, the Sun, or Mercury.

Mercury in the 4th: Some of the influences of this transit include making plans for the home, talking about important family matters, talking about past events, talking about moving to another house or making repairs or renovations at home. This is also a period for reviewing future plans and taking cautious and smart steps. The native should reorganize his private life during this transit. He may also take the necessary decisions for restructuring himself. These matters are more significant when transiting Mercury makes positive aspects with the lords of the ASC, MC, 4th, or with the Sun.

Mercury in the 5th: This house is related to children, love, fun, hobbies, and sports: so, the native's mind is focused on these issues during this transit. For instance, he may think about having a baby and even make a decision about that. This transit is also good for setting up a healthy communication platform with children. The native may convince children easily during this transit. He may also talk about love and sexuality. He may get news from his partner or he may flirt of propose dating, especially if transiting Mercury is in positive aspects with natal planets. If transiting Mercury is in positive aspects with the lords of the ASC, 5th, 7th, and Venus, the native may benefit from this transit. This is also a good period for producing creative mental or artistic projects.

Mercury in the 6th: Communication and agreements in the areas of illness, daily routine, and subordinates increase during this transit. This transit is suitable for new job applications and agreements. The native may find success through the aid of good relations with his coworkers. He may get the benefit of his colleagues' skills. This transit is helpful for being organized in the working environment. The native may review his duties, identify his mistakes, organize his daily work, and make new agreements that are connected to his working conditions. He may make plans for solving problems in working conditions. This is also a good time for reviewing one's health. Due to the busy pace of the working environment, the native's nerves may be shot. This transit is also beneficial for taking care of pets.

Mercury in the 7th: Mercury's transit in the 7th house activates partnership issues. As the 7th is also related to agreements, this transit brings issues related to signatures: the native may sign some agreements concerning business contracts, buying or selling a house, or marriage. The native may be successful if he acts with others and develops tactics and strategies in one-on-one relations. As this house is also related to customer relations, the native may develop new sales strategies and take part in important negotiations. The native may get news regarding his business or romantic partner. This is a good period for talking about important issues with one's partner. It is also a good period for making new partnerships and traveling together.

Mercury in the 8th: This transit is a proper period for discussing and planning financial matters. The native may build financial partnerships with others, and easily find support for his projects. To avoid any possible problems and protect his rights, he should put everything in writing and carefully read all terms of any agreement. The native may also deal with other people's money, or credits and debts. For better results in these areas, the native may prefer to act when transiting Mercury is in positive aspects with the lords of the 2nd or 8th, the lord of the 7th, or with the Sun (in diurnal charts) and the Moon (in nocturnal charts). This is one of the ideal transits for delving into the occult and metaphysics. Death and inheritance issues are also pertinent during this transit.

Mercury in the 9th: Mercury's transit in the 9th is suitable for all kinds of educational purposes. Education abroad, publishing, and broadcasting issues are on the agenda. It brings a new perspective which may change the native's whole life. The native may come together or make contacts with people who may enlighten him. When transiting Mercury makes aspects with the lords of the ASC, 3rd or 9th, or with Mercury, the native may attend trainings, give seminars, or make international speeches. When transiting Mercury makes positive aspects with natal planets, the native may make plans for the future, make decisions, and find solutions for problems. He may attend some training which helps his future career.

Mercury in the 10th: During this transit the native may sign some agreements or attend some training related to his profession. As short distance travels are ruled by Mercury, the native may travel for business purposes. He may also learn new techniques, share his ideas with people in authority, and get advice on his career, especially when transiting Mercury makes positive aspects with the lords of the ASC, MC, 11th, or with the Sun. He may also schedule meetings, or get in touch with, VIPs.

Mercury in the 11th: During this transit, the native's interaction with his social circle increases. It is suitable for all kinds of social activities and organizations, and the native may come together with people who share the same ideals. It is good for considering his plans for the future. The native may review his old friendships and experience some changes in his social environment. He may get some advice and consult his trusted friends. He may be surrounded by smart, talented, and communicative people. He may even be busy with too much communication. This transit is suitable for the exchange of ideas, charitable activities, commercial ventures, and investments, especially when transiting Mercury is in positive aspects with the lords of the ASC, MC, or 11th, or with the Sun or Mercury.

Mercury in the 12th: The native wants to spend his time in a reserved way during this transit. Working alone helps him, and after developing his mental skills in this period, he will employ them when Mercury enters his 1st house. This is a preparatory period, so the native now collects necessary information and material. When Mercury transits the 12th, the native cannot express himself clearly. His hidden enemies may gossip about him. Events from the past may annoy him once again. As Mercury is related to slyness, lying, and gossip, the native may feel depressed because of such actions around him. The native may now know who these people are and why they act that way.

Moon transits

The Moon circles the zodiac in about 28 days and spends approximately 2.5 days in each sign. Her transit represents the direction of our emotional life. The Moon is also related to daily routine and factors in our inner circle. By following the Moon's transits, we may easily understand how we are affected by daily changes. The house where the Moon is placed on a daily basis tells us about the theme that will prevail during that time. The transits of the Moon are generally valid for a few hours: they do not have permanent influences. However, these transits may trigger other elements in the natal chart. As the Moon generally represents women, her transits may bring communication with women.

Moon transits in natal houses

Moon in the 1st: During this two-and-a-half day period, personal issues come to the forefront. Personal needs, emotional expressions, empathy and sympathy, the need for belonging, and the give-and-take of feelings are intensely felt. The native may easily find the attention he needs if his expectations are not very high. During this period, the native is successful in understanding others but objectivity might not be maintained. The native may get involved in personal enterprises to express his feelings.

Moon in the 2nd: During these days, the native defines his possessions and the things he values in an emotional way. The need for financial security is dominant. The native may identify himself with the things he has, but he cannot be objective about financial matters and may make emotional decisions. While the Moon transits in the 2nd house, if she makes positive aspects with natal planets, the native may engage in some financial ventures. The theme of these days always revolves around financial themes.

Moon in the 3rd: During this period, communication traffic gets busy. The native's bonds within his inner circle become emotional. Speaking with people is also emotional, and so is important for the native. If he is good at controlling his emotions in a conscious way and knows how to be objective, then he may build healthy and meaningful communication with others. This transit is good for learning, sharing information, writing and speaking, and travelling.

Moon in the 4th: During these two-and-a-half days, the native may need to withdraw. He may enjoy spending his time at home and with his family, or he may just want to rest. During these days, the native may take a look at his own attitudes and emotions and how he displays them to the outer world. The native may realize how his habits and past conditioning influence his life now. Events of the past may come to the surface. This is an ideal transit for moving or making some changes at home.

Moon in the 5th: During this period, issues like love, sex, children, creative skills, hobbies, spare time activities, and fun have priority. Emotions are so aroused that they are hard to hide. As a result, emotions may be displayed in an exaggerated way. As the native is so wrapped up in his feelings, he cannot recognize the feelings of other parties. The native may be fond of children, so that he makes efforts related to them. These days are good for fun and sports.

Moon in the 6th: During these days, one's daily routine and responsibilities have priority. Matters related to coworkers and subordinates and daily work are the most boring things on the agenda at this time. This transit is a bit short for indicating disease, nevertheless the native should take care of his health. The native does not care about himself but is always at the service of others.

Moon in the 7th: During this period, one-on-one contact in both personal and professional relationships is important. The native tends to express himself on the emotional level. This transit affects the native's marriage, relations with his enemies, and other emotional conflicts. (Of course, being objective is hard under this influence.) This transit may be used for setting up partnerships, enhancing one-on-one relations, having important meetings, and making agreements (as long as the native can control his emotions).

Moon in the 8th: During this two-and-a-half days, issues like common possessions, money owed and debts, death and inheritance, metaphysics and the occult, are on the agenda. The native may long for things that belong to another or may want to have more control over common possessions. Some changes related to other people's money may occur. On the positive side, the native may receive money he lent to others, or make his own payments easily. If the transiting Moon makes hard aspects with natal planets, the opposite may be true and the native may not get his money back or have difficulties in making his own payments.

Moon in the 9th: During this period, the native may want to get away from his daily routine. Traveling is a good idea. If the native cannot get away physically, he may do the same virtually: he may be involved in religion, philosophy, higher education, and communication with people who are based abroad. He may acquire new ideas and a new perspective. He may make friends with people from foreign countries or he may come together with different people.

Moon in the 10th: At this time the native may be focused on his career, work projects, goals, and social status. The native's inner life may come out through this transit and he may have difficulties in hiding some truths about his private life. If he has nothing to hide, then he may feel better. The native may also establish emotional bonds with people in authority and have sincere relations. This transit is ideal for expressing oneself within society. It is also good for public relations and sales.

Moon in the 11th: This transit brings a need for socializing. The native wants to spend time with his friends and people from his social groups. He feels fine in such environments. He feels comfortable when he is with those who have common ideals, and he gets their support. This period is a good time to evaluate one's goals and check if they are aligned with one's ideals. This is a good transit in terms of social cooperation and lively activities. It is also good for professional gains.

Moon in the 12th: During this time the native feels a need to withdraw. He may feel more comfortable when he is reserved, and may not want to be involved in social activities. This is a good time for being alone and facing the negative traits of the self. This transit is also good for dealing with mystical and spiritual disciplines, because such teachings require an emotional understanding, not a mental one. On the other hand, some outer conditions that the native does not have a control over, and some hidden enemies, may come to the fore. The native may also have some psychological problems during the Moon's transit in the 12th house.

Transits of the Nodes

The Nodes take approximately 18.5 years to circle the zodiac. The mean Nodes are always retrograde and move an average of 20° per year. When they are in contact with a planet or reference point, events proceed in a pre-destined way and we do not have the chance to change the course of events. The transits of the North Node bring opportunities for making necessary changes in life and to evolve, while those of the South Node bring traces of past problems to the surface. The transits of the South Node describe experiences of déjà vu.

Four examples

The most significant transit in the example chart below (for the time I left the my career at Grand Bazaar for good, in 2003), is Saturn's transit from the natal MC. Cancer is on the MC, and Saturn is in detriment in that sign. So, his transit from that house cannot bring satisfying developments in terms of profession and career. This is the date when I left Grand Bazaar, the center of trade in Istanbul where I had worked for 20 years. Saturn's transits in the 10th bring changes in the professional life. This period also brings responsibilities and worries about the future.

My decision to quit that job was a sudden one. When I made the decision, transiting Mars had just passed over my natal Sun and was in square with my natal Moon. This is an important transit, as the Moon is the lord of my 10th house. Mars makes the same transit once every two years, in this case passing over my Sun and squaring my Moon—but this time, transiting Saturn was also passing over my MC. Minor transits always trigger major transits and so they work together in an integrated way.

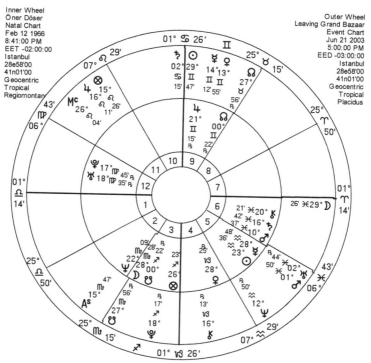

Figure 20: Öner Döşer, transits for June 21, 2003

Next is the transit chart of the day I went to a mundane astrology seminar in Vancouver taught by my teacher Robert Zoller (October 2004). Here, transits can be seen in the angular houses of my chart.

Jupiter, in the 9th house of my natal chart, is transiting over my natal ASC degree. For this I would say, "the 9th house came to me." Transiting planets manifest the themes of their natal placement, and this is more significant when they transit the angular houses. Transiting Jupiter is in his triplicity in Libra, so his transit from my ASC was very beneficial, enlightening, and educating. During the eight days I stayed in Canada, I really learned a lot. Jupiter in the natal 9th represents my teacher. The ASC represents me and the events around me. I spent two days with him after the seminar, learning many things. On the other hand, my natal Jupiter is retrograde motion and in square with Saturn. So I should admit that my educational plans in life never worked out as good as I had planned: I always felt Jupiter's support, but I also felt his restricted capacity in my natal chart. In those same days, transiting Saturn was in aspect to my natal Moon. This represents a period which helped me become more mature but challenged me emotionally. Although this is a trine, we should keep in mind that Saturn makes this aspect from Cancer, where he is in detriment.

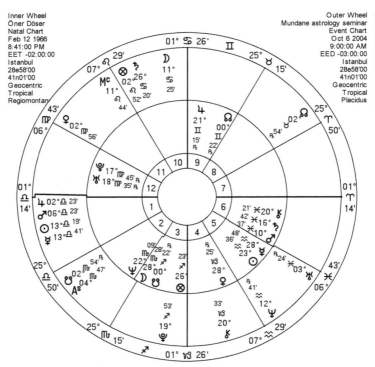

Figure 21: Öner Döşer, transits for October 6, 2004

Another example is my wife's transit chart below, when she traveled to the USA (June 2006). When my wife began her trip it was very important for her career: Mars, the lord of her career house (the natal 10th) was transiting her ASC degree. (Mars is also in the natal 10th, by the way.) This means that 10th house themes are now about to gain importance in her life. As Mars means action, this transit also points to an undertaking such as a journey. At the same time, transiting Saturn is also on her natal ASC. So, some significant events may be seen. What types of events could they be?

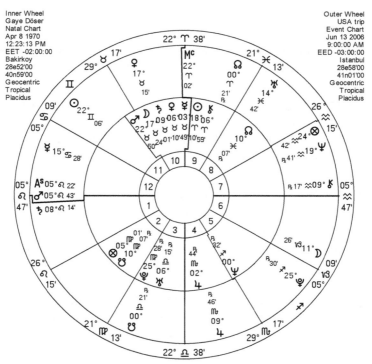

Figure 22: Gaye Döşer, transits for June 13, 2006

First of all, as Saturn is a natal 10th-house planet, and now transiting in Leo where he is in detriment, we might not think of it as a very satisfying period in terms of career. She had quit the company where she had worked for five years, and due to Saturn's transit on her ASC she felt restricted. Although she had worked hard and was highly talented, she could not achieve rapid progress. These are some influences of transiting Saturn on the natal ASC in Leo. It was the end of a trend, as Saturn had already started to separate from that degree and would not come to it again by retrogradation.

Another significant theme was related to health, because the 6th house fell on Capricorn and the two lords of this sign (Saturn by sign, Mars by exaltation) were in conjunction with the natal ASC. Transiting Saturn was also in a square with the natal lord of the 6th house (Saturn). So, she had to be careful in matters of health. Saturn represents cold, Mars represents fevers.

I advised her to take care of herself on the plane and take a lot of medicine with her. However, preventing some events are really difficult. As she had too many flights (8 flights) and the air conditioning was always on, she caught a cold. Then as she felt weak, she had a fever. Saturn and Mars placed in her natal Taurus (which signifies the throat and neck) also represent throat problems. Now, these problems came to the surface because both malefics were transiting on the ASC degree. Saturn had not yet made an aspect to the natal Moon, the lord of the 12th house. That means she might still be prone to diseases related to the breasts, lungs, and stomach (which are signified by Cancer and the Moon).

My wife's travel is also a good example of the transiting Nodes. When we place her transit chart on my natal chart, we see that the North Node, which is transiting in her 9th (travel) is also placed at the entrance of my natal 7th (spouse). The North Node shows that she may travel a lot. Of course, this is not ordinary travel: it has a fated importance in her career. Let's also emphasize that her transiting Sun (the victor of my natal 7th) is now transiting in my natal 9th, the house of long distance travels (and is conjoining my natal Jupiter there).

Fourth, when transiting Saturn opposes natal Saturn, the native questions life, eliminates unnecessary things from life, and has to make important decisions about his relationships and focus. Saturn's return to his natal degree is a time for maturing. These returns may bring positive or negative consequences, based on his natal placement.

In the example chart below, transiting Saturn makes an opposition with the natal Saturn. Natal Saturn is in the 6th house, in Pisces, and is the lord of the 4th and 5th houses. As the nativity is nocturnal and Saturn is the lord of the 4th, Saturn may be related to the native's father. The native's father married for the second time 1.5 months after this opposition: so, Saturn's transit from the 7th house of its natal position shows that the father experiences an important phase of life in terms of relationships.

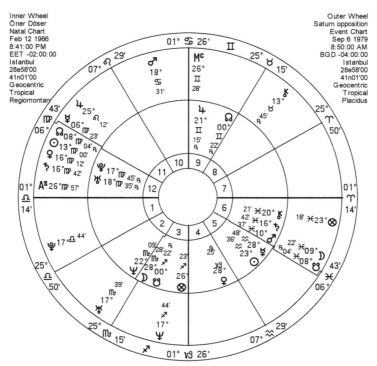

Figure 23: Öner Döşer, Saturn opposition

Repetition of the natal symbolism through transits

According to Morin in his work on transits,[3] we should compare the influences of transits and progressions upon the natal chart, because only what the natal chart promises, can be realized. If combinations similar to the nativity occur in the transits, their influences are more powerful. Let's illustrate this important principle with a few examples:

On the day of Princess Diana's death (see Chapter 3), the Moon was in square to transiting Mars. She also had a similar combination in her natal chart: the Moon, lord of the natal 8th, was opposed to the natal Mars in the 8th house. So, the natal chart promises a Martian death (as a result of an accident or operation). The same combination was in the sky at the time of the accident. This shows us that the native is open to risks.

---

[3] See for example Morin 2004, Ch. 12.

Another example is James Dean's death.[4] His natal Moon, the lord of the 8th house, has a close square with natal Mars in the 8th house. This means his death would be a harsh one. At the time of the accident which caused his death, there was a sharp opposition between the Moon and Mars. Of course, this is not the only significator—we should also examine other transits, too. However, here I want to direct you to the similarity between the chart's symbolism and the transiting symbolism in the sky.

As another example, let's have a look at the nativity of President John F. Kennedy, who was assassinated on September 22, 1963.[5] Natal Mars in the 8th represents the possibility of a harsh death. The natal Moon, being placed on the cusp of the 12th and being the victor over the position of Mars, is in trine with him. Mars is also in sextile with the 10th-house Saturn. When we examine the transit chart of his death, we see that the transiting Moon was again in contact with Mars, and Mars was in contact with Saturn. The alignment in the sky on that day was similar to his natal chart. The square between transiting Saturn and natal Mars in the 8th house, as well as the opposition between transiting Mars and Venus, the lord of the ASC (which signifies life), is significant. Again, the symbolism in the sky was similar to the symbolism in the natal chart.

Transits and Solar/Lunar returns

Robert Zoller likewise states[6] that transits should not be considered alone, but should be evaluated along with other techniques: "Transits are…triggers of underlying causes, things that are being produced by other factors in the chart, such as the *firdaria*, the profections and solar returns, primary directions, and progressions…They are conceived of as modifying other influences and they are the last thing that is considered."

Let's consider an example: let Jupiter be in the natal 9th house, in 10° Aquarius. Now, Jupiter may also be in 10° Aquarius in a solar return chart. This is a magnificent return, in the sense that he has returned to his natal degree at the very time of the solar return, so his meaning in the natal chart becomes much more prominent. The native may now have the opportunity

---

[4] According to Solar Fire, Dean was born February 8, 1931, 2:11 AM, in Marion, Indiana, USA. He died on September 30, 1955, around 5:45 PM Pacific Time.
[5] According to Solar Fire, Kennedy was born on May 29, 1917, 3:00 PM, in Brookline, Massachusetts.
[6] Zoller 2003, Lesson 17, p. 12.

to deal with religious and spiritual subjects, travel for education, and will be successful in higher education and foreign trade (based on Jupiter's condition.)

If a transiting planet in the solar return reaches its natal sign but not the exact natal degree (such as Jupiter reaching only 1° Aquarius), this is also important, as it aids the realization of the promised things. Although a transiting Jupiter returning to his natal sign is not exactly in conjunction with his natal position, his influences are still felt extensively.

If a transiting planet in the solar return comes to the exact degree of a different natal planet (that is, not itself), we should evaluate whether these planets are benefic or malefic, and if this conjunction is positive or negative.

Finally, transits should be evaluated together with primary directions and return charts, since transits often provide the triggering effect and timing that shows when and how a direction or solar return will manifest. For instance, a transit that indicates illness will be particularly effective if a primary direction also shows illness around that time, especially if the transiting planet aspects its natal position or that of the promittor. Or, if a planet shows success and good reputation in a solar return, these good effects should be more manifest when it transits the natal ASC during that year.

GUIDO BONATTI

CHAPTER 6: SOLAR ARC DIRECTIONS

IN THE SOLAR ARC TECHNIQUE, ALL SIGNIFICATORS IN THE CHART ARE ADVANCED BY AN AMOUNT EQUAL TO THE SUN'S PROGRESSION OVER A CERTAIN TIME. THE SUN, AS THE CENTER OF OUR SOLAR SYSTEM, IS THE CELESTIAL BODY THAT REPRESENTS OUR EXISTENCE. HIS DAILY PROGRESS SYMBOLIZES THE DEVELOPMENT THAT WE WILL ACHIEVE THROUGHOUT OUR LIVES. IN SOLAR ARCS, ONE DAY OF SOLAR MOTION IS EQUAL TO ONE YEAR OF LIFE, AND WE EVALUATE THE CONTACTS BETWEEN THE PROGRESSED AND NATAL CHARTS.

The solar arc technique

The Sun is the center of our solar system and this same symbolism is reflected in our charts. The Sun is the most important celestial body that symbolizes our existence. The daily progress of the Sun also represents the development we achieve over a lifetime. This is expressed by the formula "one day of Solar motion equals one year of life," which is then applied to the other planets. There are three ways of calculating this motion. The third way is the most accurate.

First, one may use the Sun's average daily motion, 59' 08". However, because his daily motion varies day by day, this average measurement may deviate from his true position 1° for those over 30 years old (i.e., over 30 days of his motion). One reason for this is that the Sun's motion shows seasonal differences: the Sun moves more slowly between March and September, and faster between October and February. So, carefully-timed predictions should really be based on his true daily speed (which is calculated automatically by computer programs), but for a broad overview this average motion is useful.

Second, one may use the easy and widely-used "degree for a year" calculation. Here, one simply advances the Sun by 1° for each year of life (beginning with the natal position of the Sun), and likewise the other planets. For instance, to progress a chart to age 27, add 27° to the natal Sun's degree, forward in the zodiac. (There is no retrograde movement in solar arcs). Then do the same for the other planets. So, when the native is 27 years old, the whole chart is progressed by a solar arc (or SA) of 27°. The planets, MC, and ASC may all be directed to each other or to the angular houses. This is often used for rectification.

Third, we should remember that even the "degree for a year" formula is an average. So, for greatest accuracy the true daily speed of the Sun should be used, which differs between 57' and 1° 01'. For example, if you wanted to know about age 45, then simply find the actual difference between the Sun's position at birth and his position 45 days later: this is the arc or amount you will add to the rest of the points in the nativity.

After erecting the SA chart, we should compare it with the natal chart and observe the conjunctions and other major aspects between the planets, axes, and midpoints. The orb is 0° in solar arcs, and 1° equals one year. When these precise points are triggered by transits and by the secondary progressed Moon, important events occur.

As Saturn and the other generational planets move very slowly, when these planets are directed to the axis and other planets they may bring important events. For instance, when SA Saturn is directed to the natal ASC, the native may feel restricted and hindered; he may be faced with some health problems, or he may feel pessimistic and depressed.

To make accurate predictions using SAs, we should consider what is being directed to what. For instance, if we consider the example just mentioned, there is a difference between the SA Saturn conjoining with the ASC, and the SA ASC conjoining with Saturn. For while the SA Saturn being directed to the natal ASC brings restrictions and possible health problems, the SA ASC direction to natal Saturn brings maturity and progress towards wisdom.

However, the most important point in making predictions is the position of the natal planets. Considering the same example of the SA ASC directed to natal Saturn, the dignity, house placement, and aspects of the natal Saturn show us in which area of the native's life this maturity will take place, and what its qualities will be. As the planets and other sensitive points will also change place, they should also be considered.

Keywords and interpretation hints

Here we will only give brief lists of words, without further comment. The symbolism of the planets will be very useful for quick analyses.

☉	Enlightenment, progress, development.
☽	Emotions, emotional approaches.
☿	Intellect, ideas.
♀	Beauty, love, goodness.
♂	Energy, effort.
♃	Progress, prosperity, expansion.
♄	Seriousness, discipline, challenges, restructuring, death, planning, control.
♅	Individualism, higher ideals, contradiction, reform, sudden changes.
♆	Cloudiness, losing one's purpose or goal, melting into universality, inspiration.
♀	Transformation, power.
MC	Professional life, career plans, aim of life, early childhood, mother.
IC	Home, family, moving (including buying and selling property), new beginnings, early childhood, father.
ASC	Identity, personality, tendencies of character.
DSC	Spouse, partners, relationships.

The first 14 years of life are the most important period in the development of the personality: so, investigate to see if there is any significant event within the first 14° of solar arcs. These events may also be related to some conditions in the parents' life.

Saturn's, Uranus's, Neptune's, and Pluto's conjunction, square, and opposition with the angular houses are always important.

If more than one arc is active at the same time, a critical period is likely. When these arcs are triggered by transits and especially by the progressed Moon, we find the timing of events.

If you use the actual speed of the Sun for your arcs, then assume that the events will take place within about 3 months of the exact direction. But if you use the "degree for a year" method, then assume about 6 months.

In solar arcs, we do not interpret the houses that the SA planets progress through. However, if the points involved emphasize something in the natal chart, then we may mention them. For instance, when the lord of the MC is directed to the MC, an emphasis on the career is likely.

The analysis should be in line with the spirit of the time and the nature of the events. For instance, you should not predict a marriage for a seven-year-old child. Such a direction at that time would rather reflect something in the life of the parents.

When studying midpoints, pay attention to SA directions to the midpoint of the Sun-Moon, and the midpoints between Saturn and the outer planets (Saturn-Uranus, Saturn-Neptune, Saturn-Pluto). When the chart is directed, if the outer planets form conjunctions or other aspects with these midpoints, they emphasize important periods in the native's life. You should identify these points beforehand. For instance, the Uranus-Pluto midpoint brings turmoil, changes, and transformation; Saturn-Pluto brings losses and rebirth after destruction, and Jupiter-Pluto brings gains and power. If any directed point makes an aspect to these points, the analyses should be done in accordance with the nature of the directed planet or axis. For instance, the Saturn-Mercury midpoint is related to depression: so if directed Neptune makes a contact with that midpoint, and Neptune is also related to the 12th house, then the native may be in therapy due to a mental problem or depression.

Finally, due to the cause-and-effect principle of the Divine order, if a potential is not promised in a chart it will never be realized. So, before starting prediction, the potentials of the natal chart should be well defined.

Example

In an SA directed chart, since each planet, cusp, the Nodes, and the Lot of Fortune will be directed at the same rate as the Sun, nothing in the chart can be interpreted alone. Although the planets, Nodes, and Lot of Fortune are directed in the signs, their house positions are considered to be the same as in natal chart's house positions.

Let's examine a chart which has been directed by SA for a specific date, and project it onto the natal chart. Below, an SA chart for May 15th, 1991 is projected onto the natal chart. The SA Venus at 23° Aquarius is in conjunction with the natal Sun. Also, the SA Moon at 23° Sagittarius is in a sextile to the degree with the natal Sun. These directions show us that the social status[1] and relationships of the native will be well affected (SA Venus – SA Moon affects the Sun positively); and as the Sun is the lord of the 11th house and

---

[1] **BD**: The Moon rules the natal 10th.

the victor of the 7th house and the Lot of Marriage (16° Leo), it shows that the native will have some experiences like marriage (Venus, Moon). The native was engaged on that date and was married nearly one year later.

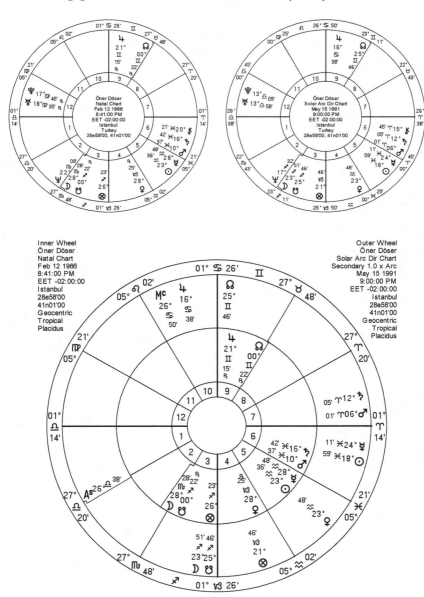

JOHANNES SCHOENER
(REGIOMONTANUS)

CHAPTER 7: SECONDARY PROGRESSIONS

SECONDARY PROGRESSION IS AN IMPORTANT PREDICTIVE METHOD. IT IS BASED ON THE PLANETS' "SECONDARY" MOTION, WHICH IS THEIR MOTION IN THE ZODIAC (AS OPPOSED TO "PRIMARY" MOTION, THE DAILY ROTATION OF THE HEAVENS). IN SECONDARY PROGRESSIONS, ONE DAY IS EQUAL TO ONE YEAR: SO, THE ACTUAL POSITIONS OF THE PLANETS 24 HOURS AFTER BIRTH COMPRISE THE SECONDARY PROGRESSION CHART FOR AGE 1. EACH PLANET PROGRESSES ACCORDING TO ITS OWN PARTICULAR SPEED.[1] SECONDARY PROGRESSIONS ARE RELATED TO THE NATIVE'S INNER DEVELOPMENT, AND HELP US UNDERSTAND HIS POSSIBLE RESPONSES.

Differences between secondary progressions and transits

In terms of interpretation, transits represent outer dynamics, whereas secondary progressions represent the psychological development of the native. Transits refer to outer events because a transiting planet actually appears a certain place of the sky: it can be observed. But secondary progressions cannot be observed directly since they are measured based on some symbolic assumptions. Nevertheless this technique is highly successful in evaluating the psychological process of the native. In a psychological context, everything begins on the level of thought and the emotions which accompany them, and they are then reflected in one's attitudes. As a result, secondary progressions can accurately predict attitudes.

Transits are also universal: in other words, any transit of a planet is valid for everyone on earth.[2] However, the secondary progression of a planet into a sign, its aspect to a natal planet, or its retrograde motion, does not affect everyone at the same level because the effects depend on its contacts with each natal chart. Secondary progressions have individual effects: all influences of the progression—the sign and house changes of the planets, their retrograde and direct movements, and all contacts between the progressed chart and the natal chart—are personal.

The most significant technical difference between transits and secondary progressions is the speed of the planets. As a result, slow planets are important in interpreting transits, while fast planets play the leading role in

---

[1] For the progressed MC and ASC, see below.
[2] **BD**: For example, if Mercury is currently in Gemini, it is in Gemini for everyone.

secondary progressions. The speed of the Moon in the progressed chart is 13° per year, Mercury and Venus 1°, Mars 1° in two years, but Jupiter 1° in 6-7 years and Saturn 1° in 9-10 years (when moving fast and direct).

The orb is +/- 1° in secondary progressions. For applying aspects, the last 12' are more effective because it shows that the beginning of the event is very close. When the exact aspect is realized, the psychological needs and the emotions accompanying them increase. The effects of applying aspects are always more powerful than those of separating aspects.

In order for secondary progressed effects to manifest properly, transits may be needed to trigger them. So, secondary progressions should always be evaluated together with transits. Additionally, instead of evaluating the secondary progressed chart on its own, it must be interpreted in light of its aspects to features of the natal chart. Finally, the aspects of progressed planets to each other should be considered. Contacts between the progressed Sun and Moon are especially important.

In the case of contacts between progressed and natal positions in particular, the native has the opportunity to manage events.

The meanings of progressed planets

The Moon shows our changing emotional needs and emotional tendencies.

Mercury shows changes in the cognitive structure and communication style.

Venus shows changes in the native's attitudes in his social relations and aesthetic values.

Mars shows changes in how the native manifests himself and how he gets involved in actions.

The ASC points out that the habits, primary motivations, and style of the native are changing and developing, with newly added features. For instance, when the progressed ASC is in Libra the native will have a superficial approach towards events, but it will deepen when the progressed ASC enters Scorpio. Aspects between the progressed ASC and the progressed planets will inform us about that style and approach.

The MC, as it represents social status, is less personal as compared to the ASC. Basically, the MC tells us about the native's career, goals, and the path he takes to reach them. As the MC is progressed, the goals of the native and his social image will change. For instance, a native with a Cancer MC tends not to enjoy taking risks for his goals; but when the MC progresses in Leo, the native may become bolder and more decisive.

The Sun represents developments in one's creative expression, the manifestation of will, and organizational structure. The progressed Sun generally represents the course of life. For instance, someone with an Aries Sun will experience Taurus and Gemini characteristics in turn. As consecutive signs have the ability to develop the potentials of the previous ones, the progressed Sun will help the native develop individual integrity and spiritual maturity as he moves from sign to sign.

- What is the lunar phase between the progressed Sun and Moon?
- What is the sign and house of the progressed Moon?
- What is the sign and house of the progressed Sun?
- Does any progressed planet shift to another sign or house?
- Does any progressed planet change direction?
- Is there an exact aspect in the progressed chart?
- Aspects between progressed planets or between them and natal planets.
- The effects of transits on the progressed chart.
- Contacts between the natal chart and the progressed house cusps, particularly the angles.

Aspects to the natal chart

In order to manifest their effects, secondary progressions should apply to the exact aspect by no more than 1°; the effect's duration changes according to the speed of the planet. For example, since the Sun progresses by about 1° per year, he will apply to the exact aspect one year before exactness and will be fully separated one year afterwards. Moreover, note when planets already in aspect in the nativity make those aspects exact by secondary progression.

Conjunctions represent the manifestation of energy. For instance, conjunctions of the Sun raise related motivations to the conscious level: Sun-Uranus represents a kind of enlightenment, Sun-Moon places family issues front-and-center, and Sun-Saturn represents extra responsibilities and maturity.

Squares represent challenges, conflicts, ambitions, and actions.

Oppositions represent contradictions, disaffection, and complementarity between opposed ideas. For instance, Mars-Venus represents conflicts in relationships and Sun-Moon refers to conflicts between emotions and reason.

Trines represent easy flows, opportunities, balance, and harmony. For example, Moon-Saturn refers to a harmony between career, responsibilities, and family life.

Sextiles represent sharing, support, and learning: Sun-Venus represents the support of one's social relations.

Quincunxes represent fated crises and neurotic stresses which need to be transformed. For instance, Sun-Moon represents an incompatibility between the conscious and unconscious mind, and the crises that may occur as a result.

Following are some important things to observe about aspects:

- The natal chart should be well examined and evaluated for its potentials.
- Aspects may be evaluated and understood in light of similar aspects in the past and what they have manifested.
- Aspects between the progressed and natal charts are important and have long-term effects. One should especially examine the aspects of the natal Sun and the lord of the ASC.
- Note when the natal aspects are activated. For example, the progressed Sun may be intersecting the angles of a natal T-square. Or, progressed Venus may square natal planets which are already in opposition and thereby create a new T-square.
- One aspect alone may not cause a significant manifestation. Transits, solar returns, and other techniques should always be used to confirm any prediction.

House and sign shifts

When a planet shifts from one sign to another, the element and quadru-plicity of that sign gains importance. For instance, when the Sun shifts from Pisces to Aries, the element of Fire and the Cardinal quadruplicity will as-sume the stage. The native will give up the quality of self-sacrifice (Pisces) and begin to display a self-oriented attitude (Aries). His self-confidence and vitality will increase. Instead of depending on other conditions, the native will now display strategic attitudes, and need to take action. Moreover, as the Sun is exalted in Aries, the Sun will easily display the Aries functions (identi-ty, creative expression, will power, etc.).

When a planet shifts to another house, we may conclude that the energy of that planet now flows into another field of life. Also, if a planet shifts from a cadent house to an angular one, the power of that planet will increase.

The progressed Sun

The Sun symbolizes vitality and the native's style of manifesting will pow-er, as well as his needs for acceptance and creative expression. The progressed Sun represents development in all these themes. The spirit of the native does not change, but he integrates new characteristics into his person-ality. For instance, a native with the Sun in Aries will experience Taurus and Gemini in turn: so, in addition to the characteristics of Fire, he will later add the features of Earth and then Air to his individuality. When the Sun pro-gresses from a Fire sign to Air, the native will use his previous Fire and Earth qualities in his communication and will express himself by sharing his opin-ions. Finally, when his Sun progresses to the Water element, he will learn how to express his emotions spontaneously and spiritual values will gain im-portance.

The Sun progresses by an average of 1° per year, but is faster in winter and slower in summer. Therefore, for those who were born near the equi-noxes (April and September), the annual progression is virtually 1°, but for those born near the winter and summer solstices (December and June), it will be greater or less than this.

The progressed Sun in the signs

Aries: The Sun is exalted in this sign, and so can display his functions easily and becomes stronger. This progression brings an ability for direct expression, leadership, entrepreneurship, the joy of love, self-confidence, and courage. On the negative side, it may bring impulsiveness, selfishness, and aggression. The native may be more focused on his own wishes instead of being sensitive to others' rights: this may create problems in the stability and harmony of his relationships. If the Fire element is lacking in the native's chart, then when the progressed Sun enters into Aries it will bring a certain sense of adequacy; the native may then easily understand and use Fire energy, perhaps displaying extroverted attitudes and acting with self-confidence and courage.

Taurus: This helps the native in continuing the ventures that he initiated in Aries. He will now have a more peaceful energy and will aim at reaching concrete results by acting in silence. Material needs will take center stage and the native will need to feel financially secure. On the negative side, this progression may bring stubbornness, a resistance to change, and monomania. If the Earth element is lacking in the native's chart, then when the progressed Sun enters Taurus, that inadequacy is compensated for to a certain degree: the native may then easily understand and use Earthy energy; he may act in a practical way and achieve concrete results.

Gemini: The adaptation and learning capacity of the native increases. Communication and mental activities begin to gain more importance in his life. He may be more talkative and restless than before. He is able to shed his stubbornness and monomania, integrating flexibility and versatility into his personality. On the negative side, the native may have some mental obsessions and he may be easily distracted. If the nativity contains much of the Mutable quality, the native may have difficulties in maintaining the continuity of his ventures.

Cancer: Entering Cancer after Gemini, the native learns to listen to others, since Cancer is related to listening to others in an empathic way and giving emotional support. The native now maintains emotional bonds, loves unconditionally, needs emotional security, and increases his capacity for introspection. Family and maternal issues gain importance. The native wants to spend more time with his family during this period. On the negative side, he may display shyness, touchiness, and exaggerated emotions, as he is afraid of being rejected and being unloved.

Leo: After entering Leo, the native needs to be accepted, appreciated, and express himself in a creative way. He wants to manage his life through his will power in order to attract the attention of others and be appreciated. He may display more energetic, confident, and extroverted attitudes. On the negative side, he may be selfish, highly egocentric, overly proud, and patronizing.

Virgo: Here the productivity and performance of the native increase, as well as the need for analysis and the talent for solving problems. In contrast to Leo, Virgo is interested in the demands of others; he wants to help other people. He may be involved in detailed analysis so as to be more productive in life. Due to excessive self-criticism, he may have some issues with his self-confidence: he may avoid risky ventures for fear of making mistakes. Work and health issues will be on the native's agenda, and he may also want to diet and pursue physical fitness.

Libra: When the progressed Sun enters Libra, the native would like to have social bonds with others, and his need for aesthetics, balance, and harmony increases. He may be able to establish permanent and balanced relationships. Partnership issues and marriage may be on his agenda. However, as the Sun is detriment in Libra, the native may experience some difficulties in organizing his life and manifesting his will power. As he is very conciliatory, he may ignore his own wishes and lose his sense of inner balance while trying to put his outer world into balance. During this period, he must learn to get rid of relationship addictions and take the initiative.

Scorpio: The native will need to eliminate the unnecessary structures in his life, focusing instead on renewal, becoming stronger, and transforming. Depth, desires, and spiritual themes will gain importance. During this period the native may use his intuitions to better effect and transform crises into opportunities. However, due to the fixed nature of this sign, the native may have some difficulties in displaying a flexible attitude; he may act in an all-or-nothing manner. Moreover, due to his excessive suspicion, obsession, and desire for revenge, he may find himself engaged in power struggles. He will need to curb his desire for attaining power.

Sagittarius: Here the native will need to discover life, find the meaning of existence, have an original philosophy, and gain wisdom. He enjoys viewing life from a broader perspective and sharing his experiences with others. However, on the negative side, he may be faced with some unwanted results due to taking risks and his excessive optimism. He may also become arrogant, dogmatic, and exaggerate. The native should learn how to take acceptable risks.

Capricorn: The native will need more success, authority, order, and control. During this period, business and responsibilities will be highlighted and the native will be a perfectionist, ambitious, planned, and goal-oriented. He will be more patient and quiet. On the negative side the native may be pessimist and anxious, as he will be afraid of being unsuccessful and inadequate.

Aquarius: Here the native will need change, progress, enlightenment, and obtain a more social identity and perspective. He may be involved in new social groups during this period. He may need to become more free. On the negative side, due to his emotional distance from others he may experience some separations and incoherence in his relationships.

Pisces: The native will need transcendence, devotion, and holistic love. Spiritual and mystical themes will be more important for him, and he will be able to use his creativity and imagination actively. However, on the negative side the native may lose his way; he may be confused and loosen his ties with reality (which he should try to avoid doing).

Aspects of the progressed Sun

Sun-Mercury: As the Sun and Mercury cannot separate from each other by more than 28°, there are not many major aspects between them. A long time is needed for a sextile to form, but when it does the native will have opportunities related to the areas of education and communication. He may make effective decisions, he may form new projects, his mental abilities may increase, and he may travel frequently.

Sun-Venus: Social relations, the joys of the senses, marriage, partnership, artistic activities, and aesthetic values gain importance. When interpreting these aspects, we should focus on the house where the natal Venus is and the houses she rules. For instance, if she rules the 7th then the themes she naturally represents will be more significant because in modern astrology Venus is the natural lord of the 7th house.[3] When the Sun and Venus conjoin, the sign in which they conjoin is important. For instance, if the conjunction

---

[3] **BD**: Döşer means that in the "astrological alphabet" of modern astrology, Aries and its lord Mars are archetypally assumed to represent the 1st house, and so Libra and Venus represent the 7th. Of course in traditional astrology Venus also represents 7th house matters like relationships, but there is no equation of *Libra* and the 7th.

takes place in Scorpio then desires in relationships and some power struggles may come to the surface. As Venus and the Sun cannot be separated from each other by more than 48°, their contacts represent critical periods. However, these two may progress together as their speeds are nearly equal. When they make an aspect of 45°, some stress and conflicts may be seen in social relations.

Sun-Mars: Leadership and entrepreneurial qualities are dominant. When interpreting these aspects, we should focus on the house where Mars is and the houses ruled by him. The Sun-Mars conjunction may increase the native's strength but also the risk of accidents. Positive aspects (the trine and sextile) may increase the native's capacity for competition and undertaking action. The native may also express himself in a direct and clear manner. Negative aspects may bring stress and conflicts. The native may have difficulties in anger management. If the hard aspects occur in the 6th, 8th, or 1st houses, the native may have some health problems.

Sun-Jupiter: Personal development, optimism, hopes, luck, prosperity, having a broader perspective on life, religious and philosophic subjects, are all the themes of these aspects. We should focus on the house where Jupiter is and the houses ruled by him. Positive aspects bring happiness and joy for the native; he may express himself in a creative way and spread his life philosophy to others. He may meet with many opportunities which assist his development both spiritually and physically. Negative aspects may bring risks, exaggeration, arrogance, dogmatism, and adventurousness. If the hard aspects occur in the succeedent houses, the native may be too lavish or may experience financial loss due to taking excessive risks.

Sun-Saturn: Career, responsibilities, success, authority, the need for order, and restructuring are the themes of these aspects. We should focus on the house where Saturn is and the houses he rules. With positive aspects, the native may easily restructure his life. He may achieve success and stability in his career. He knows his responsibilities and focuses on his goals in an organized way. Negative aspects may bring difficulties in his creative expressions, as he may feel stressed and depressed. The native may lose his self-confidence during this period and be easily demoralized. He may also have some health problems.

Sun-Uranus: Changes, developments, enlightenment, and a potential for extraordinary creativity are the main themes. We should focus on the house where Uranus is and the houses he rules. With positive aspects, the native may make some important changes in his life, gain advantage from team-work, and explore new environments. Creativity and dynamism prevail during this period. If these aspects occur in the 1st or 5th houses, the native may manifest his creativity in an extraordinary and original way. Negative aspects may bring some sudden and shocking developments, ups-and-downs, and inconsistencies. If these aspects occur in the 6th or 12th, the native may have some health problems; in the 1st and 7th he may have some separations in his relationships, as well as some financial ups-and-downs if in the 2nd and 8th.

Sun-Neptune: Spiritual and mystical matters, idealism, creativity, inspira-tion, transcendence, and submission are the themes of these aspects. Focus on the house where Neptune is and the houses he rules. With positive as-pects the native may get rid of his ego, overcome duality, and reach holistic love, submission, idealism, inspiration, intuition, and creativity. If these as-pects occur in the 1st or 5th houses, the native may manifest his imaginative power in creative projects. Negative aspects may bring uncertainty, confu-sion, loss of direction, and isolation. If these aspects occur in the 12th, the native may have a drug or alcohol addiction; in the 1st and 7th, he may have some problems and disappointments in relationships, and some health prob-lems if in the 6th and 12th.

Sun-Pluto: The native may experience some important changes and a pe-riod of gaining power and transformation. Focus on the house where Pluto is and the houses he rules. With positive aspects the native may transform crises into opportunities, or he may display his charisma and gain power through the support of authority figures. He may experience a symbolic re-birth. Negative aspects may bring obsessions, skepticism, manipulation, jealousy, hatred, and power struggles. This transformational period may also include serious crises. If the progressed chart is in a balsamic lunar phase, this period may be a strenuous one.

The progressed Moon

The progressed Moon helps us with good timing and planning; she has a triggering effect. As she is the fastest planet, she is able to make contacts with every feature of the chart: so, her progression is a most important tool for astrologers. It shows the subjects the native is focused on emotionally.

The progressed Moon changes signs every 2.5 years, and progresses approximately 1° each month. Her speed changes, being sometimes rapid, sometimes slow, but the annual average speed of the progressed Moon is 13° 10'. Her progression magnifies the nature and house of the planet she aspects, and also the houses which that planet rules. When her aspect triggers aspect patterns in the natal chart, it may bring important events. For instance, she may convert a square to T-square.

The house of the progressed Moon represents the field of life where the native feels a need for change, while her sign represents the quality of his emotional expectations. If the progressed Moon moves from the upper hemisphere of the chart to the lower (or vice versa), it brings important developments.

The progressed Moon in the houses

The delineations below illustrate progressions through the houses using the Moon, but can be applied in principle to the other planets:

1st house: The native initiates a new, individualistic cycle, gaining a subjective perspective and focusing on his own wishes. He cares about his primary motivations, habits, personal development, and physical appearance. His urge is to make changes in his life, and now is the time for action. The motive for realizing himself is based on the element and quadruplicity of the sign in the 1st house.

2nd house: Here the native is focused on his financial resources and values. He needs financial freedom, but may experience some ups and downs in such issues. He may make some investments and take some financial risks. As a result her squares with planets in the 5th house or oppositions with planets in the 8th are important, because the 5th rules risks and speculations, and the 8th rules investments held in common with others.

3rd house: The energy of change is focused on mental processes. This is a good opportunity for engaging in mental activities and for educational purposes. Short distance travels may also be on the agenda, as well as relationships with siblings and neighbors. Communication is also important during this period.

4th house: Emotional security, the need to be rooted, elements related to the family and home, are important issues. The native may want to move to another place or make some renovations at home. He may buy and sell property. It is a time for introversion and looking for inner peace. The native may reappraise his family bonds: some separations may be experienced, or he may come together with family members.

5th house: The native enjoys expressing himself in a creative way. Issues like children, hobbies, fun, love, and sexuality are emphasized. Romantic travels may also be on the agenda.

6th house: The native wants to help others, solve problems, and be productive during this period. He may be involved in activities which help him develop his talents. However, his tasks and the number of problems he has to deal with, increase. This is an ideal period for going on a diet and starting athletic and fitness activities, but the native should be careful about his health. Some issues related to the working environment and one's subordinates may be important. It is also a time for making some adjustments in the working environment and the approaches that are used in it.

7th house: Relationships become important in the native's life. Marriages, divorces, and partnership issues may be a topic of action. The native may develop new attitude patterns in his relationships. Open enemies and conflicts may also come to the surface. The native gets involved in social activities, more so than before.

8th house: Shared resources are emphasized. Topics like credit, mortgage, common investments, and inheritance may be on the agenda. The native may have a tendency towards metaphysics and mystical themes. He may find himself in power struggles and subject to excessive desires. He may also suffer from some emotional crisis.

9th house: The native needs to question existence and become wiser, with a broad perspective. He wants to attain knowledge that will provide meaning to life and form his own philosophy of life. He may evolve through alternative studies. He may also give lectures or write in order to share his knowledge and experiences. Beliefs, spiritual and philosophical themes, all gain importance. He may also travel with the aim of discovering life and foreign cultures.

10th house: Goals, career, social status, and the native's image in society is emphasized. He may have a serious approach towards life and take on more responsibilities. His visibility in society increases and his social status may change; he may get a raise or become famous.

11th house: Radical ideas, changes in the social environment, being involved in charities and clubs, and making new friends, are the themes of this period. The native wants to act together with those who share the same ideals. On the other hand, as the 11th house is the second from the 10th, the native may earn money due to his career achievements.

12th house: Creativity, imagination, inspiration, isolation, and mystical themes will gain importance in the native's life. He may be interested in alternative therapies, meditation, and humanitarian issues. He may prefer to stay behind the scenes. On the negative side, he may run away from reality and lose his direction: so the native must be careful.

The progressed Moon in the signs

The ingress of the progressed Moon into another sign does not mean that the native will totally acquire the qualities of that sign: rather, he emotionally needs the characteristics of that sign.

Aries: The native is focused on taking action and initiative. He likes challenges. He may display his leadership qualities easily. He is more interested in his own desires instead of others' needs. He feels an enthusiasm for life, he begins to act rapidly. On the negative side, he may be over-impulsive, he may rise up in anger and be forced to sit down with a loss, being faced with unwanted results because he acts without thinking.

Taurus: The native is focused on obtaining concrete results and stability. He only feels safe when he is financially secure. He needs more quiet and peace. He does not respond without thinking; he displays silence to those around him. On the negative side, he may be stubborn and resist change. However, as the Moon is exalted in Taurus, these negative possibilities will not be emphasized a lot.

Gemini: The native is focused on taking and giving concrete knowledge, communicating, and engaging in research. He is more curious now. He is fed by knowledge. As he is more extroverted and social during this period, he will not enjoy sitting still and will always act quickly. On the negative side, the native may be nervous and uneasy. As he is multifaceted, he may easily be scattered in his mind.

Cancer: The native is focused on family matters, emotional bonds, and emotional security needs. During this period, he wants to spend more time at home and focus on family problems. The potential of maintaining empathy, emotional support, and emotional bonds, increases. On the negative side, the native may be overly sensitive and resentful. However, as the lord of this sign is the Moon herself, its negative sides are not emphasized much.

Leo: The native is focused on expressing himself in a creative way, and being accepted and appreciated by others. He is optimistic, extroverted and he has the talent for acting self-confidently. He displays his leadership features and his authority easily. On the negative side, he may be selfish and too proud of himself.

Virgo: The native is focused on being productive and making detailed analyses. Issues related to daily work and health are emphasized. The native has a mechanical approach to emotional issues; he only focuses on solving such problems in a mechanical way. As he is too keen on details, he may not see the big picture; and as he is more obsessive, he may feel himself under great stress. He may also lose his self-confidence. Sometimes the native may be obsessive about certain health issues like diets and exercise.

Libra: The native is focused on aesthetic values, relationships, and marriage. He needs to know himself through relationships and maintain one-on-one as well as social bonds. Since he wants to establish a stable and balanced relationship, he will display a conciliatory attitude or act as a reconciler between others. He does not like debates. Aesthetic values gain importance and the native wants to be beautiful as well as make the environment a beautiful place.

Scorpio: The native is focused on eliminating the unnecessary things in life, renewal, gaining strength, and transformation. On the emotional level, he may have a deep, passionate, and sharing attitude. His intuitions develop and he wants to learn everything by examining things deeply. He may be secretive and introverted. On the negative side, the native may be obsessive, skeptical, jealous, and vengeful because the Moon is not in a good position in this sign.

Sagittarius: The native is focused on discovering life, belief systems, and personal expansion. He is optimistic, hopeful, and adventurous. Education, foreign relations, travel, and legal issues are the main themes. On the emotional level he may display a broad perspective towards events but without much depth. On the negative side, he may be faced with unwanted results due to taking too many risks and being too optimistic. He may also be dogmatic and arrogant.

Capricorn: The native is focused on career, success, authority, and order. During this period, work and responsibilities have priority because the native may be cold at the emotional level. The native may suppress his feelings and maintain an emotional distance from others. As it is not a good place for the Moon, the native may be pessimistic and anxious. In any event he may not be able to achieve the success he desires.

Aquarius: The native is focused on changes, progress, reform, enlightenment, and new perceptions. As he needs to have a social identity, he makes new friends and expands his circle. Due to his desire for freedom and being extraordinary, he may have some conflicts with authority and may even rebel. As Aquarius is not a good place for the Moon, the native may experience some emotional ups and downs, and instability. On the positive side the native may make changes during this period, as he is open to new ideas.

Pisces: The native is focused on spiritual and mystical themes. He needs transcendence, submission, and holistic love. He is devoted, emphatic, caring, and sharing with others. His intuitions are strong. On the negative side, due to over-idealizing he may be disappointed and confused, and lose his direction in life.

Progressed Mercury

Mercury represents the native's perception of the world, his communication style, and cognitive process. Mercury's progression shows us what the level of the native's mental development is like. When there are many aspects between progressed Mercury and other planets, the native needs to acquire concrete knowledge, he becomes busy with learning activities, and he is busy with too much communication. As Mercury is also related to travels, commercial activities, transportation, and siblings, those themes are also emphasized.

The aspects of progressed Mercury

Mercury–Venus: Sociability, love, happiness, romantic expressions, creative processes, and artistic themes are emphasized. However, relationships may be superficial. Positive aspects bring harmony in relationships, effective communication, and education. Negative aspects bring disharmony in relationships and problems in communication.

Mercury–Mars: Ventures related to communication and education, and combining physical and mental efforts, are emphasized. The native is successful in producing projects via mental activities and putting them into action if he has the help of positive aspects; he acquires the skills for expressing himself in a direct way. Their negative aspects bring nervous stress, tactlessness, and making decisions without thinking. The native may have problems related to anger management.

Mercury–Jupiter: Education and the integration of concrete and abstract knowledge are emphasized. Positive aspects between these two planets bring opportunities in the fields of education and communication; the native may easily express himself to great masses and discover the world via travelling. On the other hand, negative aspects may bring mental stress, exaggerated or inapplicable ideas, dogmatism, and arrogance. As the native may take risks in the areas of education and communication, he may experience some problems.

Mercury–Saturn: Seriousness and consistency are emphasized in education and communication. The native may take serious steps in his educational life, make effective decisions, and increase his power of concentration with the help of positive aspects between these planets. He may be well-organized and disciplined, and use his planning skills to find success in his career. On the other hand, negative aspects may bring pessimism, anxiety, problems in education and communication, difficulties in concentration, and obsession. He may have difficulty attaining the success he desires because of his shyness and lack of self-confidence.

Mercury–Uranus: Transformation and enlightenment in education and communication are emphasized. The native may produce extraordinary and radical ideas, develop a quicker understanding of things and experience positive development in educational matters through the influence of positive aspects between these two planets. Negative aspects may bring unexpected developments in education and communication, utopian approaches, and rebelliousness. The native may possibly have some nervous disorders.

Mercury–Neptune: Cognitive processes such as creativity, inspiration, and imagination are reflected in communication. With positive aspects, the native may benefit from a limitless imagination and the blessings of his intuition. On the other hand, negative aspects bring confusion, difficulties in making decisions, escaping from reality, and in extreme cases delusion.

Mercury–Pluto: This aspect represents a transformation in educational and communication issues and also in cognitive processes. Positive aspects between these two planets bring an increase in observational ability, the elimination of useless mental patterns, and transforming one's existing cognitive process, becoming a charismatic and effective communicator with positive developments in education. Negative aspects may bring obsession, skepticism, and the fear of death, and power struggles in communication. The native may force others to accept his ideas.

Progressed Venus

Venus is related to aesthetic values, harmony, balance, joy, sexuality, relationships, and sociability. Venus also represents the native's capacity for self-appreciation. In general, this progression shows us the native's style in his one-on-one and social relationships.

The aspects of progressed Venus

Venus–Mars: Creativity and assertiveness in sexuality, desires and male-female relationships, and artistic matters, are emphasized. Positive aspects between these two planets bring harmony in one's sexual life, an easy flow of energies between the two sexes, and creativity in artistic matters. Negative aspects may bring conflicts, competition, and aggression in relationships, extreme desires and an overly impulsive sexual life.

Venus–Jupiter: Opportunities are emphasized, as well as luck and prosperity which arrives due to relationships. Their positive aspects bring important opportunities in social relationships, new friends, and financial opportunities. Negative aspects may bring exaggeration in social relationships, extravagance, big-headedness, and an excessive appetite for sexuality and other sensory pleasures.

Venus–Saturn: Seriousness and stability in social relationships, traditionalism in aesthetic values, and control over pleasures and sexuality are emphasized. With their positive aspects the native may have distant relationships; he is loyal and trusted, and he prefers permanent relationships. He knows his responsibilities in relationships and he may control his sexual desires. Negative aspects bring difficulties in relationships, pessimism towards love, a lack of self-love, a lack of sexual drive, and the suppression of pleasures. The native may also suffer from Venusian health problems (diabetes, diseases of the kidneys and reproductive organs) and financial difficulties.

Venus–Uranus: Innovation and humanism in social relations, sensory pleasures and aesthetic values are emphasized. Positive aspects of these two planets bring sensitivity towards the rights of social groups, and possibly too many friends. As the native has an original approach towards the aesthetic values and sensory pleasures, he may be involved in extraordinary artistic activities. He is also open to new experiences in his sexual life. Negative aspects bring instability, shocking developments, sudden beginnings and endings in social relations, ups-and-downs in financial conditions, and a perverse sexual life.

Venus–Neptune: Romanticism, submission, holistic love, Divine love, and creativity in artistic activities are emphasized. The positive aspects bring devotion, forgiveness, submission in social relations, and a highly romantic love life. The native may also seek Divine love through mysticism. He has the capacity to love everyone without discrimination. As he may use his strong imaginative power in his approach to aesthetic values and pleasures, he may be involved in artistic activities. Negative aspects bring excessive idealization or forgiveness or devotion in social relations, and as a result the native may suffer from disappointments, confusions, and deception. He may be addicted to drugs or alcohol, since such substances help him escape from the realities.

Venus–Pluto: Transformation through relationships is emphasized. The positive aspects bring depth and possessiveness, but the native may transform crises into opportunities. He may see financial and emotional support from influential people and take on some powerful position within society. He uses his power and charisma in his relations with others. Negative aspects bring skepticism, obsession, jealousy, hatred, and power struggles. The native may experience degeneration in sexual relations, which may (at the extreme) lead to sadism. He may also experience a serious financial crisis.

Progressed Mars

Progressed Mars and his aspects show that the native is about to manifest himself, take the initiative, undertake new ventures and actions, and use his energy in a new style.

The aspects of progressed Mars

Mars-Jupiter: Sports, the opportunity for new ventures, and attempts at personal development are emphasized. Positive aspects bring enthusiasm and courage, so that the native may display such attitudes and also use his leadership skills effectively. During this period he may be interested in athletic activities and begin some ventures related to education. He may also be involved in activities which aid his personal development. He may be faced with many opportunities. Negative aspects bring risky ventures, fanaticism, dogmatism, and arrogance. The native may be involved in activities which will later affect him negatively.

Mars-Saturn: Permanent ventures and anger management are related to the harmony of the "id" and "superego," because Saturn represents the social rules and our inner judge (the superego), while Mars represents our primitive sides (the id). Positive aspects between these two may bring effective anger management, permanent and stable ventures, being goal-oriented, and decisive. Negative aspects bring problems in anger management, passive-aggressiveness, and difficulties in taking the initiative. Some problems with physical health may be evident.

Mars-Uranus: Ventures which leads to changes, courage, innovative activities, and independence are emphasized. Positive aspects bring new beginnings, changes, independence, and innovation. Negative aspects bring accidents, resistance to change, incoherency, bursts of anger, and rebellious actions.

Mars-Neptune: Struggling for spiritual values and spiritual goals and idealism are emphasized. Positive aspects bring imagination and creativity in the native's ventures: he may create new artistic projects or manifest himself in spiritual activities. Negative aspects bring a loss of direction, laziness, disappointments due to failed endeavors, and a lack of motivation. As Mars represents the power of survival, the native may experience some health problems (which may be especially related to the immune system).

Mars-Pluto: Ventures which help convert crises into transformations are emphasized. Pluto is like the higher octave of Mars, so when these two planets make positive aspects they bring charisma, courage, leadership, ventures which bring permanent changes, and a talent for beating one's competitors. Negative aspects may bring the misuse of power, cruelty, sadism, and serious crises in one's ventures.

The Moon-Sun relationship

All of the aspects between the progressed Moon and the progressed Sun will create a contact that incorporates both of their natural meanings: such as the feminine-masculine polarity, the conscious-unconscious, emotions-logic, and so on. The houses in which these aspects form, are important.

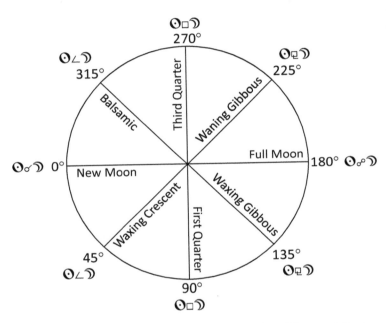

Figure 24: Aspects and phases in the Sun-Moon cycle

This diagram shows the phases between the progressed Moon and progressed Sun. When the Moon and the Sun conjoin (0°), this is the point of the symbolic New Moon. As the Moon is faster than the Sun, she continues her tour and makes different aspects with the Sun until the next conjunction. When the distance between the Sun and the Moon is 45° we have a waxing crescent, 90° is the First Quarter, 135° is waxing gibbous, 180° is the Full Moon, and 315° is the balsamic phase. When the Moon completes this cycle of 360° and reaches the Sun's degree again, it is another New Moon and a new cycle is formed.

Put simply, the period from the New Moon to the Full Moon is a time for initiating and establishing, while the period from the Full Moon to the New

Moon is a time for completion and resignation. Taking each phase individually, the New moon is initiation, the waxing crescent is expanding and concretizing, the First Quarter is action, waxing gibbous is accomplishment, the Full Moon is satisfaction and harvesting, waning gibbous is sharing one's capacities with others, the Third Quarter is reorganizing, and the balsamic Moon is the release period. Let's examine each phase in detail:

New Moon (0°–45°): The progressed Moon and Sun conjoin every 29.5 years. The native may make a new beginning at this time, but as this phase's course is still unclear, the native may not know which direction to take. He may not know the results of his steps. He asks, "Am I doing the right thing?" Nevertheless he wants to take a course of action and leave the past behind, since he has already felt the need for change in the previous balsamic phase. The house where the New Moon occurs is important, because the new beginnings will be related to the needs of that sign and house.

Waxing Crescent (45°–90°): This phase emphasizes the obtaining of feedback for the ventures which were begun at the New Moon, as well as materializing the goals and stabilizing them according to this information. Now the native may rid himself of the effects of the past and be decisive: he may take conscious steps to reach his goals and be ambitious in preserving his own resources. Although it is a difficult phase at the beginning, once the aspect reaches 60° it will be easier to be organized and attain the result.

First Quarter (90°–135°): This is a testing period; the native should be ambitious and disciplined, and make efforts to show his progress. He should actively work at laying a sound foundation for the new steps taken at the progressed New Moon (above). The native should take the initiative and fight for his own existence during this period. It is the time to protect the ventures which were begun under the New Moon. The native should also be approved of by others, even though he may sometimes feel that he is not well understood and not appreciated. Because this aspect starts with a square, some difficulties may be experienced at first, but when the aspect reaches a trine these difficulties should begin to fade and the energy will flow easily.

Waxing Gibbous (135°–180°): During this phase, the native begins to display his creativity, productivity, and he begins to present his works to society. He may be working to find new methods which will increase his productivity and use his resources in an effective way. This is a time for expanding business. The native may make efforts at doing his best and may easily see the results of his efforts. Now the goals are more significant. The native asks himself, "Are there any details of my goals which I have ignored?" He should have confidence in himself and his goals, because the quincunx (at 150°) may cause mistrust and indecisiveness. As a result, the native may experience some crisis which should be transformed into opportunities.

Full Moon (180°–225°): The native may see the results of his efforts to which he gave a start about 14 years ago at the New Moon. So, this is a time of harvest. If the native made positive attempts, he now reaches success; if he was not productive and mature enough, the results he gets may be disappointing. The native is more objective and sharing during this phase, and he may develop with the help of his relationships. Marriage or partnership issues may be on the agenda during this period.

Waning Gibbous (225°–270°): After the Full Moon phase, the energy in the native's life will decrease. Personal ambitions begin to fade. The native now shares his experience with society, wanting to share his philosophies, vision, and—now—wider perception of life with others. During this phase he asks himself, "What have I done for society while trying to reach my goals?" Additionally, he may experience some changes in his life: for instance, he may leave or change his job.

Third Quarter (270°–315°): After the waning gibbous phase, the native wants to present his works to society. He may be busy with his working life and look to obtain concrete results. The native may achieve success and reputation during this phase. He may need to make more efforts and struggle more when the phase reaches the degree of the square. By the end of this phase the native may ask, "What shall I do after this?"

Balsamic (315°–360°): It is the time for purification and recovery from the effects of the past. The native may have difficulties in taking the initiative and may be confused. He may have difficulties in leaving his old habits and addictions behind. Although he resists, he is hardly able to protect his possessions. Some fated losses may be seen. The native needs to be alone and listen to his inner voice: he may then achieve a sense of moving smoothly along with the flow of things. He may enjoy studying spiritual subjects, meditating, and praying.

Progressed retrograde planets

All planets in our solar system are in direct motion, but as observed from the earth most planets appear to slow down, stop, and move backwards. (The Moon and Sun do not retrograde.) This retrograde motion of the planets causes their energies to be blocked: they cannot be utilized well. So, the energy flows inwards and finally the native's capacity for introspection increases. The dates or years when these planets station retrograde or turn direct again are very important, as well as the houses they rule.

Mercury retrograde: Progressed Mercury represents changes in cognitive processes and one's communication style. When the progressed Sun and progressed Mercury are in different signs, the native may feel some conflicts between his spirit and his style of expressing it. When progressed Mercury is retrograde, the native may have some difficulties in communication, learning, and decision-making processes. Consequently, the native may feel that he is misunderstood or that cannot express himself sufficiently. This period lasts for about 19-23 years. On the positive side, the native has the opportunity to turn inwards and observe his own being. When Mercury turns direct, he starts to express himself easily and implement the ideas he composed during Mercury's retrogradation. The houses in which Mercury turns direct, and the houses he rules, are important.

Venus retrograde: Progressed Venus retrogrades for approximately 42 years. During this period, the native may have problems in one-on-one and social relationships. Delays and dissatisfaction may be seen in Venusian themes like marriage, sexuality, and partnerships. When Venus retrogrades, her energy flows inwards and as a result one may see platonic love. On the positive side, the native may develop an awareness of self-love, and his artistic creativity may increase. Aesthetic values carry importance for him, and he may have an original approach towards love and aesthetic values.

Mars retrograde: Progressed Mars retrogrades for approximately 80 years. During this period, the native may have some difficulties in taking the initiative or new steps, and in anger management.

The planets beyond Mars cover longer periods in human life which are not as easily applicable or interpretable. For instance, Jupiter retrogrades for 120 years and Saturn for 150 years.

The progression of house cusps

One may observe the progression of intermediate house cusps in their sign changes as well as their contacts with natal and progressed planets. However, as the MC and ASC are the most personal indicators, they should be emphasized.

Finding the progressed MC is easy: it is progressed at the same rate as the Sun. Because the ASC is a function of the MC and the birth latitude, the progressed ASC is found by first progressing the MC to the desired position, and then finding the corresponding ASC calculated from it, using a table of houses or computer program. For example, one may display the chart in a computer program, and advance or animate the chart over time: the program will automatically calculate the ASC for whatever MC position one chooses.

Progressed MC: This represents the native's goals, his way of manifesting himself, his career, social status, and social image. When the MC progresses, its contacts with planets represent events and changes in the native's life. For instance, when the progressed MC conjoins with the natal Moon, it is a time for making *changes* in one's business life and one's goals, because the Moon represents changing conditions. When it squares the natal Moon, the changes also bring emotional crisis. When it trines the natal Moon, the native may find support from women or from his mother.

Progressed ASC: This represents the native's primary motivations, talents, and habits. When the progressed ASC makes contacts with planets, important events and changes occur that are related to those contacts: the energy of that planet is reflected in the native's life in terms of 1st house themes. With sextiles and trines the energy flows easily, whereas with squares and oppositions some challenges and stresses may come to the surface. For example, the conjunction of the progressed ASC and natal Mars means that the native should be involved in new ventures and take the initiative. However, as the ASC represents the body and Mars rules accidents, this period may be risky in terms of health issues; this risk is greater when the progressed ASC squares natal Mars. Moreover, the native may need to fight for his projects and he may be aggressive because he is under stress. With the trine of the progressed ASC and natal Mars, the native may easily take the initiative, since the flow of energy helps him to take action.

JOHANNES SCHOENER

CHAPTER 8: DIRECTING BY BOUNDS OR TERMS

DIRECTING OR DISTRIBUTING BY THE BOUNDS OR TERMS IS ONE OF THE OLDEST PREDICTIVE TECHNIQUES. BOUNDS ARE DIVISIONS OF EACH SIGN INTO FIVE UNEQUAL PARTS, EACH RULED BY ONE OF THE FIVE TRADITIONAL PLANETS (EXCLUSIVE OF THE LUMINARIES). THESE BOUND LORDS ARE THE KEY FACTORS IN THE TECHNIQUE: WHEN THE ASC OR OTHER POINTS ARE DIRECTED THROUGH THE BOUNDS, THE BOUND LORD DESCRIBES THE TYPES OF EVENTS AND DEVELOPMENTS THAT WILL TAKE PLACE DURING THAT TIME PERIOD.

The table of Egyptian bounds is used for this method (see below).[1] As an example, an Ascendant of 1° 14' Libra falls in the bound of Saturn, which stretches from 0° - 5° 59' Libra. So as we direct the Ascendant, Saturn will be the bound lord for as many years as correspond to the remaining 4° 46' of his bound, until we reach the next bound at 6°. Then the Ascendant will enter Mercury's bound and he will rule the native's life for the years corresponding to 6° - 14° Libra. Jupiter is the next bound ruler, between 14° and 21° Libra. Venus is the next bound lord to dominate the native's life, between 21° and 28°. Finally, Mars will rule the bound between 28° Libra and 0° Scorpio, then Mars again from 0° - 6° 59' Scorpio, and so on.

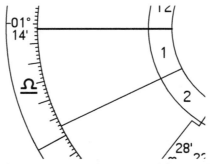

Figure 25: The Ascendant in the bound of Saturn in Libra

---

[1] **BD**: Historically there were several versions of the bounds or terms, but the "Egyptian" was the most widespread from antiquity up through the medieval Arabic period.

♈	♃ 0°-5°59'	♀ 6°-11°59'	☿ 12°-19°59'	♂ 20°-24°59'	♄ 25°-29°59'
♉	♀ 0°-7°59'	☿ 8°-13°59'	♃ 14°-21°59'	♄ 22°-26°59'	♂ 27°-29°59'
♊	☿ 0°-5°59'	♃ 6°-11°59'	♀ 12°-16°59'	♂ 17°-23°59'	♄ 24°-29°59'
♋	♂ 0°-6°59'	♀ 7°-12°59'	☿ 13°-18°59'	♃ 19°-25°59'	♄ 26°-29°59'
♌	♃ 0°-5°59'	♀ 6°-10°59'	♄ 11°-17°59'	☿ 18°-23°59'	♂ 24°-29°59'
♍	☿ 0°-6°59'	♀ 7°-16°59'	♃ 17°-20°59'	♂ 21°-27°59'	♄ 28°-29°59'
♎	♄ 0°-5°59'	☿ 6°-13°59'	♃ 14°-20°59'	♀ 21°-27°59'	♂ 28°-29°59'
♏	♂ 0°-6°59'	♀ 7°-10°59'	☿ 11°-18°59'	♃ 19°-23°59'	♄ 24°-29°59'
♐	♃ 0°-11°59'	♀ 12°-16°59'	☿ 17°-20°59'	♄ 21°-25°59'	♂ 26°-29°59'
♑	☿ 0°-6°59'	♃ 7°-13°59'	♀ 14°-21°59'	♄ 22°-25°59'	♂ 26°-29°59'
♒	☿ 0°-6°59'	♀ 7°-12°59'	♃ 13°-19°59'	♂ 20°-24°59'	♄ 25°-29°59'
♓	♀ 0°-11°59'	♃ 12°-15°59'	☿ 16°-18°59'	♂ 19°-27°59'	♄ 28°-29°59'

Figure 26: Table of Egyptian Bounds

According to 'Umar al-Tabarī, the degree of the natal ASC should be directed for making predictions about the native's life as a whole.[2] After specifying the exact degree and minute of the ASC, the bound lord should be identified, and number of zodiacal degrees between the ASC and the next bound should be converted into oblique ascensions.[3] "Oblique" ascensions (or more often, simply "ascensions") are degrees of the celestial equator that pass across the Ascendant-Descendant axis: they are *not* simply zodiacal degrees. Thus a bound that is 6° long in the zodiac will not last for 6 years, but will last for the period corresponding to how long the bound is in *ascensional* degrees. These depend highly on the birth latitude. Once we know the number of ascensions, each 1° of ascensions will equal 1 year of life. Easy mathematical instructions will be given below for determining the ascensions of each bound at any latitude.

The lord of whatever bound the ASC is in, is called the *jārbakhtār* by 'Umar al-Tabarī, which is a Persian word meaning the "distributor" or "divisor" of time.[4] The first bound lord will rule the native's life for the years, days, and hours corresponding to those remaining degrees, minutes, and seconds of the bound, the next bound lord will rule for as many years as correspond to its bound, and so on.

---

[2] **BD**: See my translation of 'Umar's book on nativities, in my *Persian Nativities II*, Ch. II.5.
[3] **BD**: See below.
[4] **BD**: See 'Umar's book of nativities in my *Persian Nativities II*, Ch. II.6.

Interpreting the bound

In order to interpret the period of the bound, the nature of the distributor and the bound's position in the zodiac should be considered. If this planet is a benefic or is in contact with the benefic planets, these years will be spent in tranquility, enlargement, and prosperity. On the contrary, if the bound lord is a malefic planet, or in detriment, or in a bad place, the native will be faced with difficulties and dangers during that period of his life.

Guido Bonatti also states[5] that we should evaluate the planets that are in aspect to the bound, and the nature of that aspect. In the chart below, let's assume that the direction of the Ascendant has reached 21° Libra, the bound of Venus, with the natal Jupiter being at 21° Gemini. Jupiter's trine to that bound, which is a positive aspect to a benefic bound, points out that the native will have a prosperous and good time in regards to his relationships. Indeed, the native below (me) got engaged at that time and married when he was 26. Marriage is a Venusian event, and since Jupiter is in a good aspect to the bound, we may conclude that the native is about to enter a happy period in his life.

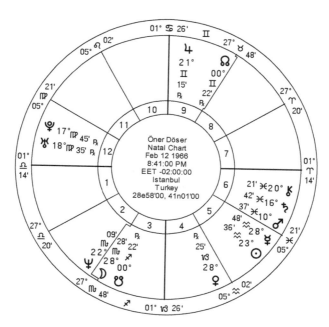

---

[5] **BD**: See Bonatti's *Book of Astronomy* (or *Bonatti on Nativities*), Tr. 9, Part 2, Ch. 6.

188 ASTROLOGICAL PREDICTION: A HANDBOOK OF TECHNIQUES

By directing the longevity releaser or *hīlāj* through the bounds,[6] we may also make predictions. Let's assume that the releaser is in 16° Gemini, which is the bound of Venus. When we direct that degree to 18° Gemini, the health conditions of the native will change because the bound lord will shift from Venus to Mars. The native may experience some more health problems when the releaser's bound shifts from Mars to Saturn. According to Bonatti, if the releaser's bound lord proceeds from one malefic planet to another malefic, the result may be fatal. Of course, we should always consider the placements of these planets in the natal chart and their aspects. If the malefic planets are well placed in a chart or if they rule good houses, the interpretation changes accordingly.

Example: Öner Döşer Ascendant

As I said above, the number of degrees between the ASC and the next bound must be converted from zodiacal degrees to oblique ascensions (OA). This means we must know the OA of both the ASC (or OA ASC), and the beginning of the next bound. The difference between these OAs will be the length of the period we want.

The OA ASC is always the RA of the MC (or RAMC) + 90°. So if we know from our computer program that the RAMC is 91° 34' 35", then this number +90° gives use the OA ASC:

For ASC 1° ♎ 14':
OA ASC = RAMC + 90°
OA ASC = 91° 34' 35" + 90°
OA ASC = 181° 34' 35"

Now we need to find the OA of the beginning of the next bound, that of Mercury at 6° Libra. Although we could calculate this directly using trigonometry, the easier way is to advance the native's chart (using the electional

---

[6] **BD**: *Hīlāj* (also spelled *hyleg*) comes from a Persian term meaning "releaser," which translates the Greek term *apheta*, "releaser." In general, a releaser is nothing more than some point which we direct. But in particular, it refers to a point in the chart which indicates the native's longevity and life force: so directing it will have significations for the native's health and well-being. Ptolemy's instructions for finding this releaser are in *Tetrabiblos* III, Ch. 10 or 11 (depending on the edition). 'Umar al-Tabarī's are in his book on nativities, in *Persian Nativities II*, Ch. I.4. Not every releaser can be directed in exactly the same way.

or other timing function on your computer program) until 6° Libra is rising. Then, look up the RAMC for that chart and add 90°. The RAMC when 6° Libra rises at the native's latitude, happens to be 97° 35' 04".

For 6° ♎ 00' (Bound of Mercury):
OA ASC = RAMC + 90°
OA ASC = 97° 35' 04" + 90°
OA ASC = 187° 35' 04"

The time between birth and when the Ascendant enters the bound of Mercury, is the difference between the two OAs: 187° 35' 04" – 181° 34' 35" = 6° 00' 29". How long is this exactly? The ancients used a year of 365 days for calculations, with an assumed 30 days per month. Therefore:

1° = 1 year
5' = 1 month
1' = 6 days
10" = 1 day

The distance of 6° 0' 29" is 6y 0m 3 days: Therefore, the native will enter the Mercury period shortly after turning 6 years old.

The following calculations show the OA at the beginning of two more bounds and the total time elapsed from the birth OA, showing us how old the native will be when he enters each bound. Cast the natal chart above and use your own computer program to put the successive bounds on the Ascendant, and verify the RAMC and OA ASC for those times:

For 14° ♎ 00' (Bound of Jupiter):
OA ASC = RAMC + 90°
OA ASC = 107° 42' 43" + 90°
OA ASC = 197° 42' 43"
Time elapsed: 197° 42' 43" – 181° 34' 35" = 16° 08' 08" = 16y 1m 15d from birth

For 21° ♌ 00' (Bound of Venus):

OA ASC = RAMC + 90°

OA ASC = 116° 35' 36" + 90°

OA ASC = 206° 35' 36"

Time elapsed: 206° 35' 36" − 181° 34' 35" = 25° 01' 01" = 25y 0m 6d from birth

With the help of these calculations, it is possible to determine the planetary age of the native and his distributor or bound lord for any age. The table below shows the values for this client until about 74 years old, beginning from his ASC in the bound of Saturn:

BOUND	SIGN	LONG.	OA OF BOUND	YEARS FROM BIRTH
♄	♌	(1° ♌ 14')	(181° 34' 35")	0y – 6y 3d
☿	♌	6° ♌ 00'	187° 35' 04"	6y 3d – 16y 1m 15d
♃	♌	14° ♌ 00'	197° 42' 43'	16y 1m 15d – 25y 0m 6d
♀	♌	21° ♌ 00'	206° 35' 36"	25y 0m 6d – 33y 11m 11d
♂	♌	28° ♌ 00'	215° 31' 24"	33y 11m 11d – 36y 6m 1d
♂	♏	0° ♏ 00'	218° 04' 49"	36y 6m 1d – 45y 5m 19d
♀	♏	7° ♏ 00'	227° 02' 47"	45y 5m 19d – 50y 7m 6d
☿	♏	11° ♏ 00'	232° 10' 38"	50y 7m 6d – 60y 10m 10d
♃	♏	19° ♏ 00'	242° 26' 19"	60 y 10m 10d – 67y 3m 0d
♄	♏	24° ♏ 00'	248° 49' 36"	67y 3m 0d – 74y 10m 11d
♃	♐	0° ♐ 00'	256° 26' 21"	74y 10m 11d

Ages 0 - 6 (Bound of Saturn)

During this time, the native had many inflammatory diseases, especially due to throat infections. He had a weak constitution. Saturn is in the 6th, in a conjunction with Mars: this is an indication of inflammatory diseases. Saturn squares Jupiter, the lord of the 6th: this also threatens health.

Ages 6 - 16 (Bound of Mercury)

In this period, the native was interested in scientific subjects and especially in the space sciences. When he was small, he wrote many stories. He had athletic tendencies, playing football in his early years and basketball after 13. During that period, sports were the only important thing in his life. Although he was talented and successful in them, he did not attain the level he hoped for. (On the other hand, many of his teammates became famous basketball players.) His health was still poor until age 13. There were also some problems related to his mother, who died when he was 13.

Mercury is in trine with Jupiter, which shows his interest in scientific subjects and writing; the 5th house, where the Mercury is placed, shows his tendency toward sports. His Mercury is separating from the Sun, but is combust: this means he is still weak and cannot attain the level of success he desires in athletics. The Sun is the lord of the 11th, so his conjunction with Mercury shows that the native is friends with many famous basketball players. Mercury square Moon represents the problems with the mother, and the Moon square Sun shows the unrest between his father and mother. Finally, Mercury is placed in the 8th house from the 10th (the house of mother): this shows the death of the mother.

Ages 16 - 25 (Bound of Jupiter)

The native was still highly fond of sports. In 1982, he failed a class because he forgot the exam, and decided to take a break from school and work with his father. His father was an extreme disciplinarian during that period. In 1984, the native had jaundice; after that he had a stomach hernia operation, then another small operation on his foot, and finally some diseases related to his kidneys. After graduating from high school, he started his business in commerce. During the same period, he took some language and computer courses. Due to a discussion with his father on the night before the university entrance exam, he canceled all of his applications and attended long-distance learning courses. He continued helping his father. He graduated from the long-distance program in 1991, but was never content with that degree: he always believed that he would have been more successful if he had attended a formal university.

The bound lord Jupiter is the lord of the 6th, which indicates illnesses in general. He is in Gemini, in the 9th, in trine with the Sun and Mercury in his 5th house. This shows his athletic talents. Saturn (the lord of the 4th) squaring Jupiter in the 9th house represents the difficulties in academic environments; his dissatisfaction in that area stems from the Saturn square as well as the retrograde motion of Jupiter. However, the Mercury-Jupiter trine explains his desire for a better education. Jupiter in detriment explains the jaundice, as Jupiter rules the liver. Pisces on the cusp of the sixth house represents the problems related to the feet. His early business life in commerce is indicated by Jupiter, as Jupiter is the exalted lord of the cusp of the 10th house.

Ages 25 - 34 (Bound of Venus)

Here, he began flirting with his future wife. After completing his military service, he got married at age 26. He continued working with his father, setting up a partnership together in 1995. Then in 1996, he began manufacturing apparel and got active in a wholesale business with a different partner. He was busy with that business and also with his father's activities until 2002. He was badly affected by the economic crisis in 1995. He moved his house four times after getting married, until he was 34 years old. In 1997, his father died in a traffic accident.

The bound lord Venus is in Capricorn, in her own triplicity and in retrograde motion. She is in aspect to the Moon and the North Node. The sextile between the lord of the ASC (Venus) and the Moon represents marriage. Also, Venus indicates partnerships generally, and the 4th house where Venus is placed is the house of the father. So, a partnership with the father is likely. Venus is in the 10th house from the 7th house: this shows us his partner in the apparel manufacturing business. Venus in the 4th and in a cardinal sign explains why he moved to different houses,[7] while her retrogradation represents dissatisfaction in finding the right one. Retrograde Venus also represents the economic turbulence during the crisis. His father's death is emphasized due to Venus' placement in the fourth house. As Saturn (the dispositor of Venus) is in conjunction with Mars in the 6th, we may conclude that his father's death will have a Martial nature (a traffic accident).

---

[7] **BD**: Movable or cardinal signs show quick changes from one thing to another.

Ages 34 - 45.5 (Bound of Mars)

The native was badly affected by an economic crisis in 2001, and ended his involvement in the manufacturing business in 2002. In 2003, he started studying astrology. In 2005, he founded the AstroArt school of astrology as well as an art business with his wife. He supported his wife financially.

The bound lord Mars is in Pisces in the 6th, in conjunction with Saturn. Mars is the lord of the 7th house as well as the 2nd house by whole signs. Mars ruling the 2nd must have brought negative developments due to the financial crisis. The Mars-Saturn conjunction in the 6th represents his change of occupation and escape from the family business. Both of these planets ruling the 4th house (Saturn by sign, Mars by exaltation): he soon started working from an office at home.

The technique of directing by bounds should be used together with other interpretive and predictive techniques. More explanatory data may be maintained by using profections, primary directions, solar and lunar return charts, and transits.

JOHANNES KEPLER

CHAPTER 9: PRIMARY DIRECTIONS

PRIMARY DIRECTIONS ARE BASED ON PRIMARY OR DIURNAL MOTION (THE APPARENT DAILY ROTATION OF THE HEAVENS AROUND THE EARTH). IN THIS TECHNIQUE A PLANET OR ITS ASPECT IS DIRECTED TO AN ANGULAR CUSP OR TO ANOTHER PLANET. THIS IS ONE OF THE STRONGEST PREDICTIVE TECHNIQUES OF TRADITIONAL ASTROLOGY, AND IS USED FOR PREDICTING IMPORTANT EVENTS IN A NATIVE'S LIFE.

Basic concepts

Primary directions are an ancient technique, which were probably first used in calculating longevity, and are described in the earliest sources, such as Nechepso-Petosiris and Dorotheus. One of the most famous and influential descriptions came from Ptolemy (ca. 150 AD), in his chapter on calculating longevity.[1] Martin Gansten's work on the history and theory of primary directions (2009) is a fascinating discussion of how different astrologers used, adapted, changed, and misunderstood primary directions. They were particularly popular in the Western Renaissance and Early Modern period (15th-17th Centuries). Famous names in this area include Regiomontanus (1436-1461), Naibod (1527-1593), Morin (1587-1656), Lilly (1602-1681), and Placidus (1603-1668).

Each of these astrologers had his own preferred method, and certain people's primary directions can be very complicated. We will stick with the basic method described by Ptolemy, and described in a somewhat simpler way by al-Qabīsī in the 10th Century: both give the same results as Placidean Semi-Arcs.

Basic definition of directions

Primary directions are based on primary motion, which is the earth's rotation on its axis every 24 hours. The planets, fixed stars, and luminaries all rise from the east, culminate at the meridian, set in the west, and anti-culminate at the IC. Throughout that daily motion, each one makes all possible aspects

---

[1] *Tet.* III.10 (Robbins edition).

with all other planets, stars, luminaries, and Lots, all of which are considered to be fixed in place (see below).

The distances between points are measured in arcs of degrees, but those of right ascension (RA) along the celestial equator, rather than in longitudinal degrees in the zodiac: the whole aim of primary direction is to measure these arcs. The size of the arc determines when (how many years, months, and days after the birth) the events will be experienced. The character of an event is based on the nature of the "significator" and "promittor," their positions in the zodiac, and their house placements.

Because primary directions are based on primary or diurnal motion, they are different from secondary progressions, which are based on secondary or zodiacal motion. In secondary motion, the planets move in the zodiac from west to east; likewise, secondary progressions are measured by longitude in the zodiac (on the ecliptic), instead of the equatorial degrees or right ascension (RA) used in primary directions.

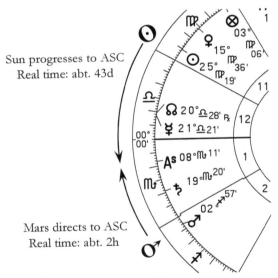

Sun progresses to ASC
Real time: abt. 43d

Mars directs to ASC
Real time: abt. 2h

Figure 27: Primary directions and secondary progressions

The diagram above partly illustrates the difference. If we progress the Sun (at 25° Virgo) to the ASC (at 8° Scorpio) by secondary progressions, this will take about 43 days, simply because it takes that long for the Sun to move there in real time. Since progressions equate one day of actual motion to one year of life, we should expect an event of a Sun-ASC type around age 43. But we can also move Mars (at 2° Sagittarius) to the horizon or ASC by primary directions: this is based on the rate of the daily rotation of the heavens. In this case, it will take somewhere around 2 hours of real rotation after birth for his body to reach the horizon or ASC. The actual distance on the celestial equator needed to do this, is converted into years of life.

The significator and promittor

In primary directions, one point is directed to another point: the point that remains still (such as the Ascendant above) is considered passive, while the point which moves by primary motion is the active point (such as the body of Mars). Since medieval times these were called the *significator* and *promittor*, but not every author used these terms in the same way. We will follow Martin Gansten's understanding of how these were understood by ancient authors.

The significator is a planet or point in the chart which indicates some area of life: it is the passive element which remains still. Ptolemy[2] and other authors used 5 significators, which were sometimes called "releasing" (or "hylegiacal") points: the Ascendant, Midheaven, Sun, Moon, and Lot of Fortune. They believed that all important events of life might be predicted by using primary directions. However, some astrologers disagreed: al-Rijāl, Morin, and Lilly used all 7 traditional planets as significators.[3]

On the other hand, the promittor is the active element which is brought to the significator by primary motion, and it defines the nature of the events indicated by the significator. All 7 planets, and their aspects, are the traditional promittors. Some astrologers include the fixed stars, too.

Important: because the astronomical reality is different from how it looks on paper, confusion can arise when reading books on directions. On paper, people often imagine that a significator like the Ascendant is moving forward or counter-clockwise through the zodiacal signs, to meet the promittor (such as the body of Mars). So in the diagram we might think of the Moon (significator) being directed forward in the zodiac to the square of Mars (promittor) at 2° 57' Virgo. But in reality it is the other way around: the square of Mars (promittor) is being directed clockwise by diurnal or primary motion toward the significator (Moon).

---

[2] *Tet.* III.10 (Robbins edition).
[3] Gansten, pp. 5-6.

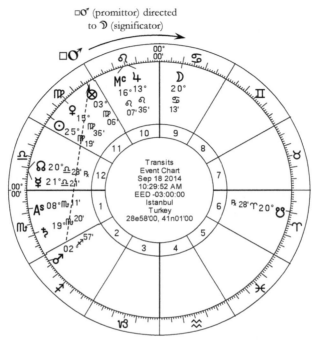

Figure 28: Square of Mars (promittor) directed to Moon (significator)

Direct and contrary motion

As Gansten points out, Ptolemy distinguished two types of direction when predicting the length of life.[4] The first type is exactly what we described above (although in Ptolemy it only occurs when the planet indicating longevity is on the eastern hemisphere of the chart): the promittor is directed by primary motion, from east to west, towards the stationary significator (the planet indicating longevity). But because on paper it is easier to visualize the significator as moving counter-clockwise through the signs towards the promittor, Ptolemy called this "motion towards the following signs." This came to be known as "direct" directions.

In the second type, Ptolemy's longevity planet is on the western side of the chart, and instead of remaining still, he directed the *significator* itself with

---

[4] Gansten, pp. 109-11. **BD:** Please note that Ptolemy *only* described this for the length of life technique: he did *not* discuss contrary motion in his general account of directions for normal annual predictions (i.e., directing or distributing through the bounds/terms), in *Tet.* IV.

diurnal motion, towards the *promittors*. This time, Ptolemy called it "motion towards the previous sign," and it came to be known as "contrary" directions. *Nevertheless, it still involved primary or diurnal motion, not motion through the zodiac.*

After the 19th century, the meaning of contrary directions changed greatly, and one may read Gansten's book to understand what changes took place. By that time as well, retrograde planets and Lots were being directed in special ways, sometimes by people who did not completely understand the techniques.

In mundo and in zodiaco directions

A major division of primary directions is between *in mundo* ("in the world") and *in zodiaco* ("in the zodiac") directions, and aspects associated with them.

In zodiaco directions involve positions on the ecliptic itself, with no ecliptical latitude. For instance, since the Sun's path defines the ecliptic, his directions are always *in zodiaco*. In the diagram above, an *in zodiaco* direction of the body of Mars would be a direction of 2° 57' Sagittarius *on the ecliptic or zodiac itself,* not of the actual body of Mars: for, he probably has some latitude north or south of the ecliptic.

In mundo directions take planetary latitudes into account. If Mars has some latitude north or south of the ecliptic, his position will be slightly different than 2° 57' Sagittarius on the ecliptic itself: so, the direction of his body *in mundo* will lead to a somewhat different arc of direction. This can sometimes create years of difference between the same *in zodiaco* and *in mundo* direction.

Because aspects are measured on the zodiac, a promittor like the square of Mars can be directed *in zodiaco* (as in the chart above). But it can also be measured *in mundo*, or on the celestial equator. Because of the obliquity of the ecliptic, a square on the equator (*in mundo*) can correspond to a degree on the zodiac that is closer to a zodiacal trine, and vice versa.

In this book we will not direct any aspects at all. We will also use only *in mundo* positions: this is because when most computer programs list planetary positions (such as right ascension and declination), they automatically use the *in mundo* positions, which will make our work easier. For more information on primary directions, with numerous formulas, see Gansten (2009).

Why do we direct certain points?

In the medieval tradition, the following points are directed for the following purposes:[5]

- **ASC**: health and physical conditions.
- **Sun**: reputation and recognition.
- **Moon**: physical and spiritual conditions, and the spouse.
- **Lot of Fortune**: wealth and earnings.
- **MC**: the native's occupation.
- **Pre-natal lunation:**[6] if the native was born with a waxing Moon, events up until middle age; if a waning moon, events after middle age.

Three kinds of directions

Below I will explain certain specialized terms, but in general there are three ways to calculate a direction, based on what the significators and promittors are:

- If one of the two points is the MC or IC, then the arc is measured purely in RA: it is the difference between the significator's and promittor's RAs. This is the easiest to calculate.
- If one of the two points is the degree of the Ascendant or Descendant, the arc is measured purely in oblique ascension (OA) in the case of the Ascendant, and oblique descension (OD) in the case of the Descendant. The arc is the difference between the OA/OD of the two points. This is the next easiest to calculate.
- In all other instances, we must use a kind of adjusted OA or OD based on a ratio to be described below. This is trickier, but still not difficult.

---

[5] See Bonatti, *Bonatti on Nativities*, pp. 1401-03.
[6] **BD**: That is, the degree of the New or Full Moon which more closely preceded the native's birth.

Terminology and symbols

Many people are intimidated when calculating primary directions, and they may seem complicated. But by using *in mundo* positions taken directly from the computer, most of our work will be adding and subtracting, with only one equation to solve at the end. Following are a few abbreviations we will use in the formulas:

Φ = Birth latitude
λ = Zodiacal longitude
β = Zodiacal latitude
RA = Right Ascension. "RAMC" is the RA of the MC, and "RAIC" is the RA of the IC.
OA / OD = Oblique Ascension (used for the eastern side of the chart) and Oblique Descension (used for the western side of the chart).
δ = Declination of a point, expressed as a positive (northern) or negative (southern) value.

Key of Time: The value for converting the arc of direction into time. Ptolemy's key is a common one: 1° of arc = 1 year, 5' of arc = 1 month, 1' of arc = 6 days. Other keys include Naibod's, which is used by followers of Regiomontanus directions.

Calculation examples

As I stated above, there are three ways to direct, based on what the significator and promittor are. We'll take each in order:

1. If the MC/IC is one of the points: use RA only

In the example chart below, the MC is directed in a contrary manner to Jupiter.[7] Since the MC is one of the positions, the arc is simply the difference in RA between them (otherwise known as the MD, or meridian distance):

---

[7] **BD**: This would not normally be allowed in strict classical practice, because the Midheaven is a fixed circle: so, it could not move with diurnal motion towards Jupiter. In this case, Döşer is really directing the *degree* of the MC. We could also look on this as a converse direction of Jupiter to the MC. Either way, we only need the RA of both positions.

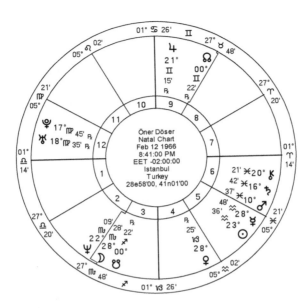

	MC	Jupiter
RA (from computer)[8]	91° 34' 35"	80° 30' 11"

Arc of Direction = RA MC (91° 34' 35") – RA Jupiter (80° 30' 11")
              = 11° 04' 24"

Using Ptolemy's key of time, the arc is 11 years, 1 month (approximately). Since I was born on February 12, 1966, the direction comes to March, 1977. In March 1977, I took the exams to attend secondary school. I was highly successful in all the exams I took, and started to attend one of the best schools at the time.

Important: computer programs usually only give the RA of the MC (RAMC), not the RA of the IC (RAIC). If we had directed something involving the IC, we would use the RAIC instead. The RAIC is always 180° from the RAMC, so you would simply add or subtract 180° to or from the RAMC to find it. If the value is greater than or less than 360°, then add or subtract 360° to it to get a number between 0° and 360°.

---

[8] **BD**: These are values from the astrology program Janus, accurate to the second. They are found from the main screen: Calculate > Planet Positions.

Pt	Name	Sg	Hs	R.A.	Decl.
☽	Moon	♏	3	236° 16'	-19° 37'
☉	Sun	♒	5	325° 55'	-13° 39'
☿	Mercury	♒	5	331° 35'	-13° 33'
♀	Venus	♑	4	298° 57'	-13° 01'
♂	Mars	♓	6	342° 28'	-08° 26'
♃	Jupiter	♊	9	080° 30'	+22° 55'
♄	Saturn	♓	6	348° 30'	-06° 58'
♅	Uranus	♍	12	169° 49'	+05° 15'
♆	Neptune	♏	2	230° 12'	-16° 36'
♇	Pluton	♍	12	174° 50'	+18° 32'
⚷	Chiron	♓	6	349° 34'	-00° 07'
☊	North Node	♊	9	058° 40'	+20° 19'
☋	South Node	♐	3	238° 40'	-20° 19'
ASC	Ascendant	♎	1	181° 08'	-00° 29'
MC	Midheaven	♋	10	091° 34'	+23° 26'
⊗	Pt. Fortune	♐	3	266° 03'	-23° 36'
DSC	Descendant	♈	7	001° 08'	+00° 29'
IC	Imum Coeli	♑	4	271° 34'	-23° 26'

Figure 29: Table of right ascensions and declinations, Öner Döşer

2. If the ASC/DSC is one of the points: use OA/OD only

Now, let's direct the Descendant in a contrary manner to the body of Mars. Because the Descendant is one of the points, the arc is simply the difference between the OD DSC and the OD of Mars.

The OA of the Ascendant is always RAMC + 90°, and the OD of the Descendant is always RAMC - 90°. Since the RAMC is already given by the computer program, it is easy to calculate. Let's find the OD DSC first:

$$OD\ DSC = RAMC - 90°$$
$$= 91°\ 34'\ 35" - 90°$$
$$= \mathbf{1°\ 34'\ 35"}$$

If the result is greater than or less than 360°, then add or subtract 360° to it to get a number between 0°-360°.

Now let's find the OD of Mars, which is a bit more complicated. First we need to get some data on Mars from the computer, then make two calculations:

	Mars
RA (from computer)	342° 28' 56"
δ (from computer)	-08° 26' 36"

In order to use this information to find the OD of Mars, we must find his ascensional difference (AD), which is always found using this equation:

$$AD = \arcsin (\tan \delta * \tan \Phi)$$

AD Mars $= \arcsin (\tan \delta * \tan \Phi)$
$= \arcsin (\; (-.14844004) * (.869797567) \;)$
$= \arcsin (-.129112785)$
$= -7.418326626 \; (\text{or } \textbf{-7° 25' 06"})$

Important: Preserve the negative or positive polarity of the AD, and use it in the next step.

Now we add or subtract the AD, based on whether we want OA or OD, and where the birth took place:

	OA	**OD**
Northern hemisphere	RA – AD	RA + AD
Southern hemisphere	RA + AD	RA – AD

The birth was in the northern hemisphere, and we want the OD of Mars:

OD Mars $= \text{RA Mars} + \text{AD Mars}$
$= 342° \; 28' \; 56" + (-7° \; 25' \; 06")$
$= \textbf{335° 03' 50"}$

The arc of direction is the difference between the ODs: 1° 34' 35" (or 361° 34' 35") - 335° 03' 51" = **26° 30' 45"**. By the key of Ptolemy this is 26 years, 6 months (and about 4 days).

According to traditional rules, a marriage is likely when the lord of the 7th house is directed to the cusp of the 7th. Here, Mars (the lord of the 7th) has been directed in contrary fashion to the cusp of the 7th. If we add 26 years and 6 months to my birth date, we find approximately August 1992. Well, I was married at May 7th, 1992. We do not expect absolute precision in the timing, so a difference of a few months is normal.

3. Direction by all other degrees: use mixed or adjusted degrees

In the previous examples, the directions all involved one of the axial degrees: the ASC/DSC or the MC/IC. We found a single value for each point (either RA, or OA/OD), and the arc was the difference between them. But for all other directions, we need a few other values which we will put into a final equation.

In this example, we will direct the Sun as promittor (moving point), to Venus as the significator (stationary point). The table below shows all the values we will need. Values from the computer are in normal typeface, but values we will calculate are in **bold**—starting with the equatorial positions of the axes, which were already described above as being additions or subtractions of 90° or 180° from the RAMC:

RAMC: 91° 34' 35"
RAIC: **271° 34' 35"**
OA ASC: **181° 34' 35"**
OD DSC: **1° 34' 35"**

	Venus 28° 25' 20" ♉	Sun 23° 36' 22" ♒
λ	298° 25' 20"	323° 36' 22"
β	7° 36' 15" N	0° N
RA	298° 57' 47"	325° 55' 54"
δ	-13° 01' 40"	-13° 39' 16"
MD	27° 23' 12"	54° 21' 19"
AD	-11° 36' 37"	-12° 11' 55"
OD	287° 21' 10"	313° 43' 59"
HD	74° 13' 25"	47° 50' 36"
SA	101° 36' 37"	102° 11' 55"

Figure 30: Table of values for directing the Sun to Venus

Step 1: Find the MD or meridian distance for both planets. This is the difference in RA between them and the RA or IC, whichever is closer. Since they are closer to the IC, we use the RAIC:

MD Venus = RA Venus (298° 57' 47") – RAIC (271° 34' 35")
= (**27° 23' 12"**)

MD Sun = RA Sun (325° 55' 54") – RAIC (271° 34' 35")
= (**54° 21' 19"**)

Step 2: Find the OD of each planet.[9] As in Example 2 above, we first need the ascensional difference of each:

$$AD = \arcsin (\tan δ * \tan Φ)$$

AD Venus = arcsin ((-.231378902) * (.869797567))
= arcsin (-.201252806)
= **-11.61022928 or -11° 36' 37"**

---

[9] Since Venus and the Sun are on the western side of the chart, we use OD rather than OA.

AD Sun = arcsin ((-.242931542) * (.869797567))
= arcsin (-.211301264)
= **-12.19862058 or -12° 11' 55"**

Again, we use our rule for OD and the location of birth, which we used in the second example:

	OA	OD
Northern hemisphere	RA – AD	RA + AD
Southern hemisphere	RA + AD	RA – AD

OD Venus = 298° 57' 47" + (-11° 36' 37") = **287° 21' 10"**
OD Sun = 325° 55' 54" + (-12° 11' 55") = **313° 43' 59"**

Step 3: Find the HD or horizonal distance. This is the difference in OD between each of the planets and the Descendant. (If they had been on the eastern side of the chart, we would have used their OA and the OA of the Ascendant). Note that we must add 360° to this particular OD DSC, so that we can effectively subtract the other planets' OD from it.

HD Venus = OD DSC (361° 34' 35") – OD Venus (287° 21' 10")
= **74° 13' 25"**

HD Sun = OD DSC (361° 34' 35") – OD Sun (313° 43' 59")
= **47° 50' 36"**

Step 4: Find the semi-arc (SA) of the planet, which is the total amount of the arc between the horizon and meridian—in this case, between the Descendant and the IC. It is nothing more than the sum of the planet's MD + HD.

SA Venus = MD Venus (27° 23' 12") + HD Venus (74° 13' 25")
= **101° 36' 37"**

SA Sun = MD Sun (54° 21' 19") + HD Sun (47° 50' 36")
= **102° 11' 55"**

Step 5: Calculate the arc. Now we use the MD and SA of each planet, and make the following calculation. Remember that Venus is the fixed point, the significator (Sig); the Sun is the moving point, the promittor (Prom).

$$\text{Arc} = \text{Prom MD} - [\,(\,\text{Sig MD} / \text{Sig SA}\,) * \text{Prom SA}\,]$$

$$
\begin{aligned}
\text{Arc} \quad &= 54° \ 21' \ 19" - [\,(27° \ 23' \ 12" \ / \ 101° \ 36' \ 37") * 102° \ 11' \ 55"\,] \\
&= 54° \ 21' \ 19" - [\,(.26952654) * 102° \ 11' \ 55"\,] \\
&= 54° \ 21' \ 19" - [\,27° \ 32' \ 43"\,] \\
&= \mathbf{26° \ 48' \ 36"}, \text{ or 26 years, 9 months, and about 18 days}
\end{aligned}
$$

This date takes us to about November-December 1992. I was married in May 1992. Such an event was expected because the Sun is the victor of the 7th house and rules the 11th. Venus is related to marriage by her own nature, and the Sun, being the victor of the 7th (marriage), is in the 5th house (pleasure, children, good fortune). My intended wife was my friend since 1988. The Sun here links the 7th and 11th house, and I met my wife in a cafeteria (a place related to the 11th house) and through my wife's friends.

Although there is about six months' difference between the actual wedding day and the Sun's direction to Venus, this does not mean that the direction is unrelated to the marriage. In primary directions, we do not expect to see day-to-day correspondences between directions and events. Here in particular, one planet is being directed to another (rather than to an angle), and contacts between two planets in primary directions cannot be used to time an event exactly—for example, they cannot be used in rectification. However, they are closely related to the symbolism of the event showing that a related kind of *period* is being experienced in the native's life.

Interpreting primary directions

First of all, the natal chart should be well understood before using primary directions or other techniques: for, predictions answer "when" something will happen, but the natal chart itself says "what" it will be. The natal chart shows us all possible experiences during a lifetime, but both positive and negative ones appear mixed together in it. Directions and other predictive techniques put them in temporal order, but we must also understand what types of things they will be. Nothing is realized or predictable if it is not promised in the natal chart.

Even if similar directions give us different results with different natal charts, we may still see similarities in the directions which include the same planet, since each planet acts in accordance with its own nature. For instance, Mars means heat, battle, and violence; Venus means love, beauty, and fun. So, two Mars directions in different charts will still have Martial qualities, but the details may differ greatly depending on what each chart is like. The primary thing that changes is the relationship each planet has with the houses and signs, but the dignity or detriment of the planets also affects the quality of the results, as well as how its aspects with other planets affect those house relationships and qualities.

Now according to Robert Zoller,[10] a planet in a primary direction acts differently when it is the significator, as opposed to being the promittor. The promittor (along with its condition in the zodiac and rulerships) represents the outer conditions and the specific nature of the event, while the significator is a universal indicator for some topic. So, when reading a chart we must first understand what the promittor promises: that promise is specific to the chart, and is brought to bear upon the general significator. For instance, when a planet is directed to the Sun (he being the general significator of reputation), it may bring reputation, but of a particular kind depending on the nature and situation of the promittor. However, when the Sun is used as the promittor, he may refer to the conditions pertaining to the father specifically, and bring them to bear on some other planet's general meaning. By using this technique, the events experienced by the native may be evaluated wonderfully.

A word of caution: primary directions may be used in rectifications, but remember that an event does not necessarily occur exactly on the predicted day and hour. As we have seen, it may occur within some months of the time indicated by the arc of direction. Moreover, since many techniques may be active at the same time (such as primary directions, directions through the bounds, *firdaria*, and profections), primary directions may not be suitable for understanding every possible event. So, directions should not be relied on for day-to-day concerns.

---

[10] Zoller 2002-03, pp. 61-63.

JEAN-BAPTISTE MORIN
(MORINUS)

CHAPTER 10: ECLIPSES

SOLAR AND LUNAR ECLIPSES ARE USED FOR ANNUAL PREDICTIONS, AND ARE OBSERVED IN BOTH MUNDANE AND NATAL ASTROLOGY. SOLAR ECLIPSES CAN ONLY OCCUR AT A NEW MOON, AND REQUIRE THE MOON TO PASS BETWEEN THE SUN AND EARTH, SO THE SUN'S LIGHT TO THE EARTH IS BLOCKED. LUNAR ECLIPSES CAN ONLY OCCUR AT A FULL MOON, AND REQUIRE THE EARTH TO COME BETWEEN THE SUN AND MOON, SO THE SUN'S LIGHT TO THE MOON IS BLOCKED. IN BOTH CASES ALL THREE BODIES ARE ARRANGED IN A STRAIGHT LIGHT.

Basic principles of eclipses

To understand the mechanism of eclipses, let's consider the Sun as a light source, the Moon as a reflective curtain, and the earth as a lightproof object which sometimes stands at the back of that curtain, and sometimes in front of it. When the Moon (the curtain) is between the Sun and earth, it prevents the Sun's rays from reaching the earth, so the earth is left in darkness: this is a solar eclipse. But when the earth is between the Sun and Moon, the earth's physical body casts a shadow on the curtain (the Moon) so as to prevent the Sun's rays from reaching it: this is a lunar eclipse.[1]

During each New and Full Moon, these three celestial bodies are aligned in the same zodiacal longitude and vertical plane, but not on the same horizontal plane: eclipses can only occur when they are in the same vertical and horizontal plane, so that the shadows fall in just the right place. Therefore, not every New Moon is a solar eclipse, and not every Full Moon is a lunar eclipse.

Again, solar eclipses can only occur with New Moons, and lunar ones with Full Moons. Now, each year we have at least four eclipses: two solar and two lunar. And in some years, we may have more: for instance, in 2011 there were four solar eclipses and two lunar ones; in 2013 we had three lunar and two solar ones. However, we may experience a limited number of eclipses in each year, and many of these will not be total. If we consider solar eclipses, the Moon circles the zodiac 12 times in one year, but she does not pass through the middle of the Sun on each tour because of the 5° inclina-

---

[1] **BD**: At other times, the Moon would reflect the Sun's light and so be visible (the "reflective" aspect of her role as a curtain).

tion of her orbital plane away from the ecliptic (that is, she has zodiacal latitude). Consequently, we will have at least two, but at a maximum five, eclipses in a year. At most two of these eclipses may be total eclipses, which are astrologically the most important ones to observe.

Lunar eclipses

As we mentioned before, during a lunar eclipse the shadow of the earth's body is cast onto the Moon's body. As the earth is smaller than the Sun, it sends a shadow in the form of a cone: a "shadow cone." As the light travels in direct lines, they form another shadow with the dimensions of the earth. When the Moon reaches that portion of space where the shadows fall, a lunar eclipse takes place.

But the Moon does not always reach the plane where these shadows fall. As the Moon circles the Earth, she will approach one of the Nodes, and the Full Moon occurs between 12° and 24° of these. The more the Moon approaches the Node, the greater the eclipse will be. If the Full Moon comes within 12° 15' of the Node, there will be a partial eclipse: for instance, within 9° 30' of the Node, the eclipse will be partial; within 3° 45' and 6° 00', the eclipse is both partial and total.

Lunar eclipses emphasize emotional themes. These periods are suitable for taking care of one's emotions, completing unfinished projects, and leaving unnecessary things behind.

The ancients believed that lunar eclipses were malefic: they awaken irrational responses. As the Moon represents the family, home, and emotional issues, lunar eclipses trigger inner changes as compared with solar ones. However, their influences are still felt in the social and political arena as well. Lunar eclipses may bring some insecurity in private life. The native should avoid making important decisions, as maintaining emotional balance may be difficult. Instead of being active and extroverted, the native may prefer to be alone and observe his own inner dynamics. As he may find some complicated responses to this even from his loved ones, he may easily get discouraged.

Solar eclipses

The Nodes are the points where the Moon's orbit crosses the ecliptic. If the New Moon appears at least 18° 31' from the Node, there will be a partial solar eclipse. Between 0° and 9° 55', it is a total eclipse. If the distance is between 9° 55' and 11° 15', the eclipse is both partial and total.

Solar eclipses are useful for starting new ventures and for maintaining rapid progress. This is a beneficial period for identifying new goals and leaving old patterns behind. Solar eclipses have very powerful influences, as they occur close to the Earth. Since both luminaries will be in the same sign, the features of that sign are highly emphasized.

Influences of eclipses

According to the ancient astrologers, eclipses were negative events because they cause tragic conditions, and certain existing things come to an end. Eclipses bring stress and sudden problems. However, modern astrologers tend to perceive eclipses as a chance for rapid changes and development. According to modern astrology, eclipses give us the energy we need to make the changes we want. They help us reorganize our lives, even though they accelerate the occurrence of both negative and positive consequences.

The native should always remember that everything has a reason even if matters are complicated and stressed on the surface. Eclipses are designed to bring better things to our lives. Progress cannot be achieved without change. Eclipses force us to give up certain things or act differently than before, which can be painful but is necessary for growth. By being aware of the influences of eclipses, we may realize that better things may come to our lives, and we may minimize the effects of any possible crisis.

Eclipses begin manifesting their effects a few months before they occur, and their effects continue to be felt for a few months afterwards. According to a common view, lunar eclipses are effective for six months afterwards, while solar ones are effective for one year. But based on the duration of the eclipses, some astrologers claim that the influences will last as long. For instance, if a lunar eclipse lasts for four hours, it is influential for four months. Likewise, if a solar eclipse lasts for two hours, its effects will be felt for the coming two years.

Important eclipses leave a kind of "trace" of influence in the sky: future transits and progressions trigger the effects of that eclipse. Some astrologers claim that the effects of such eclipses are mainly felt after such triggers. For example, if an eclipse falls on one's natal Sun at 15° Gemini, the eclipse will be felt more strongly when (say) Mars transits 15° Gemini, or the progressed Moon reaches that degree or its opposite.

Each planet affects this process in conformity with its own nature:

Sun: Leadership, authority, power struggles.
Mercury: Communication, important talks, education, short-distance travels.
Venus: Peace, love, diplomacy.
Mars: Competition, conflicts and fights, great tension, wars.
Jupiter: Beliefs, moral and ethical values, legal issues, long-distance travels.
Saturn: Critics, restrictions, responsibilities, delays.
Uranus: Sudden and unexpected changes, surprises, ups-and-downs.
Neptune: Disappointments, spiritual issues, imaginative power.
Pluto: Power struggles, charisma, transformational crises, restructuring.

The effects of eclipses manifest themselves according to the house they occur in. Moreover, the axes of eclipses tend to move backwards in the natal chart. For instance, an eclipse which occurs in the axis of the 2nd-8th, will be followed by eclipses in the 1st-7th, and then the 12th-6th.

Saros cycles

By 747 BC, the Babylonians were able to predict when eclipses would occur. By the 4th century BC, they confirmed that eclipses occur in series. Series of solar eclipses were later called "saros" series or cycles, after a medieval Greek encyclopedia called the *Souda* or *Suda*: each solar eclipse belongs to a particular eclipse cycle, which repeats important features every 18 years and about 11 days. The Babylonians also discovered that lunar eclipses occur two weeks before or after solar ones.

As these series also tour around the chart, the native experiences a similar eclipse every 18 years, with a distance of approximately 10° from the previous one, often in the same sign and house. If these eclipses conjoin with natal planets, then the native may have experiences similar to those 18 years before.

Summary

Every year there are at least two lunar and two solar eclipses, but some years we may experience more (although the total eclipses are the most important). No eclipse is exactly the same as another, though they belong to a family of eclipses with a particular cycle. The time between eclipses within a particular Saros cycle, is 18 years and about 11 days.

Astrologically, the difference between solar and lunar eclipses is that solar eclipses have more outer influences and are more prone to create events, having more power in our lives, whereas lunar ones trigger inner and emotional changes. In general, eclipses cast light on the dark sides of our lives. Things that were hidden before become apparent, and what we have postponed or ignored before, must be changed now. Eclipses are like earthquakes: they shake us up and tell what should be cleaned out, ended, and destroyed. Some eclipses may bring permanent influences in the native's life. Although the tension lasts for a few weeks, its influences may be effective for longer.

As for the aspects and orbs to be used in interpreting them, astrologers have stated different opinions. Some astrologers use all aspects which the eclipse makes to natal planets, while others use primarily the conjunctions and oppositions, with squares being optional (I myself see squares as being effective). Some astrologers claim that the orbs used should be as 2.5° for conjunctions, 2° for oppositions, and 1° for squares; on the other hand, others state that the orb may be 5°. I myself believe that an orb of 3° is ideal.

Important interpretive questions for eclipses

1. In which house does the eclipse occur?
2. Is the eclipse close to the ASC, MC, or any natal planets within a 5° orb?
3. Does the eclipse affect any aspect patterns?
4. Is the eclipse in contact with any transiting planet?

5. Is the lord of the sign where the eclipse takes place being contacted by a transiting planet? Or, are the lord of the sign and this transiting planet contacting any other planet in the natal, progressed, or solar return charts?
6. Is the eclipse in contact with any fixed star?
7. Is there any clue to the current solar eclipse in events which happened 18 years ago?

In general, eclipses in cardinal signs change the course of events more rapidly, in approximately two weeks' time. Eclipses in fixed signs bring slow but long-lasting influences. Eclipses in mutable or common signs have fewer effects. They just bring adjustments and changes to our daily routine.

Finally, remember that the themes of the eclipse will be related to (1) the nature of the planet which the eclipse is in contact with, (2) the house where the eclipse occurs, and (3) the house which is ruled by the planet contacted. The general information below will help you in applying these principles more concretely in prediction.

Contacts between eclipses and planets

Contacts with the Sun: Eclipse contacts with either luminary, are important. When an eclipse makes contact with the natal Sun, naturally it reflects its influences upon the Sun. So, events will be focused on the father or others who represent authority, people who are important to us, our personality, situations we need in order to manifest ourselves, and recognition and leadership issues.

Contacts with the Moon: When an eclipse is in contact with the natal Moon, we may experience events related to female figures like the mother or wife, our health, our emotional life, our subconscious, our family life, our eating habits (and other habits), elements of the past, and changing situations related to home and family issues.

Contacts with Mercury: In a contact with natal Mercury, the native may go on short-distance travels and experience some sudden and rapid changes in issues related to his close circle (like siblings, cousins, or neighbors), young people, and educational and intellectual activities. This contact may influence our intellectual side as well as our behavior and communication style.

Contacts with Venus: When an eclipse makes a contact with the natal Venus, we may experience important changes in our approach to relationships, our values, and what gives us pleasure, as well as our style in having fun and clothing. We may also experience changes in maintaining harmony with others, sexuality, and our relations with younger female figures.

Contacts with Mars: When an eclipse contacts natal Mars, we may experience important changes in the way we act and on the things that motivate us. We may need to take the initiative and make rapid and strong decisions, we may be given a challenge and so need to act boldly, or we may be pushed towards over-direct and inconsiderate behaviors. We may also be open to accidents, quarrels, and competition. We may need to make a huge physical effort during such contacts.

Contacts with Jupiter: Contacts with the natal Jupiter indicate that sudden and unexpected developments related to religious or spiritual issues, and foreign travel, may take place. The desire for expansion and growth is emphasized. New opportunities may arrive. On the other hand, being careful and prudent may be hard: the native may exaggerate and be overly expectant. One's life perspective may expand, and growth in spiritual or financial matters may be maintained. The native may be overly idealistic.

Contacts with Saturn: With contacts to natal Saturn, we may experience new responsibilities and unexpected difficulties, or an economic crisis. As Saturn is related to death, sudden deaths may take place. We may face situations which make us anxious, so that we need to be cautious. We may work harder than before but earn less.

Contacts with Uranus: Contacts with the natal Uranus mean that sudden separations, accidents, or changes may be seen. The native's need to express his freedom and individuality increases. Uranian themes like technology, astrology, and alternative healing methods may show progress and we may be faced with weird and unexpected attitudes. The house where the Uranus sits is important: if it is close to the axes, these influences may be more prominent.

Contacts with Neptune: When an eclipse contacts natal Neptune, the native may experience situations related to sensitive, creative, and artistic issues. He may be drawn away from reality and find himself within an illusion. This may bring disappointments, separations, and abase or lose oneself in devotion. The native may also experience problems due to alcoholism or drug addiction.

Contacts with Pluto: When an eclipse makes a contact with natal Pluto, the native may experience sharp and deep influences which require him to restructure his life. Violence, death, obscurity in relationships, and deep passions may bring difficult experiences. On the positive side, this contact may bring support from influential people and a desire for success, no matter what the current conditions are and even if it is impossible to achieve.

The house axes of the eclipses

The natal house where an eclipse takes place is important in making predictions. During solar eclipses, the Sun and Moon are within the same sign, so they are in the same house. During lunar eclipses, the Sun and Moon are in opposite signs, so they form an axis in opposite houses.

Axis of 1st-7th: If the eclipse takes place in this axis, the native may experience situations related to relationships, marriage, or partnerships, situations which highlight his personality, the health of the native or his partner, or new beginnings and ventures for the native and his partner. This is a situation of mutual cause-and-effect or give-and-take.

Axis of 2nd-8th: This eclipse may bring profits or losses. The native may experience restrictions or sudden opportunities in personal or common resources and savings, and also in debtor-creditor relationships. As the house of death is a focus, inheritance issues may also be part of the financial influences.

Axis of 3rd-9th: Issues related to education, mental activities, siblings, relatives, travel, ideas, writing and publishing activities, lecturing, and legal issues are emphasized.

Axis of 4th-10th: Issues related to the balance between family and professional life, housing, career, and vital decisions about the future (and some ups-and-downs in it) are emphasized.

Axis of 5th-11th: Issues related to one's style of having fun, social life, close friends and social environment, children, love and romance, hopes and expectations, and issues related to the support we rely on from others are emphasized.

Axis of 6th-12th: Diseases, weaknesses, the uncontrolled and troublesome sides of life, fields in which we cannot display our ego, or where we work harder but earn less, problematic situations, losses, and compulsory works are emphasized.

Practice example: two solar eclipses

To illustrate these important influences, let's have a look at two important eclipses in my life and their effects on it.

In my natal chart the two malefics, Mars and Saturn, are in the 6th house (diseases, weaknesses and daily routine), in conjunction with Chiron, and also in opposition to Uranus and Pluto in the 12th house (losses, uncontrolled events, hospitals). This indicates that themes related to the house containing Mars and Saturn, as well as the topics which these planets rule, will be prominent in my life, bringing stress and difficulties.

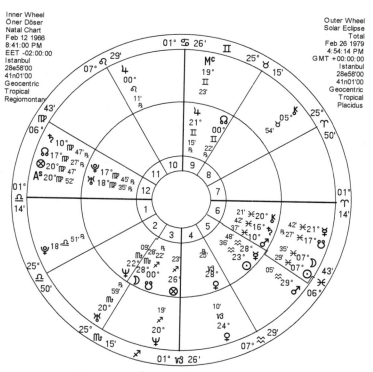

Figure 31: Öner Döşer, 1979 eclipse

Mars is the lord of the 3rd, 7th, and 8th houses of my chart. So, he is related to siblings, the spouse and relationships, and death. As Saturn is the lord of my 4th and 5th houses, issues related to family, children, and love are also emphasized. Mars is the exalted lord of the 4th, and Saturn is the exalted lord of the 1st and 2nd. So, both Mars and Saturn are lords of the 4th house, which is related to family and parental issues. The Moon, a natural indicator for the mother, is in Scorpio, so she is also ruled by Mars. This means that in my chart, the positions of Mars and Saturn are related closely to the mother and father.

When I examined the celestial events at certain critical dates of my life, I was shocked to see that two eclipses in Pisces (where Mars and Saturn are placed) with an 18-year interval between them, were related to the deaths of my mother and father. In the chart above, you may see the projection of the solar eclipse of February 26, 1979 onto my natal chart. The eclipse took place in 7° Pisces, which is very close to Mars (who sits at 10° Pisces). Two months after this eclipse, my mother died. Remember that Mars is one of the lords of the 4th house and also the lord of the Moon.

After a period of 18 years, on March 9, 1997, I again experienced a solar eclipse in Pisces, this time occurring close to Saturn (see diagram). Three months after this eclipse, my father passed away. Here, remember that Saturn was one of the lords of my natal 4th house, and also the dispositor of my natal Sun (a general significator of the father).

These examples illustrate the importance of eclipses which occur in 18-year intervals, which can help us make predictions about crucial events in the native's life. Of course, we do not necessarily face negative outcomes. Some eclipses may bring births, marriage, career, or success and profit, while some others do bring deaths, separations, failures, and losses.

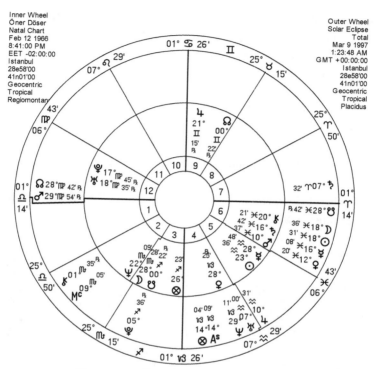

Figure 32: Öner Döşer, 1997 eclipse

Prenatal eclipses

Prenatal eclipses, which occur while the native is still in the mother's womb, have a special importance. The sign and house of the eclipse is important, as is any planet which is close to the degree of the eclipse. The prenatal solar eclipse shows us our gifts and the lessons we need to learn, the social mission which we share with others born in that group. The prenatal lunar eclipse shows influences coming from past lives, the lessons we took from them, and what we need to balance and fix during this lifetime.

If the prenatal eclipses are in good aspects with our natal planets, then we may reach our goals easily; but if they are in harsh aspects, then we may face challenges and difficulties. In synastry charts, if the prenatal eclipses make contacts with natal planets or other important points, this may indicate the partnership is a fated and karmic one.

Let's clarify the issue by observing my chart again. I was born in February 12, 1966. The nearest solar eclipse to my birth date was on November 23, 1965, when the Moon and Sun conjoined in 0° Sagittarius.[2] Now, I have to analyze these two issues:

1) What is the sign of the eclipse, and in which natal house does this sign fall?
2) Is the degree of the eclipse in contact with any natal planets or Nodes or reference points (like the ASC and MC)?

In the chart below, you may see the projection of the celestial position of this solar eclipse moment on my (future) natal chart.

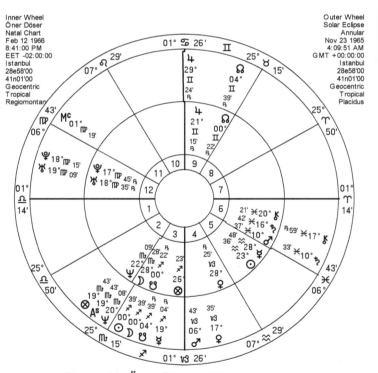

Figure 33: Öner Döşer, 1965 solar eclipse

---

[2] **BD**: Note that this is an "annular" eclipse, which is similar to a total eclipse but with the Moon appearing slightly smaller than the Sun.

Again, the prenatal eclipse took place in Sagittarius. This indicates that Sagittarian themes like education, publishing, religions and beliefs, philosophies, a passion for expansion and a larger perspective, a motivation for reaching more people and over long distances, and optimism, are important features of my spiritual infrastructure. The eclipse was in my natal 3rd house, which means that I must spread my knowledge to as many people as I can reach. As the eclipse was also in conjunction with my natal South Node, it points to wisdom that I brought from my past lives.

In the chart below, you may see the projection of the most recent prenatal lunar eclipse upon my natal chart, from December 8, 1965.[3]

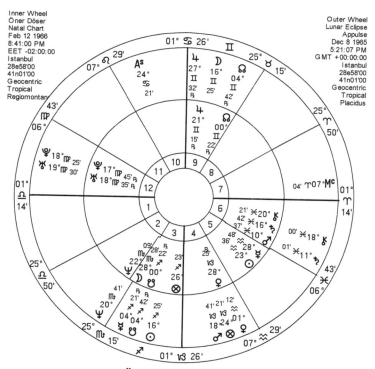

Figure 34: Öner Döşer, 1965 lunar eclipse

The prenatal lunar eclipse took place in Gemini. This means that I have to fix or complete some duties related to communication and sharing infor-

---

[3] **BD**: This is an "appulse" or penumbral eclipse, in which the Moon is dimmed by going through the penumbra, but not eclipsed by the umbra itself.

mation. As the eclipse was in the 9th house of my natal chart, these duties are related to 9th house themes such as religions, philosophies, astrology, education, etc. This eclipse was close to Jupiter in the natal 9th: this signifies that the duties I must complete are related to Jupiterian themes (again: beliefs, philosophies, education, etc.), and that Jupiter in my natal chart would help me. As this eclipse was in a square with my natal Saturn in the 6th, I will need to overcome some challenges and obstacles while on that path.

To summarize: as the prenatal eclipses were in Sagittarius / Gemini and the 3rd house / 9th house axis, the things I need to realize for myself, and which I need to fix and complete in order to achieve success, are of the nature of these signs and houses.

WILLIAM LILLY

CHAPTER 11: SOLAR AND LUNAR RETURNS

RETURN CHARTS ARE CALCULATED FOR THE EXACT MOMENT WHEN A CERTAIN PLANET RETURNS TO ITS NATAL POSITION. THEY MAY BE ERECTED FOR ALL PLANETS, BUT IN ASTROLOGY WE PRIMARILY CAST SOLAR AND LUNAR RETURNS. SOLAR RETURNS CHARTS MAY BE CONSIDERED AS AN ANNUAL NATAL CHART, AND MAY BE CONSULTED FOR THE PREDICTION OF ANNUAL EVENTS.

A solar return (SR) chart is calculated for the exact moment when the Sun returns to his natal position: so, the common reference point between the natal chart and the SR is the degree of the Sun (since other planets are usually in degrees other than their natal positions). With the help of SRs, we may evaluate the events of the year ahead.

The solar return is also called an annual chart, or more traditionally a "revolution" of the nativity. The moment of the SR may occur slightly before or after the calendar date of the native's birthday. Some astrologers assert that the effects of the coming SR begin 3 months beforehand, while others state that they begin one month before and last for one month after the year is completed.

As for where to cast the chart, some modern astrologers erect the SR for the native's birthplace; many others prefer to erect it for the place where the native actually is at the time of the SR—this could be accepted as being more valid if the native has been there on a permanent basis. Unlike Morin and Volguine, who erect SRs for the place where the native happens to be at that very moment, I prefer to use the place where the native spends most of his year. Also, I follow Morin and Volguine in that I do not adjust solar returns for precession; I get very good results from un-precessed charts.

Rules for interpreting solar returns

There are some general rules that we need to consider while evaluating an SR chart:

Before starting to analyze the SR, we need to know the nativity thoroughly, to see what it actually promises as real possibilities. You should not make any prediction if it is not evidently allowed by the natal or progressed chart. On the other hand, if the SR does *not* indicate what *is* part of the natal influence, and the SR is not supported by primary directions and profections, then the SR is weak and the events may not be manifested at all. But if the SR's indications do support the promises of the nativity, they will manifest in a strong way.

After analyzing and delineating the natal chart, we can delineate the SR separately in its own right, and then synthesize both charts: this is just like doing synastry for two different natives.

First of all, we have to look at the ascending degree in the SR: in which natal house does it fall (or in other words, what natal house is ascending in the SR)? The central themes, main issues, and characteristic conditions of this house will be prominent for the native this year. For example, if the SR ASC falls in the natal 2nd, financial issues and possessions will be prominent for the native this year. If good natal houses are arising at the SR, this may promise a happy year; but if one of the bad natal houses is rising, it may promise an unhappy year. Of course we should also look at the conditions of the natal ruler of this house and the ruler of that same house in the SR. Volguine states that "If the Sixth, Seventh or Twelfth House of the natal chart is on the Ascendant of the Return chart, unhappiness is in the offing, and even a great deal of misfortune, if the lord of that house is afflicted at birth."[1] When the natal ASC is rising (within 5° of orb), this will be a significant year and there is a great potential to realize the natal promise.

If 29° of any sign is ascending in the SR, that means the native is about to finish something, or is about to close a door. This is also valid for the degree-position of the ruler of the ascending sign, since the SR ascendant indicates the native. (Actually, it is worth considering any planets in the last degree of a sign, as it can show that the topic which they rule will experience some important change or ending.) When the first degree of a sign ascends, it means the native is about to begin something. This is valid for the ruler of the ascending sign as well. Again, it is worth considering any planet in the first degree of a sign.

The next thing we should look at is the rising sign of the SR, because it is always a starting point in any given chart; here, it shows the atmosphere of the native's surroundings during the SR. For example, if Virgo is on the ascendant, this shows the native's need for material security; reliability, critical analysis, categorization, attending to details, perfectionism, and the need to

---

[1] Volguine, p. 15.

be organized will be prominent. Physical or emotional health problems, nervous tensions, and worrying situations are possible.

Then, we have to focus on the element and quality of the ascending sign. For example, if a fire sign rises, the native will be more active, he will prone to act with more inspiration, passion, enthusiasm, and desire this year, depending on the intensity of the fiery quality in his natal chart. We should look at the placement of the planets in elements. If the native has a strong natal emphasis of the fire element, and also in the SR, then he will be prone to act more spontaneously and impulsively, responding quickly, he may take risks, his decisions tend to be brave.

The next thing we should do is observe the quality of the SR angles, to see if they are cardinal, fixed, or mutable. Cardinal signs on the angles indicate new beginnings, fixed ones indicate the establishment of those beginnings, mutable ones indicate improving and/or altering them. If many SR planets are placed in cardinal signs, taking the initiative is easier. Cardinal angles and many planets in cardinal signs show that this will be a busy year full of events, and a desire for personal attention and impulsiveness is possible. If many SR planets are placed in fixed signs, it is easier to protect established conditions and structures, and completing projects is possible. Fixed angles and many planets in fixed signs show that this will be a steady year without great changes. If many SR planets are placed in mutable signs, it is easier to fall in step with current conditions. Mutable angles and many planets in mutable signs show that this will be a year of excessive changes, no stability, with emerging alternatives. It is hard to maintain stability and existing conditions. So the native has to remain flexible, avoid undue frustration, and be prepared for future events. All of these are general approaches, which highly depend on the SR aspects and natal placements.

The next thing we should do is to see if there is any planet placed in the SR 1st house, especially close to the ascending degree. If so, this planet shows what kind of events and situations will be easily come to the native (for good or ill), according to its nature and the houses it rules. If this planet is a malefic, it indicates difficulties and harsh situations; if benefic, then easy and good conditions will surround him and he will get support from others. This planet also shows what or who is dependent on the native: if it rules the 7th, then his partner will depend on him this year. It also shows the nature of the native's activity: if it is Mars, the native's behavior may be more impulsive, bold, and risky this year. And of course he will be prone to awkwardness and accidents, too.

After this, look at the ruler of the SR ascendant, its SR placement and aspects. The ruler of the Ascendant shows the native's agenda during this SR, the house in which it is placed gives further indications of major themes, and indicates where the native's emphasis should be and the atmosphere in which he lives this year. If it is in an angular house or a strong one (such as the 11th or 5th), then the native will have the power to dominate the events of the year, especially if it has dignity in its location as well. The aspects of this ruler will show how easy or difficult it is to do this. So, if the ruler is in a good condition, the native benefits from the things signified by that planet, and we can say this more powerfully if its own dispositor is in a good condition, strong, and dignified in its own placement. (The dispositor of a planet plays a powerful role in determining the planet it rules, and shows the resources and results of the actions which are started through its nature.) We should look at the aspect of the SR planets to the SR Ascendant, and where these aspects coming from (the nature of the aspecting planet, its SR house location, and the houses it rules).

Next, look at the SR location of the lord of the SR 10th: the house it is in indicates the results of the native's actions and undertakings, and will give information about his career and profession this year. If it is placed powerfully (in both quality and strength), then the native will have the ability to dominate his career or profession, and can achieve good results from his actions. The aspects of this ruler will show how easy or difficult to do this. If the ruler is in a good condition, the native benefits from the things signified by that planet, in terms of his career or profession, realizing his aims and goals. We can say this more powerfully if the dispositor of the ruler of the SR 10th is in a good condition, strong and dignified in its own placement. We should look at the aspects to the 10th house cusp as well.

After this, look at the other angular planets in the SR (if there are any), as angular planets have special importance. If there are many, the most angular one is the most important. According to Volguine, "The planet which is first to cross an angle in the Solar Return imprints its own individual character on the principal development of the year. For this reason, a malefic in an angle of the SR is essentially dangerous."[2]

---

[2] Volguine, p. 62.

Finally, to understand the planets, signs, and houses in SRs, we can draw on Nance McCullough, who argues that "Solar Return planets represent the native's circumstance or situation—be it activity or otherwise. Signs represent attitudes taken about these activities. Houses denote the area of the activity."[3]

Comparing the nativity and solar return

We should never read the SR chart in isolation from the nativity. After analyzing the SR in the ways described above, we should begin to compare it with the natal chart and see where the natal planets are now located in the SR: that is, for any natal planet, where was it in the nativity, and where did it move to in the SR? All natal planets carry their characteristic qualities derived from the natal chart over to the SR, so in order to understand a planet's role and effects in the SR, it is important to be aware of its role in the natal chart. For example, if Mercury is placed in the natal 2nd, but moves to the SR 7th, this indicates money through partnership this year—if that possibility is allowed in the nativity.

Increased similarity between the natal and SR placements of the planets means a greater potential for realizing what is promised for the native. If a planet which shows the same influence in both the natal and SR charts, also shows the same thing in a primary direction for that period, then it absolutely manifests its influence.

When interpreting the current SR, you should also examine those of the previous and upcoming year, since we must always consider primary directions and transits which have already, or have not yet, become exact and manifested their effects. If a good SR chart is followed by another good one, it means that events will develop in a good way; the contrary is also true.

You should note the degrees of the natal and SR Ascendants. If the ascending degree of the SR is close to that of the natal chart, the year promises to realize the significations of the natal chart. If these two degrees are in opposition to each other, the two charts work against each other and bring difficulties. If they are in a square, difficult results are likely; and if they are in trine, they bring positive results. (Of course, we should not make an evaluation based on only one criterion.)

---

[3] McCullough, p. 3.

The influence of each sign in the natal chart is realized in relation to the SR house it appears in. If a natal house (and its sign) which shows positive things in the natal chart is in a good position in both the nativity and SR, the year will be a lucky one in accordance with the themes of that house.

Again, the rising sign of the SR should also be noted, as well as the nature of the planets in the 1st house, and the zodiacal sign they are in (if not in the first sign), because the planets in the 1st house greatly influence the events of that year. Secondly, you should consider any planet placed in the 10th house.

The contacts between the ascending degree of the SR and the natal planets should be evaluated. If this degree is close to the degrees of the natal malefics, or close to the natal 8th house or the degree of the lord of the natal 8th, dangerous and harsh influences may manifest. Of course, the position of the malefics in the natal chart should be considered in terms of whether they promise death or not.

If the degree of the lord of the SR Ascendant is close to the degrees of the natal malefics, or the degree of the natal 8th or the degree of the lord of the natal 8th, it also brings difficulties. According to some authorities, if the cusp of the natal 8th house is rising in the SR and lunar return (LR), it signifies the death of the native in that year and the month.

You should also consider in which house of the SR chart the degree of the natal Ascendant is placed. If it is in the SR 6th or 12th, the native may face illnesses and should not work a lot and spend much effort. If it is in the SR 5th, it may bring themes related to children and flirtation; if it is in the SR 2nd, financial themes may take the stage.

When a planet is in an SR house which is different from the one it was in natally (which is usually the case), it manifests its natal influences through the SR house—in other words, each planet carries its natal influence into the SR chart. So you should never ignore the promises of the natal chart when evaluating the SR, even though its specific SR influences have priority in that year. Each natal planet will try to realize itself each year, through the SR house it is in.[4]

The sign of each natal planet is also important: if a planet is in the same sign in both charts, it manifests its natal promise; if it is also in the same degree, then it is called a "perfect return."

---

[4] **BD**: For example, if Jupiter is in the natal 4th, he indicates family and real estate. If he is in the SR 9th, he will not only indicate 9th-house matters, but the topic of family and real estate *as filtered through* 9th house topics.

You should also consider whether or not a planet is ruled by the same lord in both charts: if it is ruled by the same lord, then events of a similar nature may take place.

The natal house of a planet should be considered: if a planet is in the same house in *both* charts, it manifests its natal influences in a stronger way in that year.

If a planet is in the same sign and same house in both charts, then it manifests its promise in the natal chart in the most significant way.

If the position of an SR planet is in square or opposition to its natal position, its manifestations will be restricted; when it reaches the trine position, support for its manifestation will be maintained.

Contacts between natal planets and SR planets should be evaluated, and predictions should be based on their themes: positive contacts between planets bring positive results, and negative contacts bring negative results. Difficult aspects can be mitigated by mutual reception by sign or exaltation, so that their harsh influences may be decreased and bring success after great effort. If there is a conjunction between two planets, their nature should be considered, as well as the house where they conjoin and their natal positions in the natal chart.

You should evaluate if aspects between two natal planets are repeated in the SR chart. If positive aspects between two natal planets repeat in the SR, the results will be positive; if negative aspects between two natal planets repeat in the SR, the results will be negative. Such repetition indicates that the promises of the natal chart will manifest that year. If the two planets are in good aspect in the natal chart but applying in a bad aspect in the SR, then the positive potential of the natal aspect will be diminished; on the other hand, if they are in bad natal aspect but a good SR aspect, the native can find a way to slip out from under the hard effects of these planets and the themes of the natal houses they rule.

The natures of the ASC and MC, the positions of their lords, and also the positions of the Sun and the Moon should be evaluated in the SR chart. Also, the position of the Sun in SRs, and the Moon in LRs, is important: their placements help us to determine the main focus of the year or the month.

Natal houses which contain a natal stellium help us determine the lifetime focus of the native. You should then examine in which SR and LR house that natal configuration falls, as they point out the main themes of the year or the month. For example, my wife (see below) has a natal stellium in Taurus: in her 1992 SR, these planets fell in and around the SR 7th, and we married that year.

Again, the lord of the SR Ascendant is important. Its SR position should be examined and then compared with its natal position: if it is well placed in both charts, then it makes a positive influence on the native and brings success in that year. To determine where this success will come from, we should examine the SR position of the lord (as well as what natal place that corresponds with), together with the placement of the planets it is in contact with. Primary directions should also be examined to determine if the expected events are promised or not.

We should also consider where the profected lord of the year (LOY) falls in the SR chart. As described in the chapter on profections, the LOY is the planet ruling the house where the profected Ascendant lands in any given year. This is found by counting houses for every year of life, starting with the Ascendant as age 0: so, whatever age the native is, the planet ruling the house for that age is the LOY. The house and sign placement of the LOY at the SR is also important, and provides further information about the native's conditions and agenda for the year. If the LOY also happens to be the lord of the SR ASC, then its influences will be manifested even more strongly.

If the lord of the SR ASC is combust, some restrictions and malefic effects may interrupt the native's purpose, or the native may get sick or may not manifest himself properly.

If the zodiacal position of a planet is the same both in natal and SR charts, the themes of the natal chart are realized during this year.

In practice, the rising sign of the SR should be defined, and the natal chart and the SR chart should be compared first of all.

Five examples

Example #1:

In this example, the upper chart is the nativity and the lower chart is the SR for 2003. In the SR, 23° Virgo is rising, which is in the 12th house of the natal chart. This means that the themes of 2003 will be related to those of the 12th house, such as illnesses, hospitals, losses, uncontrolled factors, hidden hostility, etc.

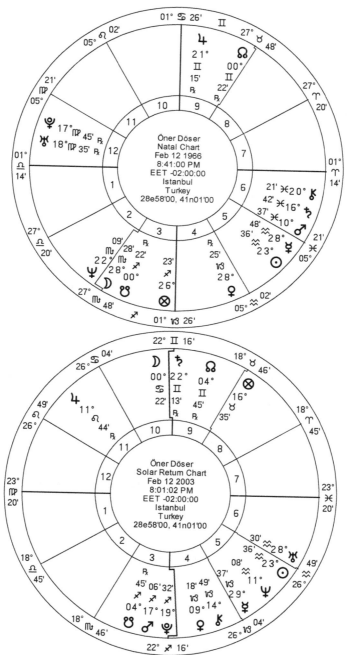

Figure 35: Öner Döşer, 2003 solar return

Next, let's see in which SR houses the natal planets are. For instance, the natal Moon is in the natal 3rd and is lord of the natal 10th; in the SR she is *in* the 10th, in Cancer, where she is strong. This means that themes related to career and goals will be important.

Venus, in the natal 4th house, is again placed in the 4th house of the SR, and again in Capricorn: this means that home and family matters will also be important. The 4th house also indicates that something in life comes to an end while other things get their start.

Saturn, in the natal 6th house, is now in Gemini and on the cusp of the SR 10th house: this means that some important changes in the working environment, working conditions, and subordinates, will change—which also affects the native's business life. The native has to take on responsibilities related to the house Saturn is placed in. As Saturn and the MC are in close conjunction, some separations, difficulties, and career discontent are likely.

Jupiter, in the natal 9th house, is in Leo and the SR 11th house: this means 9th and 11th house themes will be blended. The 11th house also represents profits coming from business activity.

Important events in 2003:

- The first half of the year was full of illnesses and hospital visits. My grandparents got sick in succession, were hospitalized, and they died within 6 days of each other. As my father was no longer alive, I had to take care of them, along with my aunt. The whole year was full of the themes of the 12th. I also need to emphasize that a Mars-Saturn opposition took place in the SR 4th and 10th: this represents the problems and death within the family, because the natal Mars represents my grandfather (he is the lord of the 7th, by derived houses the 4th from the 4th), and Saturn represents my grandmother as the victor of the 1st house (the 10th from the fourth, the mother of my father). My grandparents had some other problems before they both got sick, as my grandfather was hurting my grandmother: so, we separated them and I looked after my grandfather while my aunt looked after my grandmother.
- In June 2003, I made an important decision, leaving my work in Istanbul's Grand Bazaar and making a step towards starting a professional life in astrology. I was not happy with my work in the

Grand Bazaar: the environment and trade life there were not for me, and in addition it did not bring a satisfactory income. Astrology had become my whole life after 2 years of training, I only wanted to deal with astrology, and I had already started to ignore my existing job. I leased out my store in the Bazaar, and after guaranteeing the working conditions of my employees I transferred everything over to another employer, one of my friends. Saturn in the natal 6th house, is in Gemini in the SR 10th, explains the whole scenario: the obligations of my employees were on my shoulders, but I felt at ease after guaranteeing their new working conditions, succeeding in maintaining a secure working environment for them.

- The Moon, in the natal 3rd house and lord of its 10th, is in Cancer in the SR 10th house, where she is powerful. This emphasizes that career and professional goals are about to change. Just before starting my professional life in astrology, I had started to write a column in a newspaper, and I was on a TV news program (representing some astrological views) during the summer of 2003. I was highly satisfied by studying and dealing with astrology.

- At the beginning of 2003, I was elected as a board member of Astrology Union in Turkey. I was also receiving training from Hakan Kırkoğlu. Jupiter in the natal 9th, now in the SR 11th, indicates being active in groups which are related to astrology. In the second half of the year, I started to earn money from astrology; this is also related to the same configuration.

- I moved house twice during the year, once in July and once in November. During this period, I worked in a home-office environment. I was happy there, but lost all of my connection with the outer world while working long hours—I used to work for 14 hours a day, and could rarely engage in sports. I was panicked about the need to settle down as soon as possible. Natal Venus (who is the lord of the natal Ascendant) being in the 4th house in Capricorn with no aspect, explains being antisocial and working at home.

After this, we should see where the natal Sun is placed (since it is a solar return). In the chart below, you see that the Sun is placed between the 5th and the 6th houses, which represent hard work and interest in sports.

Then, we should evaluate two charts together as seen in the chart below: this way we are able to examine the SR chart's contacts with the axes and planets of the natal chart. I have done this by putting the SR chart in the center, with the natal positions in the outer ring.

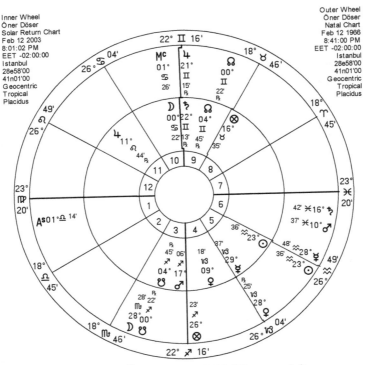

Figure 36: Öner Döşer, 2003 SR on nativity

Natal Jupiter is placed on the degree of the SR MC. This indicates astrology (natal Jupiter in the 9th) as being my profession (MC). Jupiter also stands on the SR Saturn: my discontent due to my previous job is to be resolved by astrology now. Natal Saturn is square to the SR Saturn: this means that I have difficulties due to the discontent and responsibilities of my employees.

Venus, the lord of my natal ASC, is in the SR 5th and on the SR Mercury (the lord of the SR 10th), which means that my hobbies (the 5th) will now be my profession.

The North Node of the natal chart is on the SR South Node, so my relation with astrology is a fated one.

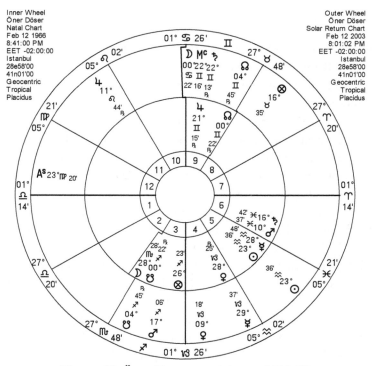

Figure 37: Öner Döşer, nativity on 2003 SR

Then, the SR chart is placed on the natal chart (with the nativity in the center) so we may examine the natal chart's contacts with the axes and the planets of the SR. Here, the SR Moon is placed on the cusp of the natal 10th, representing a change of job and new endeavors. Also, having the lord of the natal 10th (Moon) on the cusp of the natal 10th *at* the SR is a very good position. Saturn, on the natal Jupiter in the natal 9th shows that there will be difficulties in the 9th-house themes, and I did have to work hard. The SR Jupiter is in the natal 11th, which shows that there would be some group activities related to the 9th-house themes.

Next, we should examine the contacts between the planets of the two charts. If a harsh aspect between two natal planets repeats itself in the SR chart, especially between the malefic planets, this negative influence is manifested in a strong way (as Morin states).[5] The example below illustrates this.

---

[5] Morin 2003, Chapter XVIII.

Example #2:

This example is the SR for 2005. In the natal chart Jupiter squares Saturn, and in the SR this aspect is repeated. This means that the negative influence of the aspect will repeat, and the difficulties that the natal chart promises will be manifested.

In 2005, I had to wait for the exam results of my astrological training from Robert Zoller. It was a stressful period. First of all, I had written very long answers for the questions, and then my teacher was sick at that very time. But this Jupiter-Saturn square was not as difficult as it was in the natal chart, because although the aspect was the same, in this year Saturn and Jupiter were in a mutual reception by exaltation, which decreased the difficulties. During this period I had to support my wife financially in her business, because she had to make an investment. Saturn in the SR 5th house was in the 11th of my wife's chart (which is related to investments or profits related to business). Jupiter is between the SR 7th and 8th houses. As the lord of the SR ASC, Jupiter represents me and shows that I had to support my wife. As SR Jupiter is in conjunction with the South Node and is retrograde, he is not so powerful. However, he is in Libra where he is powerful and in an angular house, so he has the strength to provide support.

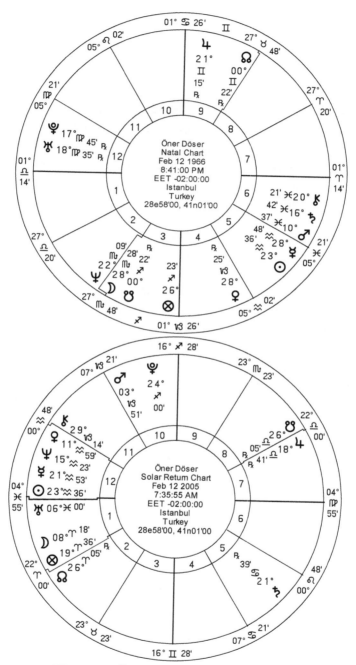

Figure 38: Öner Döşer, 2005 solar return

Example #3:

Morin was a vigorous advocate of solar and lunar returns. In his *Astrologia Gallica*, he established some rules for return charts, and we will illustrate his rules in the next few examples. For instance,[6] when the natal and SR ASCs are in opposition, this configuration brings a negative outcome, especially with an exact opposition. Let's see this in another example. Below, you see my SR for 1997. In the natal chart, 1° Libra is rising, while 8° Aries is rising in the SR chart. My father died in this year. Of course, this opposition does not alone imply my father's death. There were other indicators in the chart.

First of all, let's consider that Mars (the lord of the SR ASC) and Saturn were opposed in the 1st – 7th house axes. Saturn is the lord of my natal 4th, and in this chart he is placed between the 12th and 1st houses. He is in an opposition with Mars, with whom he was conjoined in the nativity.

The natal Saturn-Mars conjunction in the natal chart indicates that my father (Saturn) should be affected by some harsh influences such as surgery, accidents, fighting, etc. Mars is the lord of my natal 7th house, and my father's own 4th house (by derived houses). This shows that his life might end (4th) as a result of a Martial event. In the SR this influence is even more significant: Mars is in an opposition with Saturn from the cusp of the 4th house. These two planets are in mutual reception, but they are in the signs of their own detriment. All these factors increase the possibility of negative influences. In the SR chart, the Sun is between the 11th and 12th houses. After an accident, my father was hospitalized for nearly one month. We all hoped that he would get well, but he did not. Perhaps the planets in Aquarius in the 11th house increased our hopes. On the other hand, those planets were in my father's own house of death (the 8th from the 4th).

---

[6] Morin 2003, p. 130.

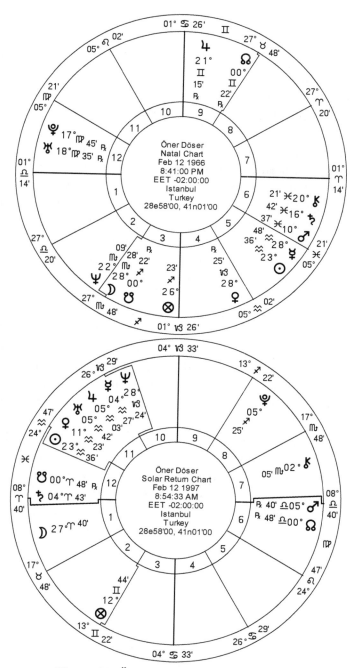

Figure 39: Öner Döşer, 1997 solar return

Example #4:

Returning to Morin,[7] he states that if the SR ASC is in trine with the natal ASC, such a configuration is a positive one in terms of the themes of the 1st house, but negative if they are in a square. (However, this is not the only criterion for judging whether the themes of the 1st house are positive or negative.)

Let's look at the SR chart for 2004. When we compare the two charts, we see that their Ascendants are in sextile (a somewhat positive but not very strong aspect). I attended the seminar of my teacher in Canada and stayed there for 8 days. I learned many things and met a lot of people there. I had long conversations with my teacher after the courses, and he even invited me to dinner at his house, along with another student. He really showed me great hospitality. However, I was not able to achieve the results I had hoped for from that journey. The lord of the SR ASC, Jupiter, is in the 9th and very close to the cusp of the 10th. This is a nice placement and represents my journey. However, Jupiter is in Virgo where he is in detriment and is also retrograding. He is also in a negative aspect to his natal position and exactly squaring the natal Saturn, which triggers the natal Jupiter-Saturn square. Because my teacher was sick, he did not accept my proposal to be his representative in Turkey: he explained that he could not support me adequately and told me that I already had the potential to act on my own. He was very realistic but I was sorry to hear it. After I returned back to Istanbul, I did not even open any astrology books for fifteen days. But then I decided to prepare my own training system without being dependent on anyone: I now know that this was the best decision I have ever made, but at the time it was disappointing. I was also stressed out because I did not yet have the results of the exam which I had taken a long time before. However, my teacher was right: he was really so sick that he could not help me.

---

[7] Morin 2003, p. 131.

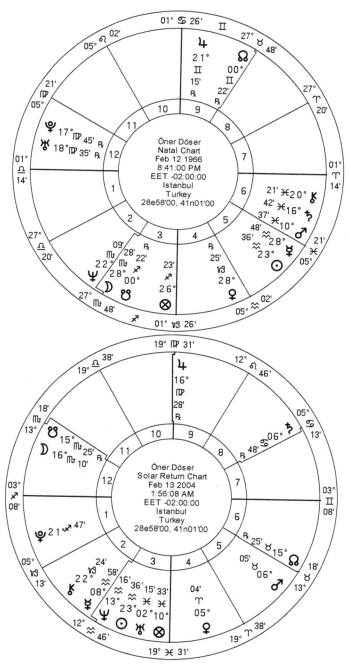

Figure 40: Öner Döşer, 2004 solar return

Example #5:

Now, Morin says[8] that the rising sign in the SR chart has an influence on the themes shown by the 1st house of the native. In the chart below, you can see the 1992 SR for my wife. In her SR chart, the 4th house of her natal chart is rising: we were married in 1992, and the 4th is related to home and family matters. Her natal Jupiter is very close to the degree of the SR ASC. We may expect this year to be a lucky one.

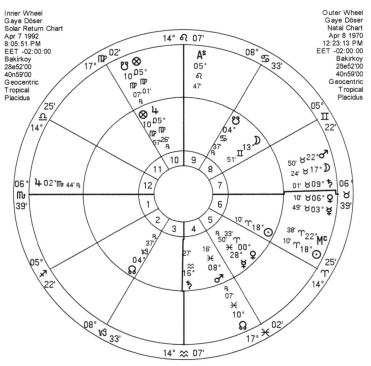

Figure 41: Gaye Döşer, 1992 solar return

Again, Morin states[9] that if a native has more than one planet in any natal house, he will experience many things related to the themes of that house, because each year those natal planets will occupy and activate the SR house they are placed in. So, the promises of this house will absolutely be realized.

---

[8] Morin 2003, p. 131.
[9] Morin 2003, p. 135.

Let's look again at the same chart. Many natal planets are gathered the SR 7th house: since the accumulation of many planets in the same SR house represents an important theme of that year, it means that in 1992 marriage and partnership issues will take center stage. Taurus is on the cusp of the SR 7th, and the natal Venus (the lord of Taurus) is also placed there. This is a marriage indication. You might think that Saturn being there will bring problems, but Saturn is ruled by Venus and influenced by her benefic qualities. The natal Jupiter on the SR ASC also helps to decrease the damages. So, there were no delays or problems related to our marriage.

Planets in the solar return chart

Solar return planets represent the native's situation in the coming year—recalling that they will also bear their natal significations by house placement and rulerships:

☉: Personal issues, the father and other authority figures, recognition.

☽: Emotional issues, the mother, family, other feminine figures, health issues, great changes.

☿: Communication, education, young people, changing from one place to another, intellectual tendencies.

♀: Relationships, women, efforts to maintain harmony, intimacy, marriage, and fun activities.

♂: Fields where energy and efforts are focused, hostility, competition, courage.

♃: Areas where we achieve expansion and progress, exaggeration, an easy flow, economic ease, academic pursuits, travels, teachers.

♄: Restrictions, responsibilities, difficulties, limitations, financial themes, lessons to be learned, death.

☊: Relationships, fated topics, group activities.

☋: Fateful events, losses, and troubles.

Review of important principles of interpretation

- After interpreting the SR, consider its planets and aspects in concert with those of the natal chart, to see how it enables or hinders the natal promise from being produced in that year.
- If the natal chart is an easy one but the SR is not, the year may bring some difficulties and lessons to learn. However, because the natal chart has good placements, the difficulties will not bring too much stress. If both charts are difficult, the year will be full of lessons to learn and some difficulties. If the natal chart is difficult but the SR easy, the native will have a good year and will overcome some of the difficulties of his natal chart during that year.
- If the harsh aspects between natal planets are now positive in the SR, then the difficulties of those planets will be overcome in that year.
- If the aspect between the angular houses of the SR and the nativity is positive (such as a trine), the year will be an easy one. If it is negative (such as an opposition), it will be full of difficulties.
- The conjunction of natal and SR Venus is generally a sign of a new love, romanticism, and happiness. If the SR Mercury is making this conjunction with his natal place, it indicates educational themes, much communication, commerce, and travel; if it is Mars, self-assertion, brave enterprises, accidents, or surgery may take place.
- If most of the planets are assembled in the 1st house of the SR, the native becomes more active and dynamic during that year. He may take the initiative. If they are in the SR 7th, the native may submit to others' wishes, acting obediently and having less initiative and control. If it is the 4th, the native has to deal with home and family matters, more so than the career and professional life. If it is the 10th, the native has to deal with outer conditions and the career and professional life.
- If cardinal signs are on the axes of the SR, the year brings new steps and beginnings, it will be a busy year full of events, and taking initiative is easier. Fixed signs show that this year is a time for completing new steps and dealing with prior changes, but is not the time to make big changes; responsibilities increase during this period, the native is now more aware about his aims in life, and he may reach success in his endeavors. Mutable signs indicate that conditions are changing and new alternatives will emerge: the native may enter a new stage of his life, and so he must flexi-

ble. The events do not occur during this year, but it is rather a preparatory phase. It is hard to maintain stability and existing conditions, and the native has to get prepared for future events.

- The triplicity (or element) in which most of the planets are found, is important.
- The SR house in which the natal ASC falls, is important, as is the natal house in which the SR ASC falls. The SR ASC shows the native's needs by means of the natal house it is in: if it is in the natal 10th, the native needs his career and future-oriented goals; it implies that 10th-house themes will come to the surface.
- The SR house in which ruler of the SR ASC is placed, represents what the native will be interested in that year.
- The SR house and sign where many planets are gathered show the focal points of the year, as conjunctions point out the native's main focus.
- SR planets have a strong connection with their dispositors: the dispositor always represents the reason for the events.
- Planets which are gathered in one house manifest the energies of the houses they rule, *through* the house they are in. That is, they establish a bond between the houses they rule and the house they are in.
- Natal transits should be evaluated together with SR charts.
- Eclipses should be evaluated together with the SR charts.
- If SR planets are close to the SR ASC or the other axes, their planetary energies are greatly manifested.
- SR planets carry their energies in the natal chart over to the SR chart. For instance, let the Moon be in the SR 11th, but natally she is in the 9th, and ruling the 10th. This means foreign friends and business themes, or friends and foreign trade themes will be brought about through the relation of these houses.
- If the degree of the SR ASC is very close to the degree of the natal ASC, the promises of the natal chart will be manifested.
- The SR position of the lord of the SR ASC represents the main theme of the year. For instance, if it is placed in the 1st house, the native will be focused on himself and his personal issues; if in the 7th, then marriage and partnership issues will take center stage.
- An SR planet placed at the 29th degree of some sign implies the end of a period, and the ending will be related to the house it is in and those it

rules. If the cusps of the angular houses are at the 29th degree of their signs, it brings the same influence.

- The place of the SR Moon shows us where the native experiences critical changes this year. If she conjoins with another planet, the house ruled by that planet also represents the area of the changes.
- If many SR planets are placed in cardinal signs or angular houses, the year becomes an active one in which the native wants to take steps in new beginnings and attract attention. He may also be involved in actions which are not thought out in detail, making sudden decisions.
- If an SR planet aspects one of the rulers of the axes, it gains more importance in the chart. For instance, if Mars (the ruler of the SR 8th) is in square with Jupiter (the lord of one of the axes), Mars gains more importance.
- If an SR planet has many aspects, it gains importance.
- If an SR planet is conjoined with the natal ASC, or a natal planet conjoins with the SR ASC, this planet manifests its influences in a strong way.
- Planets in the axes manifest their influences and characters powerfully.
- When a natal aspect is repeated in the SR chart, the SR planets emphasize the meaning of the natal configuration.
- If many planets are retrograde in the chart, there will be an increase in the topics which make us wait and delay our actions.

Let us now look at some handy rules for identifying certain topics:

Possible indications of death in the solar return:

- Natal ASC in the SR 8th, or the SR ASC in the natal 8th.
- SR ASC close to the natal ASC, *if* the natal chart promises death through the application of some *other* predictive technique at the same time.
- The ruler of the SR ASC in the SR 8th.
- The ruler of the SR 8th in the natal 1st, or the lord of the natal 8th in the SR 1st.
- Harsh aspects between the ruler of the SR 8th and the ruler of the SR ASC.

Marriage indications in the solar return:

- SR Moon close to the degree of the SR ASC degree, or in the SR 1st.
- The natal Sun in the 7th, but in the SR 1st.
- SR Moon in the SR 7th.
- SR Venus or Jupiter in the SR 1st or 7th.
- SR Venus and Moon in aspect to each other (while of them is the ruler of the 1st or 7th), or being conjoined in the SR 1st or 7th: this is because both of these planets are related to marriage (the Moon indicates the home, Venus marriage itself).
- Ruler of either the natal or SR ASC in the SR 7th.
- An aspect, and especially mutual reception, between the rulers of the SR ASC and 7th.
- The natal 7th house rising in the SR.
- Aspects between SR Venus and Jupiter, *if* Jupiter is the lord of either the natal or SR 7th.
- The degree of the New or Full moon in the 7th house.

All of the instructions we have given for SR charts in this section are also valid for lunar returns (LR), except that the indications in an LR only last for one month (specifically, 27.3 days).

Using timing techniques with SR charts:

Robert Zoller advises that we look at all of the Full Moons in the year: the place of the zodiac in which they fall, and the natal houses in which they fall.[10] For timing events, we can use them by superimposing them onto the SR houses to see what particular areas of life they light up.

I myself use New Moons, Full Moons, and the transits to SR charts for predicting the important events of the year. I give priority to the transits of the Sun for timing, especially the transits of the Sun to the SR angles. I've found that important events occurred while the transiting Sun and/or Mars trigger important aspects and aspect patterns within the SR chart.

Zoller also advises us to consider *firdaria* and sub-*firdaria* of the time.[11] As we have seen in detail while studying the important events of 2003 in my

---

[10] Zoller 2003, Lesson 19 p. 21.
[11] *Ibid.*, p. 22.

chart (during the Mars-Saturn *firdar*),[12] I find it useful to work with the *firdaria* along with solar returns. We can view the *firdaria* ruler and sub-ruler just as we do the profected lord of the year, and consider their placement in the SR chart.

I also find it useful to consider the secondary progressions of the nativity. When I was concluding my 20-year career at the Grand Bazaar, the progressed Moon's phase was balsamic, the phase which indicates endings. When I began to give astrological consultations professionally, the secondary progressed Moon was approaching the progressed Sun, and the actual New Moon occurred just a few days after my first professional consultation. In my consultations, I've seen many times that if the native is in a progressed New or Full Moon phase in the current or the next SR, I can find a New or Full Moon which confirms that the native is about to begin or end something very important in his or her life story.

Anthony Louis tells us that he finds the chart of the first solar eclipse following the solar return to be especially informative.[13] I am in agreement with him. Actually, I lean towards considering all of the solar and lunar eclipses of the year, beginning with the closest one after the native's birthday.

Now let us look at LR charts in more depth.

Lunar returns

A lunar return is calculated for the exact moment when the Moon returns to the same sign, degree, and minute where she was at birth. This takes place approximately every 27.3 days, which is a sidereal month. Each year, we have 12-13 LRs. The only position held in common between the nativity and the LR is the degree of the Moon, while the other planets are in different positions. With the help of the LR, we may observe events month-by-month.

Lunar returns are also one of the best techniques for timing SR events. Morin advises us to consider all of the LRs that occur over the year of the SR.[14] Of course, we may not have enough time to look at all LR charts in detail, but we can consider the ones which are similar to the SR chart. I find it valuable to consider the LR with the same ascending sign as the SR chart, though not necessarily the same ascending degree. It is also worth prioritiz-

---

[12] See Ch. 4.
[13] Louis, p. 11.
[14] See for example Morin 2003, pp. 67-69.

ing the LR with planetary placements that look like the current SR, or the one concordant with the current primary directions (for example, if the Moon and Saturn are in square, and they are also squaring each other by primary directions around this time).

For timing the events already delineated in the SR, it is a good idea to consider the LR in which the Moon is placed in the same house as she was in the SR: for example, if the Moon is in the SR 10th, we can give special attention to the LR chart in which the Moon is in the LR 10th.

Interpreting lunar returns:

The most important points to consider with LR charts are the axes. The sign on the ASC represents how we will manifest our individual needs and emotions, while the sign at the MC represents what we aim for and how we act to achieve it and get its results. For instance, Gemini on the ASC represents our success in communication, how multifaceted we are, and that we should quickly adapt to changing conditions; Capricorn represents the need to act in a controlled manner; Leo represents self-confidence and managerial qualities, and the need to attract the attention of others. But Aquarius on the MC represents having new and modern targets and creativity, Sagittarius represents a desire for expansion, and Taurus indicates the need for a permanent position and financial security.

The lord of the LR ASC is one of the main indicators for telling us what the native will be focused on throughout the month, how he will react to changing conditions, and to what extent he will be successful. We should also consider the ruler of the MC, which tells us how we act to achieve individual targets. However, again, this influence lasts only for one month.

Another important element in LRs is the placement of the Moon herself. By her house placement, we may understand the native's basic tendencies, main themes, and areas of emotional satisfaction in that given month (see list below).

Any planet which is close to the LR axes is important. A planet conjoined to the MC represents emotional targets in that month, and a conjunction with the ASC represents emotional needs. For example, if Mars conjoins with the LR MC, the native reaches his target or makes a step toward reaching it in that month. The native displays brave and direct attitudes toward his targets; he does not avoid discussions and competition on the path to reaching his aims. Mars's position here also represents difficulties with authority figures and the need to compete in professional life. If Venus conjoins with the LR ASC, the native needs emotional harmony and peace, and a need to act based on his relationships. If Venus has positive aspects, the native may easily reach those targets; if she has harsh aspects, the native may have difficulties in realizing his desires.

The LR house of the Sun is also important. We should examine the relationship between the Sun and the Moon: the aspect between these two may foreshadow important events.

Another important element is where many planets are gathered.

In LR charts, we sometimes see that other planets reach their natal degrees. This implies that the themes of that planet, the house it is in, and the ruler of that house, will all assume center stage in that given month.

Look also at the Moon's aspects in the LR. If her natal or SR aspects are repeated in the LR, this is a critical indicator. For instance, if Moon and Saturn are in a square in the SR, and the same aspect is repeated in the LR, the harsh influences of that aspect pattern are experienced within that given month.

We should consider further the links between the LR and the nativity or SR. The axes are critically important, such as if the natal degree of the ASC is on the cusp of the LR 7th, or the LR MC is on the degree of the natal MC.

The houses of the planets at the LR are also important, and the LR position of the natal lord of the ASC is critical.

The houses of the planets in the SR should also be compared to their positions in the LR. Examine also the situation of the lord of the SR ASC in the LR.

In all of these comparisons, we should focus on the houses which are highly emphasized.

LR charts should also be studied together with the SR, transits, progressions, and directions.

The Moon's place in a lunar return:

Moon in the 1st: The native is open to manifesting himself emotionally. He is also prone to emotional injuries as he is able to be influenced by others. Social interactions are easy. In male charts, the native's relations with female figures (mother, wife, etc.) are in the spotlight. Issues related to home and family may be on the agenda.

Moon in the 2nd: Finances are emphasized. The native needs to feel financial security; he may feel satisfied or dissatisfied due to his earnings (so the aspects of the Moon should be examined).

Moon in the 3rd: Communication issues are emphasized. Relations with siblings, other relatives, and neighbors gain importance. Intellectual issues like education, learning, reading and writing, and other mental activities are also important. This placement may represent quick changes.

Moon in the 4th: Home and family issues are emphasized. Security is also important. Issues related to the past may come to the surface. The need for belonging increases. If the Moon has positive aspects, the native feels satisfied because he feels he belongs somewhere.

Moon in the 5th: The native needs to be extraverted. Socializing, fun, love, and sexuality issues are emphasized. Activities related to children, artistic activities, hobbies, and sports may come to the surface.

Moon in the 6th: This would be a month full of work projects, in which the native needs to display his talents and work in a busy environment. He feels satisfied by working. Health issues may be central. The aspects of the Moon and the general outlook of the chart should be examined before making a firm conclusion about this.

Moon in the 7th: Relationships and socializing are emphasized. This may bring recognition. If the Moon's aspects are positive, the native may get positive reactions from others. This placement is fine for all types of social relations. Partnership and marriage issues may be on the agenda.

Moon in the 8th: The native may feel emotionally uncomfortable. Financial issues like credits, payments, and taxes may arise. Emotions are deep and the native is deeply influenced by them.

Moon in the 9th: Travel and other issues that may drive the native away from his surroundings are emphasized. Higher education and other issues that help the native's learning and evolution, legal issues, and the matters related to foreigners may arise. Teaching and learning satisfy the native. He may give lectures, be involved in publishing projects, and spread information via the internet.

Moon in the 10th: Career, profession, and social status are emphasized. The native may be recognized by others. If the Moon's aspects are positive, the native feels that he has reached his target; if not, he feels dissatisfied. As the Moon represents change, the native may experience changes in his professional and social status. As marriage is also a change of status, an emphasis on that house may represent marriage.

Moon in the 11th: Social life is emphasized. The native may feel satisfied by his relationships with friends and working for clubs and charities. Belonging to a group is important. The native may experience some changes in his friends' lives. He may be focused on his ideals and wishes for the future. He may also have some important changes in profits deriving from his career.

Moon in the 12th: The native wants to get rid of the crowd of the outer world and prefers peace. Meditation is advised. He may come across some conditions that he cannot control, or some hidden enemies. Illnesses and difficulties may be experienced. This is a hard time for making a decision. This is a time for preparation instead of acting.

The house that the Moon rules is also important, as it shows the outlet of this energy. For instance, if the Moon is in the 7th, the native is focused on one-to-one relations; but if the Moon rules the 2nd, then those relations will be career-based or financial, not romantic. The ruler of the sign on the cusp of the Moon's house also gives us clues about the reasons for the events and how they will come to the surface. If this ruler is not dignified, in detriment or fall, and if it has harsh aspects, then negative results may be expected.

Contacts with the axes in the lunar return

Planets which are close to the axes of the LR chart are also important. Natal planets whose positions fall on the axes of the LR are especially important, both in terms of the natal houses they are in, and those they rule:

☉: Personal issues, themes related to the father and other authority figures; celebrities; recognition.

☉☌ASC: Being recognized for one's personality and managerial skills, a need for recognition, having the necessary self-confidence to achieve recognition.

☉☌IC: Need for control in family and home issues, being a hidden leader, introspective.

☉☌DSC: Need for attracting the attention of others, a need for relationships and respect from others, being influential by means of common efforts.

☉☌MC: Desire to reach one's targets, recognition, attracting others' attention and being on the social stage.

☿: Communication, learning, education, young people, travel, intellectual endeavors.

☿☌ASC: Communicating, needing to talk a lot, mental activities, flexibility, expressing emotions and displaying talents.

☿☌IC: Introspection, communication within the family, reading and writing activities at home.

☿☌DSC: One-to-one communication, agreements, giving speeches, being involved in oral defense.

☿☌MC: Communication is a priority, public speeches, being recognized for one's ideas, intellectual pursuits in the career life, communication with higher-ups, commercial issues.

♀: Relationships, women, efforts to maintain harmony, intimacy, marriage and fun activities, social activities, smooth parts of life.

♀☌ASC: Maintaining harmony and balance, using one's talents to bring others together, bilateral relations and agreements, diplomatic issues, seeking peace, laziness, making changes in one's appearance, a desire to look good, nice clothing, loveliness and sympathy, socializing and fun.

♀☌IC: Seeking peace and balance within the home and family life, laziness at home, socializing at home, being with friends in the home environment (such as house parties), interior decoration and new furniture.

♀☌DSC: Socially active, relationship-centered, friends with everyone, common actions, popularity, open to invitations and new offers, romantic, seeking peace and balance in relationships, diplomatic, in sympathy with women.

♀☌MC: Attracting the employer's attention, being graceful, the advantage of looking good, good relations with higher-ups, support from people in authority about professional matters, social opportunities, recognition due to artistic themes, socializing in professional life, support from female figures in one's career.

♂: Areas where energy and efforts are focused, hostility, competition, courage, male figures.

♂☌ASC: Energetic and strong expression, a desire to display leadership characteristics, being demanding, argumentative attitudes, defiance, competition, being prone to accidents and violence.

♂☌IC: Stress and restlessness within the family, a need to be the leader of the family, an instinct to protect one's house and family, being disturbed due to past injuries.

♂☌DSC: Open enemies, keen competition, discussions and quarrels within relationships, difficulties in finding agreement, the need to take common action.

♂☌MC: The instinct to be influential in society, decisiveness in realizing one's aims, taking action, discussions with higher-ups, competition, being known for leadership and energetic features, an ambition for success, taking great risks, fighting for social goals.

Mars in the angular houses may also indicate that the time has arrived for the realization of events.

♃: Areas where we achieve expansion and progress, exaggeration, high expectations, an easy flow, optimism, economic ease, academic pursuits, travels and teachers, religious people.

♃☌ASC: Optimistic and self-confident attitudes, easily achieving one's aims, exaggeration, high expectations and demands, joyful, lucky and positive.

♃☌IC: Expansion at home and family, investment in real estate, hosting guests at home, plans for expansion, positive situations related to the father, feeling inner peace and security, travel.

♃☌DSC: Overreliance on others, positive relationships, opportunities and offers, marriage, relations with foreigners, high expectations.

♃☌MC: Positive in terms of career and professional goals, opportunities and support from higher-ups, aiming at the best, being demanding, self-confidence, social recognition, a chance to reach one's goals.

♄: Restrictions, responsibilities, difficulties, limitations, challenges, seriousness, realities, financial themes, business-related themes, lessons to be learned, death.

♄☌ASC: Serious and reassuring, responsibilities, pessimism, problems with self-confidence, emotionally uncomfortable, problems in reaching wealth and good health, realistic and critical attitudes, insecurity and skepticism, being highly disciplined and fond of responsibilities.

♄☌IC: Feeling introverted and reserved, problems in building satisfactory relations with others, a lack of confidence, worries, being antisocial, illnesses, impossibilities, problems related to the father, delays and restrictions in repairs and renovation projects related to the home.

♄☌DSC: Serious problems and responsibilities in relationships, a need to be realistic, delays and difficulties, being logical about all relationships.

♄☌MC: Being serious about goals, responsibilities related to the career and professional life, a need for hard work and being organized.

The month will be a dynamic one if there are many planets on the axes or in cardinal signs. Cardinal signs on the axes represent the need for action.

If the natal ASC is rising in the LR chart, the importance and the power of the LR increases, especially if the actual degree is very close. If the sign opposite to the natal ASC is rising, difficulties may be expected.

Return charts of other planets

Mercury returns

Natal Mercury represents our talents in communication, and his natal position gives us information about how we relate to and communicate with others. It is related to how we communicate our emotions and experiences, and how we share them with others.

Mercury returns[15] show our learning capacity and how we digest information within that year. It represents the issues that we will focus on that year. His house within the Mercury return shows us where we will be mentally focused, what we need to learn, and how we will communicate throughout the year. His aspects in the return chart represent the quality of the events and the lessons to be learned within that year. For instance, Mercury's contacts with Jupiter represent the need to be open-minded and flexible, and developments in education or adventurous thinking; his contacts with Saturn represent the need for mental concentration and being well-disciplined in mental and educational issues.

The ASC of the Mercury return represents how we would like to express our ideas and communication style with the outer world. For example, if Cancer is rising we may have emotional bonds with the issues in question, or we may express ourselves in a receptive style.

The MC of the Mercury return represents the type of communication that we would like to display and how we would achieve it. It shows which themes our mind is focused on to succeed and the direction we are heading in. For instance, if Aries is on the MC, we may be prone to be forthright in communication and be more active and decisive with respect to our ideas.

Mercury in the Mercury return houses

Mercury in the 1st: Communication is at the forefront of life. During this year, we are open to learn more. It is a time for speaking, learning, and making new contacts. Curiosity is notable.

---

[15] If Mercury contacts the natal position more than once (for example, if he then retrogrades past it again), give the first one priority, but also consider him at the time of his retrograde contact and subsequent contact when direct again.

Mercury in the 2nd: The native's mind is focused on financial issues. His ideas may bring money. He may have new plans related to financial issues.

Mercury in the 3rd: The native is mentally hyperactive; he reads and learns continuously. Relations with siblings and one's close circle are central. Exchanges of information and new research areas will attract his attention.

Mercury in the 4th: Communication related to the family and housing issues will increase. The native may move to another house. Relations with the father will be important. The native may learn new things concerning his private life and his past. Communication and action increases within the home.

Mercury in the 5th: Mental creativity will increase. Love, issues concerning children and their education will be central. Sports and hobbies which allow the native to be mentally active will be more important than before.

Mercury in the 6th: The native's mind is focused on health and work. It is a good time for any kind of mental work, the give-and-take of ideas with employees, developing new ideas or techniques about work, being more attentive to details in the work; but feeling anxious or nervous is also possible.

Mercury in the 7th: Communication with other people increases. Critical agreements may be signed. The exchange of information becomes the most important issue—consultants may have an active year, for instance. If the native is married, his spouse may experience a busy and active period.

Mercury in the 8th: Changes in financial conditions, the give-and-take of ideas with others about monetary issues, expenditures or taxes relating to commerce will surround the native. It may be a favorable time to loan money if Mercury is in good aspects.

Mercury in the 9th: A favorable placement for any kind of study or education, or travel relating to commerce, education, or religion. It is a time to be open to new ideas and experiences, or review one's own philosophy and approach to life.

Mercury in the 10th: The native is mentally focused on career and professional issues. He may be involved in businesses where creativity is important. Public relations, writing, and commercial activities may take center stage. The native may find himself making speeches in front of the public. His actions should be well-planned. If Mercury is in detriment, the native may be open to gossip and speculations.

Mercury in the 11th: This is a favorable placement for being included in any kind of social group or activity, the exchange of ideas with friends, making future plans, and talking about collective ideals, or participating in an intellectual group or one which involves young people.

Mercury in the 12th: It is not a favorable year for forming ideas about future plans, and it may be better to keep one's opinions to oneself. Secret enemies may talk behind one's back. This may be a year of withdrawing, and can be used to work alone, write, study, or research.

Venus returns

Natal Venus represents our one-to-one relations with others, how we unite with them, and the themes related to our love life. She represents what we love and how we love it, what makes us happy, what we value, and the things we find aesthetically pleasing and valuable. She represents the type of loving exchanges we hope to have and how we express our love.

Venus returns[16] represent our approach towards love and relationships, what we expect from relationships, the type of people we are attracted to, what would make us happy, and if it would be easy or not to achieve this happiness—during this specific period of time. Her place in the Venus return shows us what we expect from love, what types of relationships we would like to be in, and where we look for happiness. Her aspects indicate how the above-mentioned situations will be affected. For example, if Venus is in the 5th house of the return chart but in square with Saturn, we may be looking for love and happiness but have difficulties in finding it; even if we find it, it may only be short-term or we may experience some difficulties within it. If Venus has no aspects, the native may not find love and suffer from loneliness. He cannot establish intimate relations.

The ASC in the Venus return represents how we express ourselves through love and what we expect. If Taurus is rising, the native expects peace and security. If the degree of the ASC falls on any natal planets, the energy of that natal planet becomes more prominent and expresses its full potential.

The MC of the Venus return (and planets there) are related to the nature of our Venusian goals and the characteristics of the people we will be in relationships with. Strong planets placed in the MC represent good relationships and support in terms of career issues; they help us to determine the direction of our relationships.

---

16 Again, favor the first time Venus returns to the natal position, while direct.

Venus in the Venus return houses

Venus in the 1st: Throughout this year, we may give importance to our relationships with others and express sympathy. Marriage and partnership issues may be on the agenda. We may focus on our physical appearance, and want to look good this year. We may feel better when we are in love.

Venus in the 2nd: Financial profit and new opportunities increase, but so do expenditures because of the tendency to be extravagant. It is a favorable time for financial negotiations. We are able to get income from art, jewelry, ornaments, clothing, and entertainment.

Venus in the 3rd: We can get help from siblings, kin, or neighbors. It is a good time to get together with close friends, too. Travels may be enjoyable this year. We may get more interested in the pleasures of life.

Venus in the 4th: We expect peace and security. Home and family relationships gain importance, and we want to redesign the places we live in. If Venus is well positioned, we find peaceful relationships within the family.

Venus in the 5th: This year should be an appropriate one for fun and entertainment. It could be a year for having a child or a pregnancy, if that is promised in the natal chart. We can have good relationships with children. We are able to have time for creative arts or hobbies. Falling in love is possible.

Venus in the 6th: This is a favorable placement for all matters relating to work and profession. We can negotiate well with respect to future work. Good health and good relationships with one's employees or co-workers is possible.

Venus in the 7th: One-to-one relations gain importance. We need to be loved and admired by others, desiring harmony in our relationships; being happy also depends on the attitudes of others. If Venus is in detriment, we may experience disappointment in relationships. Marriage and partnership issues may be on the agenda.

Venus in the 8th: This is a good placement for loaning money. Financial support from others or receiving an inheritance is possible if it is promised in the natal chart and is supported by other predictive techniques at this time. One's partner or mate may experience a financial increase.

Venus in the 9th: Travel abroad may be very entertaining and satisfactory this year. We are able to make good negotiations with foreigners. This is a favorable placement relating to foreign trade. Falling in love while traveling or with a foreigner is possible.

Venus in the 10th: We build relationships based on our career life. We may attain success through the help of our good relations with others and their support. We are satisfied by success.

Venus in the 11th: This is a good placement for getting help from friends. We are able to have fun while being part of a group, and can profit from our profession or trade or with the favorable help of friends or society.

Venus in the 12th: This is not a favorable placement for any kind of relationship, but especially for private or personal ones. It may be a time for divorce or separation if that is promised in the nativity. We may withdraw from our personal or social relationships.

Mars returns

Natal Mars represents how we display ourselves and what we fight for, how we react, manifest our energy, show our anger, and complete our duties. For instance, Mars in Pisces represents fighting for universal goals; the native manifests his anger through passive and emotional reactions; he does not display spontaneous actions but prefers indirect and emotional responses.

Mars in the return chart[17] informs us about the above-mentioned themes for a period of two years. We realize how we shall survive during this period. The house of Mars in the return chart represents the field that our energy will be focused on, and what forces us to take action. We need to fight in the themes of this house; we are provoked there and called to compete. His aspects tell us if we will be successful in our competition or not: for instance, aspects with Saturn may bring delays and restrictions.

The ASC of the Mars return chart represents how we manifest our Martial energy. The sign on the ASC shows how we will react to new conditions, our attitudes during these challenges, and to what extent we may take risks.

The MC of the Mars return informs us of the quality of our goals; it also shows what message we are giving the world through our actions.

---

[17] Again, favor the first time Mars returns to the natal position, while direct.

Mars in the Mars return houses

Mars in the 1st: It is a time for progress. We may now easily display our real potential and act accordingly in order to show it to the whole world. We may be quarrelsome and argumentative. We hope to have the control over our lives in our hands. We may also be open to accidents.

Mars in the 2nd: It is a time for fighting for material things. Expenditures may rise. The houses that are ruled by Mars may tell us where we need to spend money. We may be more ambitious about earning money.

Mars in the 3rd: It is a time to focus on education. Problems with siblings and our close circle may be experienced. We may be experiencing a challenging period related to such people. We now direct our energy to learn new things. Short distance travels may take place, but we should take care to avoid accidents.

Mars in the 4th: The energy is focused on family and home-related issues. We may experience security problems at home. We may perceive our home as a battlefield. We may experience negative events like diseases and accidents within the family. Everyone seems to be interested in our private life.

Mars in the 5th: It is a time for being engaged in sports, but one must be careful if the aspects of Mars are hard in both the SR and natal charts. Physical lovemaking may be more important this year. We must be careful in relationships with children, as conflicts with them are possible.

Mars in the 6th: It is a time to work hard! Confrontations with employees or co-workers is likely. This is not a favorable time for health: infections, fevers, or accidents are possible.

Mars in the 7th: The main focus and challenge of the native are one-to-one relations. We may be faced with competition or have problems in our close relationships, including separations in marriage and other partnerships. We may have to deal with court cases and fight for our rights. Our spouse may also be faced with such difficulties.

Mars in the 8th: This is one of the most dangerous placements: accidents, injuries, or surgeries are possible if they are promised in the nativity. Conflicts in financial issues or shared possessions are probable. Expenditures may increase.

Mars in the 9th: It may not be a good idea to travel abroad if Mars has hard aspects in both the SR and nativity. Travel can be frustrating or unrewarding. Conflicts are possible because of different ideas, approaches, or beliefs. Legal difficulties with foreigners are possible, too.

Mars in the 10th: During this period we may have some difficulties related to our goals. We may quit one job and start another, have difficulties with our higher-ups, and get a raise only if we put effort into it. We may be more ambitious and energetic in this period of time.

Mars in the 11th: This placement is not very ideal for being part of a group. Conflicts with friends are possible. Cooperative enterprises should be undertaken only if Mars is in good aspects in both the SR and nativity. We should assume risks in business investments only if Mars has good aspects.

Mars in the 12th: This is a time for being careful about secret enemies, as they may be preparing something behind our backs. Surgery, accidents, injuries, and hospitalization are possible if they are promised in the nativity. This can be used as a time for working alone.

AL-BIRUNI

CHAPTER 12: RECTIFICATION

RECTIFICATION IS THE USE OF TECHNIQUES TO DETERMINE THE PRECISE BIRTH TIME. THERE ARE MANY METHODS USED TO RECTIFY A CHART, BUT THEY TYPICALLY INVOLVE USING PREDICTIVE TECHNIQUES BASED ON THE ASSUMED OR ROUGH BIRTH TIME, IN ORDER TO IDENTIFY AND TIME KNOWN LIFE EVENTS.

> *"We should realize that our judgements about time are our judgements about the simultaneous events."*
> Albert Einstein

Each birth chart is as unique as a fingerprint. The main element which creates this uniqueness is the exact birth time. The ASC and MC, two of the main points of a chart, are more sensitive to the birth time than the other elements of the chart. As they each move an average of 1° every four minutes, you can easily see the importance of an exact birth time. Since some techniques equate 1° with one year of life, a four-minute error in the birth time may create predictions that are off by an entire year.

Astrologers use rectification techniques in order to minimize the risks that may stem from an incorrect birth time. There are some techniques specific for determining the birth time directly, but predictive techniques are also used for this purpose.

Let us learn certain rectification techniques under two headings, the traditional and the modern:

Traditional rectification techniques

Traditional astrologers used several methods to determine the exact birth time, since it is impossible to interpret a chart correctly when the birth time is unknown. William Lilly uses the following:[1]

---

[1] Lilly, Vol. 2, pp. 502-23.

1. The *Trutine* of Hermes.
2. Ptolemy's *namūdār* (or "animodar") technique.[2]
3. The "accidents" of the native, which typically uses primary directions.[3]

In medieval astrology, before interpreting the chart, the longevity of the native was usually calculated. But in order to do this, one needed an accurate birth time. By using the *namūdār* technique or the *Trutine* of Hermes, the astrologer found an approximate birth time. Then, primary directions were used to match various accidents of life up with the chart, so as to find the exact birth time.

The Trutine of Hermes

In his famous *Christian* Astrology, William Lilly stated that the best way of rectifying a chart involved primary directions—but he also gave information on rectifying through the *Trutine* of Hermes. This method is based on the principle that the Moon's position at the time of conception is the Ascendant at the time of birth; likewise, that the Ascendant's position at the time of conception is the Moon's position at birth. Lilly gave a table which could be used for making calculations,[4] but the basic idea is this. The time of gestation is assumed to be between 258 and 288 days long. The specific length for the native is given by the relationship of the Moon to the ASC-DSC axis at the assumed time of birth (one must have a birth time that is fairly accurate first). If the Moon at the assumed birth time is under the earth, then if she is on or under the ASC, gestation was exactly 273 days, and the more she is distant from the ASC towards the DSC, she will indicate up to 288 days (exactly on or under the DSC). If she is above the earth, the time she indicates will be between 273 (exactly on or above the ASC) and 258 days (exactly on or above the DSC). Her exact arc from the ASC is used to get an exact number of days, hours, and minutes.

---

[2] **BD**: Ptolemy does not give a special name to this technique, but the word used by the Persians, picked up by the Arabs, and carried over into Latin, was *namūdār* (Lat. *animodar*), which means "indicator" in Persian.

[3] **BD:** "Accidents" is a standard traditional term, which simply means events experienced by the native: they are things which "happen to" him (Lat. *accido*).

[4] Lilly, Vol. 2 p. 502.

By counting backwards and looking at that day of conception in the ephemeris, Lilly figures out at what time the Moon on that day was actually at the assumed birth ASC. By adjusting the times back and forth, the astrologer is supposed to find the time when the two charts are in harmony, which yields the birth time (or the approximate time).

Ptolemy's namūdār or "indicator" technique

This is another technique[5] used to find the approximate birth time (which is then made more accurate through primary directions). It is used for clarifying the birth time when it is known not exactly, but only approximately (within two hours). It is determined by the position of the luminaries at the New or Full Moon which most recently preceded birth: if the native was born when the Moon was waxing, the prenatal lunation is the last New Moon, while if the Moon was waning we consider the prenatal Full Moon. Knowing the position of a New Moon is easy, since both luminaries are in the same place; but for the Full Moon, Ptolemy prefers the position of the luminary which was above the horizon at the time of the lunation itself.

After finding this degree, find the position of the ruler of this place (by triplicity, exaltation, bound, and phase or configuration), as it is *in the rough or assumed nativity*. If one planet rules or is related to that degree by all or most of these, then its degree in its own sign will be close to or correspond to the degree of the ASC, in *its* own sign, considered using ascensions or ascensional times. If there are two planets which seem equally dominant, take the one whose degree position in its own sign is closer to that of the assumed ASC, again by ascensions. If there are more than two, pick the one which relates to or rules the angles more, and is of the sect of the chart. But if the ruler is closer to the Midheaven than the Ascendant, then relate it to the Midheaven instead.[6]

To summarize with an example, let's assume that the prenatal lunation occurred at 23° Pisces, and in the assumed natal chart, the rough ASC is in later Taurus. Let's also suppose that Mars in the rough natal chart is at 25° Cancer. It's reasonable to say that Mars is the ruler we want: he rules the

---

[5] Ptolemy, *Tet.* III.2.

[6] **BD**: Ptolemy's discussion is extremely cramped (which is typical of his writing), and it is sometimes hard to know what exactly he means, especially in the use of ascensional times. In any case, Ptolemy's technique was understood to be relatively exact but still rough, and subject to further refinement by things like primary directions.

bound and triplicity of the place of the lunation, and trines the lunation itself. This would mean that the degree of the birth ASC is at approximately 25° Taurus: again, the position of Mars (the chief ruler or victor) in his own sign at birth corresponds roughly to the degree of the correct Ascendant, in *its* own sign.

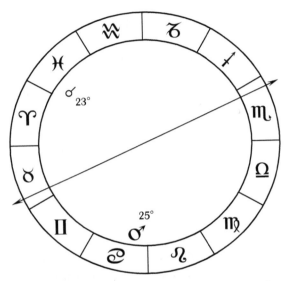

Figure 42: Illustration of Ptolemy's *namūdār*

To take another example, let's imagine that the prenatal lunation was the degree of the Sun, at 10° 22' Aquarius. Suppose that the victor over this degree in the nativity is Saturn: so, we examine Saturn's degree in the assumed natal chart. If Saturn is placed at 12° Cancer, then we adjust the rough natal ASC to be 12° in its own sign: thus if we expect Pisces to be rising, then the rising degree will be 12°.

In al-Bīrūnī's version of this method,[7] when there are two or more candidates for being the victor or primary ruler, prefer the one which aspects the ASC, or which is nearest to an angle. If the best candidates are all far away, then find the planets which have fewer dignities and are closer to the angles. On the other hand, he points out, some astrologers do not distinguish between planets which are closer to the ASC rather than the MC.

---

[7] Al-Bīrūnī, §525 (pp. 328-29). **BD**: Just as with Ptolemy, al-Bīrūnī's interpretation of this method is not crystal-clear.

It is not always clear in this method whether we should make this calculation in relation to the ASC, MC, both, or what; in my opinion, we should
consider the one which the victor or ruling planet aspects most closely. But
once we get this provisional, corrected ASC or MC, we should assume that
the true degree is within +/- 5°. So, if the adjusted ASC is 12° Pisces (as in
the example above), the true ASC should be within 7°-17°.

Let's look at another example. Heinrich Rantzau (1526-1599), an astrologer and friend of prominent Lutherans such as Philipp Melancthon, had a
prenatal Full Moon at 17° 48' Virgo, the victor of which is Mercury. Mercury
is at 7° Virgo in his natal chart. So, as his provisional MC was at 6° Virgo,[8]
we may rectify the chart to 7° Virgo. Then we may make a more precise rectification in line with the known accidents of his life.

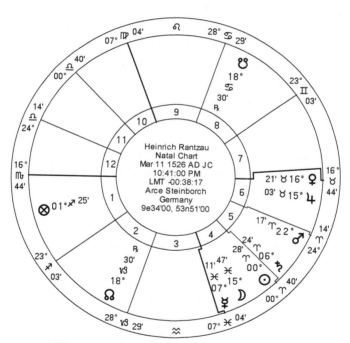

Figure 43: Nativity of Heinrich Rantzau

---

[8] **BD**: Zoller reports that several contemporaries of Rantzau calculated his chart to be at
10:31 PM, which puts the MC around 6°-7° Virgo (Zoller 2004, pp. 3-6).

The accidents of the native

Rectification is especially possible through primary directions (see Chapter 9): the calculated arcs should be made to match their related events of life. Indeed, the births of siblings, key changes of residence, deaths, marriage, the birth of children, and changes in the course of life and one's career may be predicted accurately by directing points to the angles.

By way of review, in primary directions we calculate the length of the arc (in ascensions, on the celestial equator) between two indicators, the significator and the promittor; this amount is converted into a length of time, in order to calculate when the promised event will take place. We should examine in which houses the significator and promittor are, and the houses they rule, to get a good idea of what they promise. Then we should decide which planet we should direct, and where. For instance, if we direct Saturn to the MC, and Saturn is peregrine in the 11th house, it means that a person with fewer opportunities may experience negative developments related to his career. This helps us rectify the MC of the native's chart, by aligning the arc with the date of such a known event.

The traditional astrologers limited primary directions to seven significators, and in profections they profected certain points for certain purposes. For instance, the ASC is both directed and profected to find the accidents particular to the native in his own person and life generally, but not specifically to determine the ups and downs in his career. For the career and professional life, we may direct or profect the MC instead. By directing the Lot of Fortune, we may get information about the native's financial situation, whether or not the Lot is his primary financial indicator. In fact, the directed Lot of Fortune indicates unexpected and lucky events, so it is used for that reason in rectification. For finances in particular, we may direct the primary financial indicator, planets in the 2nd house, or the lords of the 2nd. In short, each planet or point is directed for different purposes. The golden rule is: "First delineate the chart and understand what types of events it promises; then determine the timing of those promised events by using directions."

Sometimes we can direct multiple indicators to the angles simultaneously and look for possible matches by trial and error. For example, directing the body or aspects of the Sun, Venus, or Jupiter to the DSC could all indicate marriage; various directions to the ASC or IC can represent important journeys and changes of residence, directions to the MC represent changes in the career, directions with the DSC or IC can show the birth of children, and directions of the malefics to the MC, IC, or DSC can indicate the death of parents or children.

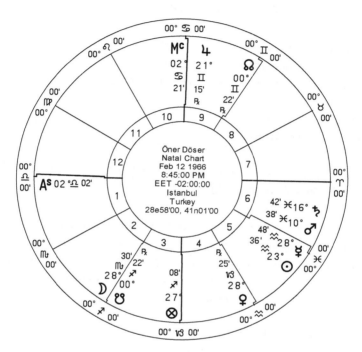

Example: Directing Mars for the date of marriage

As an example, let's use the birth time as listed on my birth certificate (8:45 PM), and see if the direction of Mars to the DSC[9] accurately shows the date of my marriage: since Mars is the lord of the DSC, his direction to that house directly represents marriage. For the formulas, please refer to the chapter on primary directions. In this case, the arc of direction is simply the difference between the oblique descension (OD) of Mars, and the oblique descension of the DSC.[10]

---

[9] **BD**: This is a "converse" direction.

[10] **BD**: Remember that oblique *a*scensions (OA) are ascensions on the eastern side of the chart. Since both Mars and the Descendant in this chart are in the west, we call them *de*scensions (OD).

To find the OD of the DSC:
RAMC (from computer): 92° 34' 45"
- 90°
OD DSC = **2° 34' 45"** (or **362° 34' 45"**, for purposes of subtraction)

To find the OD of Mars:
RA of Mars (from computer): 342° 29' 04"
Declination of Mars: (from computer): -08° 26' 33"
AD of Mars: -07° 25' 03"
RA + AD = 335° 04' 01"
OD Mars = **335° 04' 01"**

OD DSC (362° 34' 45") – OD Mars (335° 04' 01") = 27° 30' 44"
Arc = **27° 30' 44"**, or 27.5 years.

This result gives us August 1993, but I was married on May 7th, 1992, one year earlier. This means that the arc between Mars and the DSC must be about 1° smaller, since we are equating 1° of RA to 1 year. Since it takes about 4 minutes for the heavens to move 1°, let's subtract 4 minutes from the birth time (8:41 PM) and see what happens:

To find the OD of the DSC:
RAMC (from computer): 91° 34' 35"
- 90°
OD DSC = **1° 34' 35"** (or **361° 34' 35"**, for purposes of subtraction)

To find the OD of Mars:
RA of Mars (from computer): 342° 28' 56"
Declination of Mars: (from computer): -08° 26' 37"
AD of Mars: -07° 25' 07"
RA + AD = 335° 03' 49"
OD Mars = **335° 03' 49"**

OD DSC (361° 34' 35") – OD Mars (335° 03' 49") = 26° 30' 46"
Arc = **26° 30' 46"**, or 26.5 years.

The result is now within a couple of months of my actual marriage. As I mentioned before, in directions we do not look for an exact match in the days. This date is close enough, and the new time (8:41 PM) matches many other directions for life events as well.

Required information for rectification

For using this approach of identifying accidents, we need to know the dates of some important events in the native's life, like:

- Marriage and divorce. This includes the first time the partners met, if possible: this can be as important as the marriage date.
- Deaths or other important changes in the family members' lives, such as parental divorce, moving to another house, the births of siblings.
- Important illnesses, accidents, and surgical operations.
- Career changes, such as new beginnings, ventures, or losses.
- Other important successes and failures.
- Births of children.
- Important changes in the native's social status.
- Important financial gains or losses.
- Moving to a new home or office.
- Educational milestones, such as graduations, entering a university, or getting a Master's degree. This can include the date of a specific exam (and whether the native was successful or not).

Not all of those points are suitable or relevant for everyone. For instance, the native may not have a professional life, he may not be married or have children.

It is important to figure out how the native felt about specific events and how he was influenced by them.

Working with too many life events may be confusing. So, we need to work with events for which we have exact times and the best information. Exact information with fewer events is more important than numerous events with uncertain times. If the native does not remember any dates, we may at least ask him at what period of the year the event took place.

Knowing the birth time within two hours helps in rectification. If the native says that he might have been born between 12:00 PM and 2:00 PM, we may begin with 1:00 PM as an average birth time and erect the chart accordingly. If the native does not have any clue about his birth time, we may start by assigning the chart 12:00 PM or putting the Sun on the ASC.

After working with these directions, we may proceed to transits, progressions, and solar arc techniques (see below). The most critical point here is identifying contacts between the planets and the axes. Determining the axes correctly is critical: if we know the axes, then we have already rectified the chart!

If we cannot rectify the chart exactly, we may determine the axes and their lords, or the planets at the axes, in an approximate way. Aspects with such planets by transits, progressions, and solar arcs are important. Solar and lunar returns may also be helpful. We may make comparisons between those charts and the events that the native informed us about.

Modern rectification techniques

Transits

The easiest method for rectification is transits. Transits to the ASC, MC, natal planets, and house cusps represent important events: so, if we know the date of an event exactly, the transiting planets may determine where a sensitive point is. During critical events of life, transits to the ASC and MC are especially important.

For broader time periods, Jupiter, Saturn, the outer planets, and the Nodes may be used. But for more precise timing, use Mars, the Sun, Venus, and Mercury. Even if they do not make any exact aspects to the natal chart, they may be seen in axes during important events. The transiting Moon tends not to give significant results. We may also make detailed interpretations by using derived houses.

Stationary inner planets can be used for the same purpose. For instance, although Mercury is a fast planet, he often remains in his station at about the same degree for several days: so, identifying in which house Mercury retrogrades and stations may help in rectification. That is, by asking questions of the native about his experiences during such periods, we may determine the house where the associated planet turned retrograde.

If we know the exact date and time of important events, we might focus on the fast-moving planets' exact aspects or conjunctions with the axes. Since slow planets spend more time at the same degree, they are used for making predictions over longer intervals.

Indeed, determining the contacts between transiting planets and the axes is very important for rectifying the chart. For instance, contacts involving planets in the 7th house or its lord bring the themes of the 7th house to light; the native's relationships and events related to his spouse or partner are affected.

We may also consider the natural characteristics of the transiting planets for predicting the types of events that should be experienced. For example, Venus is associated with marriage and relationships, Mars with accidents, surgical operations and quarrels, Mercury with important dialogues and meetings, Saturn with responsibilities or unsuccessful ventures, Jupiter with opportunities.

We should also review the transits that are in contact with important midpoints.

If the exact time of the event is known, the chart of the transits themselves at the time may be evaluated separately and should be compared with the natal chart: for instance, the ASC at the date and exact hour of marriage may be same as the natal ascendant.

Secondary progressions

As the progressed planets move slowly, they are used for narrowing down broader time intervals in rectification. We should examine the progressed Sun, Mercury, Venus, and Mars. If we are sure that the birth time is known with a great deal of accuracy, we may use the progressed Moon. For more accurate birth times, the progressed ASC and MC may also be used. However, this should not be the first technique to be used.

Solar arcs

In this technique, all planets (except the ASC, MC, and the Moon) may be used to rectify the chart, because the planets move slowly. The daily motion of the Sun is employed, and the average speed is 5' of longitude per month. This technique is especially useful for events when we only know the year and month of their occurrence, but not the day. It gives the best results in this situation. Important events should be expected when a planet is at the axes, or when the axes are at the planets. The orb is very small.

Solar and Lunar returns

In the solar return chart, the house in which the lord of the SR ASC or the Sun is placed, represents the themes on which the native is focused in the given year. The house placement, zodiacal position, and aspects of the lord of the SR ASC tell us if the native is in control of the conditions, and if he can be successful in the topics he is focused on. So, we may begin to determine the correct ASC of a solar return chart by considering the known and important themes of that year. For instance, for the year in which the native gets married, we might expect aspects or interaction between the lord or victor of the SR ASC and the lord or victor of the SR 7th.

Evaluating the transit chart for a given event along with that year's solar return chart is also beneficial. Aspects and conjunctions of transiting planets with the axes and cusps of the solar return chart can help us with timing. For instance, if the native had an important surgical operation at some time, transiting Mars and Saturn may be at the cusp of the solar return 8th house. Or, for important changes in one's career, transiting planets may make aspects or conjunctions with the MC of the solar return chart.

Similarly, the lunar return house where the Moon or lord of the ASC of the lunar return chart is, shows us what the native is focused on in a given month. Transits at the time of important events may be evaluated just as with solar returns.

General approaches for the Ascendant and Midheaven

Determining the signs of the ASC and MC is also a rectification tool. The signs on these points are related to the physical appearance, attitudes, style of action, and self-expression of the native. Knowing about the physical features of the native really helps to determine the rising sign. Health problems can also offer some clues.

Influences of the planets in or aspecting the ASC on the physical body

The Sun has an authoritative attitude and image. His eyes, and powerful and direct looks, attract everyone's attention. He has a well-shaped body. He has smooth skin and pale hair. He may lose his hair at an early age. He has a significant chin and large mouth with a strong expression. His leadership attitudes are reflect in his appearance. John Lennon and Peter Sellers have the Sun in their Ascendants.

The Moon brings a round face, an upturned nose, and flat cheeks. The native is oversensitive to his surroundings. His mood changes rapidly and his emotions reflect on his face. His body is not very huge. He has small hands and feet. As an example, Madonna has the Moon in her Ascendant.

Mercury brings an oval face with high cheekbones, a sharp chin, a weak nose, a large mouth, and dainty facial features. The native has curious eyes which always seek new things. This shows that he has a sharp mind, but he may also be restless. His attractive hands move constantly. He looks younger than he is. George W. Bush and Madonna have Mercury in their Ascendants.

Venus brings a soft personality, agreeable attitudes, and a kind voice. The native has a proper nose and peaceful eyes. His eyes are generally blue or light brown. He has soft hair. He has a well-shaped body. He has kind and peacemaking attitudes. Grace Kelly and Bill Clinton have Venus in their Ascendants.

Mars brings wide eyebrows over his direct and sharp-looking eyes. The decisive and strong expression of the native is noticeable. His forehead and cheekbones are high. He has a long nose and a strong chin. He has a stocky and strong body and reddish skin. His hair is red, curly, or wavy. He is energetic. He may have a scar on his face. Tony Blair, Christian Dior, and Bill Clinton have Mars in their Ascendants.

Jupiter brings an oval and aristocratic face. The native's nose is long and his chin is significant. He has wavy hair and crescent-shaped eyebrows. He has significant and attractive eyes. The men have a fatherly expression. As he gets older, his body becomes much larger. Clark Gable and Dustin Hoffman have Jupiter in their Ascendants.

Saturn brings a serious and a harsh attitude. His chin and mouth reflects his endurance. He may have a bony and bulky structure, and curly hair. His skin is generally dark. Sean Connery and Margaret Thatcher have Saturn in their Ascendants.

Uranus gives light-colored eyes and smart looks. He has a strong and noble nose. His chin is round, fat, and even dimpled. He has sharp and original, but instable, attitudes. John Travolta, Hillary Clinton, and Carl Lewis have Uranus in their Ascendants.

Neptune brings an oval face, a small nose, and crescent-shaped eyebrows. The native has dreamy and faraway eyes. His lips are sensitive. He has a mystical charm. His face may be wrinkled at an early age due to a lack of moisture. Marilyn Monroe, Paul McCartney, Cat Stevens, and Bill Clinton have Neptune in their Ascendants.

Pluto brings dark skin. The native has sharp and attractive eyes. He may have flat and sometimes dimpled cheeks. He is physically strong and tough. His skin is soft and sensitive sometimes. Although he has rich hair on his head, he does not have much chest or body hair. Leonardo di Caprio and Glenn Close have Pluto in their Ascendants.

How to determine the Ascendant

Determining the rising sign is an important starting-point in rectification, since the chart itself is erected from the ASC. Having Gemini or Cancer on the ASC generates different experiences in terms of physical appearance and attitudes. If the Moon is the lord of the ASC, the Moon is more influential in the chart than other planets are; then, we should examine the Moon's house placement. The house shows what the native is focused on and what is important for him in his life. The native realizes his priorities through the house she is in. But if the lord of the ASC is Mercury, then the concentration of the native's energy changes totally. (This assumes of course that Mercury and the Moon are not in the same house.) Thus, if we understand the priorities of the native, then we may guess the lord of the ASC and the rising sign itself.

Since transits, progressions, and solar arcs to the lord of the ASC influence the native physically, personally, and in terms of health, we ought to discover the dates when the lord of the ASC is in harsh aspects with other planets, and ask questions about events at that time: such harsh aspects may bring accidents, diseases, and operations. For example, let's assume that we are about to make a decision between Virgo and Libra as the rising sign. If natal Mercury receives harsh aspects at the time of some mishap, then the ASC of that native should be Virgo; if Venus, then Libra.

Planets which are close to or aspecting the ASC have significant influences on physical appearance, personality, attitudes and health. Many standard physical influences are listed above, but if Venus is close to ASC, then the native may be also peaceful, harmonious, and diplomatic; Jupiter brings self-confidence, generosity, and justice; Saturn in the same position brings seriousness, melancholy, responsibility, and related attitudes.

Determining the lord of the MC and planets in the 10th is also important. Planets related to the career and profession are in the 10th house. For instance, Saturn in the 10th often brings professions related to engineering or finance. However, if the native is working in artistic areas, decoration, or topics related to fashion, then we should expect Venus. Of course, in traditional astrology we would also consider the planets in the 1st house.

If there is no planet in the 1st or 10th house, then we should consider the lord of the sign on which the cusp of the 10th house falls. For example, let's assume that we are not sure if the MC is on Gemini or Cancer (that is, between the last degrees of Gemini and the first degrees of Cancer). If so, we should consider where the lords of these two signs are placed. Let's assume Mercury is in the 9th and the Moon is in the 4th. If this person is a teacher, then having Gemini on the MC is more likely, because its lord Mercury is also in the 9th house. He may have an occupation related to education.

The house of the most significant planet of the chart also helps us to rectify the chart. For instance, let's assume that Jupiter in the 9th house is the most significant planet in the chart.[11] This suggests that the native has a tendency towards spiritual and religious themes, or a focus on higher education and issues which may expand his life-view and wisdom. If Jupiter were in the 10th house, the native could be focused on career; and if he were placed in the 8th, the native would be drawn to financial issues. By gathering some information about the native's life, we may identify the most appropriate placement for this planet.

When calculating the degree of the ASC, we should keep in mind that 1° equals about 4 minutes of time (on average). So, making a rectification of 10 minutes' difference in the birth time brings a 2.5° degree of change in the ASC. In general, allowing 4 minutes of error in a recorded birth time is rea-

---

[11] **BD**: There are several ways to evaluate the most powerful planet in the chart. For example, some methods assign points to the rulers of various places, which then point to the "victor" of the chart (see www.bendykes.com for a workshop on this topic). But we might also take the planet which is most dignified and most angular, of the sect of the chart, and so on.

sonable: birth certificates provided by hospitals may be off by a few minutes, and should be cross-checked by rectification.

Difficult aspects

In general, tough aspects bring more significant influences to important events. Those which are 4th harmonic aspects (squares, oppositions, and conjunctions) are more prominent in such events, as are aspects with the axes. We should also consider those difficult aspects which are multiples of 45° (such as 45°, 90°, 135°, and 180°), in aspect with the ASC, MC, or other natal planets by transit and solar arcs. Conjunctions, although not technically aspects, also bring the greatest influence.

Aspect orbs

For important events in the native's life, a planet which may be the significator for a certain event should have contacts with other planets and important points within the chart only within a certain range of degrees. This range can be wider for transits, but much narrower for progressions and solar arcs. We should not, however, expect absolute exactness. For instance, if such a planet is in aspect to an axis, the orb may be 2°-3° degrees on either side. Many astrologers use a 1° degree orb, since events tend to become more significant within this interval. For slow planets in transit, we should allow more degrees, while allowing less for the rapid inner planets.

Finally, we need to examine when transiting Saturn reaches the axes. Saturn's transit at the ASC-DSC axis brings more significant difficulties, problems, and responsibilities.

If we can determine a significator correctly, then we will make a better rectification based on what this planet represents or the areas in which it influences the native. Remember, in addition to investigating how the events themselves take place, we should also examine their emotional and physical influences.

Important changes in life

Career changes

For verifying these, we should examine the transits and progressions at the cusp of the 10th house, alongside those at the cusp of the 4th house. For example, the progressed Moon or Sun may be in trine, sextile or conjunction with the MC.

The progressed MC may be in aspect to the lord of the 10th or some planet which represents a career change. Aspects with Uranus may tell of sudden changes in career. Contacts between benefic planets may represent positive changes in the professional life: contacts between the progressed MC and Jupiter or Venus (being placed in the 11th house) may bring a positive change in one's career.

The lord of the 10th or a planet placed in it may have a transiting aspect to the cusp of the 10th, such as if Venus were the lord of the 10th and by transit she conjoined with the cusp of the 10th.

When a planet in the 10th returns to its natal position by transit, it may represent a time for change in professional matters.

When planets transit in the MC, important events related to the career and professional life may be on the agenda. Days when the transiting Sun conjoins with the MC are also important.

When planets transit in the 4th house, we may again expect developments concerning professional life. For instance, the native may experience difficulties when Saturn transits from the 4th house: either conflicts in the professional life itself, or difficulties within the family environment, may be reflected in one's career.

Transits of outer planets to the axes are also a critical rectification tool. For instance, Uranus's transit on the cusp of the 10th may bring sudden changes in career. Pluto's transit here may bring fundamental changes, transformation, and vital challenges. This is a forced change, not a voluntary one. It may represent power struggles to gain social status. Neptune's transit on the MC or its aspect to that cusp may bring scandals, indecision, passivity, and disintegration. Tough aspects will represent difficulties here. In general, outer planets represent fated changes.

Saturn's transit in the 10th may bring rewards, but also a period of hard work with more responsibilities. For promotions, we may examine the aspects between Saturn and the cusp of the 10th house. If the native is faced with important career opportunities, we should also examine the contacts between transiting Jupiter and the cusp of the 10th.

In a child's chart, the MC represents the professional status of the mother and father.

Marriage

Examine the cusp of the 7th house together with the cusp of the 1st. Contacts with the lord of the 7th are also important.

As Venus and the Moon tell us about marriage in a general way, their contacts with the cusp of the 7th by transit, progressions, and solar arcs may represent marriage. As Jupiter is related to happiness and expansion, his contacts with the cusps of the 7th and 4th may represent marriage and the expansion of the family as a result.

The reason for and the conditions of the marriage, are also important. So, we should not expect Venus to play an important role in every marriage. The native may have gotten married for a reason other than love. So, other planets may be more important. For example, if the native gets married for prestige, the Sun may be the leading factor. Likewise, Jupiter represents financial reasons, Mars represents sexuality, Uranus represents rebellion against the family environment, and Pluto represents power struggles.

In solar arc progressions, we may also work with the date when the partners decided to get married, and the date of a formal engagement.

If the lord of the 7th house reaches the cusp of that house or makes contact with it by transit, progressions, and solar arcs, marriage may be expected.

Contacts between the cusp of the progressed 7th and transiting planets are also important. Or, the lord of the 7th may be in contact with the planet which is the marriage indicator.[12]

The 10th house is also related to marriage. A transit or progression at the cusp of the 10th house may signify marriage.

We should also examine the aspects of the progressed MC. Progressed Moon-progressed MC conjunctions may represent marriage. The contacts of

---

12 **BD**: This is a victor over several significators of marriage: see for example *Bonatti on Nativities* p. 1287, or 'Umar al-Tabarī's *Three Books on Nativities* III.5 (in Dykes 2010, *Persian Nativities II*).

the progressed ASC with benefic planets or with the lord of the 7th house may also represent marriage.

Synastry charts may also be used in rectification. If the chart of one of the partners has been rectified, by superimposing this chart on the other and examining the houses of critical planets and their relations with the axes, we may rectify the other chart as well.

We should examine the transits to composite charts. For instance, when we superimpose the transits of the marriage moment onto the composite chart, the benefic planets or the marriage significators may be in contact with the axes.

The first marriage always helps better in rectification, with a success rate of about 95% using these methods.

Marriage indications in solar return charts

If we see the indicators below in the solar return chart for the year of marriage, then we may conclude that we did the rectification correctly:

- The Moon on the DSC or in the 7th.
- The lord of the ASC or the Sun in the 7th.
- The benefics (Venus and Jupiter) in the 1st or 7th.
- Benefics aspecting each other, and especially in opposition.
- Moon and Venus in aspect.
- The New Moon in the 1st or 7th.
- The Full Moon in the axes of the 1st-7th or 4th-10th.
- The lords of the ASC and DSC in aspect or mutual reception, and also if they are conjoined in the 1st or 7th.
- The degree of the ASC being close to the degree of the natal 7th.
- The Lots relating to marriage being in contact with the indicators of marriage in the nativity, or with Venus, the Moon, and Jupiter (which are general marriage indicators).

We could add more to this list. As the 4th and 10th houses are also related to marriage, we should examine their aspects and planetary placements as well.

Divorces

The condition of the 7th house prior to the divorce should be examined, since the nature of the planets that transit in it, and the transits of the outer planets, may be reference points. Uranus's transit in the 7th may bring sudden and unexpected separations. If the divorce brings fights and quarrels to the native's life, then we may expect a Pluto transit in the 7th. If separations occur as a result of disappointment, or if one of the partners needs to be more devoted, then we might consider a Neptune transit. Saturn's transit in the 7th may test the relationship. Tough aspects with the lords of the 1st and 7th may bring separations.

When the progressed Moon traverses the 7th house, she may be in tough aspects with other planets during a divorce. The progressed Venus and Sun may also bring divorce under the same conditions.

As marriage and divorce are also related to the native's social status, tough aspects or progressions to the MC may also indicate divorce. We should also examine the times when the solar arc MC makes tough aspects with its own lord or with planets like Mars and Uranus (which create separations).

In a solar return, oppositions in the 1st and 7th houses, and T-squares involving the 4th house, may result in divorce.

If in a chart we see that the couple divorced when an opposition was in the 6th and 12th houses, then we may rectify the chart so that the opposition occurs in the 1st and the 7th houses. If the divorce originates from or generates a specific conflict, then we may conclude that Mars and Pluto would be involved in this opposition.

Death

The following elements in a solar return (SR) may bring deaths to one's life in that year:

- The degree of the natal ASC on the SR 8th.
- The SR ASC being close to the natal ASC, if the chart otherwise promises death in that year.
- The lord of the 8th on the ASC.
- The lord of the SR 8th in the natal 1st.
- The lord of the natal 8th in the SR 1st.

- Tough aspects between the lord of the SR 8th and the lord of the ASC.
- Pluto, Neptune, and Saturn in the ASC may also bring death.

The deaths of others are predicted by finding the derived 8th from their houses: e.g., the death of the brother would be the 10th (the 8th from the 3rd).

Tough aspects or conjunctions of solar arc planets or the ASC with the luminaries, may bring the death of the father or mother.

Important accidents[13] and surgeries

Tough aspects between the ASC, its lord, and the Moon, may bring accidents.

Mars and Pluto are significant in the accidents which bring death. The 8th house is also significant in such cases. Transits in the 8th may represent accidents and surgical operations.

Contacts between the progressed ASC with planets such as Mars, Pluto, Saturn, and Uranus may also represent accidents. Bleeding and burns are due to Mars's influence. When the Moon transits the ASC and makes aspects with these planets, accidents may be likely.

Having the progressed Moon at the cusp of the natal 8th may represent important surgical operations. As such operations are followed by long periods of rest, contacts between the 4th, 12th, and their lords, are further indicators.

In solar returns, we may also see look for the above-mentioned difficult planets in contact with the ASC. For instance, suppose the native has a serious accident, and according to our provisional solar return Mars is the lord of its 8th, and is in its 12th but not very close to the degree of the ASC. We might rectify the chart so that Mars is close to the solar return ASC.

Important illnesses

Planets on the ASC and in the 1st, as well as the Moon, are related to physical health. So, tough aspects with the ASC, its lord, or the planets in the 1st may bring negative influences on health issues. On the other hand, health

---

[13] **BD**: Here we are speaking of physical accidents in the normal sense of an injury or mishap.

problems are related to the 6th and 12th. The 6th house rules lesser illnesses, whereas the 12th represents more serious diseases and hospitals. Tough aspects with the lords of these houses represent diseases.

For these reasons, we need to be sure of the positions of the planets and the signs on which the house cusps fall. For instance, let's assume that Saturn is in the 11th house of a provisional chart. If the native had an important disease or was hospitalized during a tough transit with Saturn, Saturn should be in the 12th house, so the chart needs to be rectified.

The Sun and the lord of the ASC being placed in the 6th and 12th houses of a solar return may bring important diseases.

The Moon progressing in the 6th or 12th may bring illnesses. Tough aspects between the progressed 6th house and the main natal planets should also be examined. The Moon's progression to harsh aspect patterns may bring important diseases.

The planets in the SR 6th tell us about the characteristics of the disease. Saturn may show permanent diseases which are hard to cure, Jupiter may represent liver diseases, Venus may bring diseases particular to women or diabetes, the Moon may bring hormonal dysfunction and problems with the stomach, and Mercury may represent diseases related to the respiratory and nervous systems. We also need to examine the natal chart, of course.

Childbirth

Transits in the 5th house, especially on the cusp of that house, should be considered: this goes especially for Jupiter Venus. When the lord of the 5th transits in the 5th, it may bring childbirth. When the lord of the 5th or a benefic planet transits the ASC, childbirth may be likely.

If the birth is difficult or has much bleeding, Mars may be transiting the cusp of the 5th house. Abortions or difficult births may be due to a contact between Mars or Uranus with the progressed 5th house, or the lord of that house. A hostile aspect between the natal 5th and 8th houses may represent a caesarian delivery.

Other indications of birth include the progressed Moon or Venus on the cusp of the 5th house. The progressed 5th house may be in contact with one of the benefics or its own natal lord. The solar arc Venus, Jupiter, or Moon may be on the cusp of the 5th, and any of those planets may be in contact with the lord of the 5th.

Main changes of residence

Main changes of residence may take place when the progressed IC contacts certain planets. Contacts with Uranus may bring separations, and contacts with Pluto may reveal more fundamental changes. Contacts with the Moon may also bring changes of residence. The progressed Moon may be passing through the 4th house, especially on the cusp of that house. An emphasis on the 4th house in the solar return chart is also important. When observing transiting planets in the IC, transits from the ASC and DSC may also bring changes of residence.

Education

For this, the axis of the 3rd and 9th houses should be examined.

Preparing a practice table

Preparing a practice table for important events is helpful in getting an overview of the techniques and planetary influences for each one. Below is a table of events, dates, and planetary configurations in various predictive techniques for important events in my life. The times provided are all for Istanbul:

Practice Table: Öner Döşer							
February 12, 1966, 8:45 PM (birth certificate), Istanbul, Turkey							
Year	Date	Event	Transit	Prog.	Solar Arc	☉ Return	☽ Return
1992	May 7 4:10 PM	Marriage	☊☌IC ♂t☌DSC	♂p☌DSC	♀sa☌☉		☽☌IC ♃☌ASC
1997	May 16 3:00 PM	Father's death		IC p☌♀			♄☌IC
2003	June 21 5:00 PM	Quitting job in Grand Bazaar	♄t☌MC	☉p☌DSC ☽p☌DSC	♃sa△☽	♄☌MC	
2003	July 6 11:00 AM	1st professional consultation	♀t☌MC	☉p☌DSC ☽p☌DSC	♃sa☍♀		
2003	Aug. 27	CNN Appearance		☽p☌DSC		☿t☌ASC	

The most important factor in rectification is the relation between the axes and the planets, because the axes are triggered by primary events or experiences during transits, progressions and directions. However, please note that not every direction of a planet to the axes brings an event. Of the events, the ASC-DSC axis is related to important relationship changes, but they may be triggered by aspects between planets and the MC-IC axis.

Nativities with unknown birth times

When you have nativities whose birth times are very certain, try following these steps:

1. Define a minimum of 3, and maximum of 6, important events with accurate dates, which were important in the native's life. You should know the results of the events and their personal influences on the native.
2. Define an event which is symbolized by the Moon, such as marriage, births, and issues related to the family, mother, and health.
3. Select one of the following methods: perform solar arcs of the axes for that date, or the Moon's contact with planets which have been progressed by solar arcs.

Let's assume that the important event you chose for determining the exact birth time is the birth of the native's child. Based on the general positions of the planets in your provisional birth chart, you find that the solar arc Jupiter is in close contact with the natal Moon on that date. In that case, we choose Jupiter as the planet whose solar arc indicates the child, and the Moon's position could be refined based on that.

Let's suppose that at childbirth the solar arc Jupiter was at 10° 20' Sagittarius, and the assumed natal Moon is at 15° 45' Aries. They have a difference of 5° 25'. Since we are assuming for now that the aspect is exact at the time of the child's birth, we can use the known time of the event to determine where the natal Moon would have to be in order for the solar arc to be exact. In this example we need to pull the Moon back to 10° 20' Aries, so that Jupiter will reach precisely there in the year the native had a child. Once we know at what time of day the natal Moon was at 10° 20' Aries, determine the degrees of the ASC and MC accordingly.

If Jupiter had not been at a suitable degree to make this calculation, we would have had to choose another event and make the same calculations for a different planet. And of course, we should treat other important events using the same technique, as well.

GLOSSARY

This short glossary adapted by Benjamin Dykes lists a few technical terms in this book, with references to sections or Appendices from *Introductions to Traditional Astrology* (Dykes, 2010).

- **Accident** (Lat. *accidens*, Ar. *ḥādith*). An event which "befalls" or "happens" to someone, though not necessarily something bad.
- **Aversion.** Being in the second, sixth, eighth, or twelfth sign from a place. For instance, a planet in Gemini is in the twelfth from, and therefore in aversion to, Cancer. Such places are in aversion because they cannot **aspect** it by the classical scheme of aspects. See III.6.1.
- **Detriment** (or Ar. "corruption," "unhealthiness," "harm."). More broadly (as "corruption"), it refers to any way in which a planet is harmed or its operation thwarted (such as by being burned up). But it also (as "harm") refers specifically to the sign opposite a planet's domicile. Libra is the detriment of Mars. See I.6 and I.8.
- **Dignity** (Lat. "worthiness"; Ar. *ḥaẓẓ*, "good fortune, allotment"). Any of five ways of assigning rulership or responsibility to a planet (or sometimes, to a Node) over some portion of the zodiac. They are often listed in the following order: domicile, exaltation, triplicity, bound, face/decan. Each dignity has its own meaning and effect and use, and two of them have opposites: the opposite of domicile is **detriment**, the opposite of exaltation is **fall**. See I.3, I.4, I.6-7, VII.4 for the assignments; I.8 for some descriptive analogies; VIII.2.1 and VIII.2.2*f* for some predictive uses of domiciles and bounds.
- **Distribution.** The direction of a **releaser** (often the degree of the Ascendant) through the bounds. The bound lord of the distribution is the "distributor," and any body or ray which the releaser encounters is the "partner." See VIII.2.2*f*, and *PN3*.
- **Eastern/western (of the Sun).** A position relative to the Sun, often called "oriental" or "occidental," respectively. These terms are used in two major ways: (1) when a planet is in a position to rise before the Sun by being in an early degree (eastern) or is in a position to set after the Sun by being in a later degree (western). But in ancient languages, these words also refer mean "arising" or "setting/sinking," on an analogy with the Sun rising and setting: so sometimes they refer to (2) a planet arising out of, or

sinking under, the Sun's rays, no matter what side of the Sun it is on (in some of my translations I call this "pertaining to arising" and "pertaining to sinking"). Astrological authors do not always clarify what sense is meant, and different astronomers and astrologers have different definitions for exactly what positions count as being eastern or western. See II.10.

- **Fall** (Gr. *hupsōma*, Ar. *hubūṭ*, Lat. *casus, descensio*). The sign opposite a planet's exaltation; sometimes called "descension." See I.6.
- ***Hīlāj*** (From the Pahlavi for "releaser"). Equivalent to **releaser**.
- **House-master.** Often called the *alcochoden* in Latin, from **kadukḥudhāh** (the Pahlavi for "house-master"). One of the lords of the longevity **releaser**, preferably the bound lord. See VIII.1.3. But the Greek equivalent of this word (*oikodespotēs*, "house-master") is used in various ways in Hellenistic Greek texts, sometimes indicating the lord of a domicile, at other times the same longevity planet just mentioned, and at other times a kind of **victor** over the whole nativity.
- ***Kadukḥudhāh*** (From the Pahlavi for "house-master"), often called the *alcochoden* in Latin transliteration. See **House-master.**
- **Native.** The person whose birth chart it is.
- **Peregrine** (Lat. *peregrinus*, Ar. *gharīb*), lit. "a stranger." When a planet is not in one of its five **dignities**. See I.9.
- **Profection** (Lat. *profectio*, "advancement, setting out"). A predictive technique in which some part of a chart (usually the Ascendant) is advanced either by an entire sign or in 30° increments for each year of life. See VIII.2.1 and VIII.3.2, and the sources in Appendix F.
- **Releaser.** The point which is the focus of a direction. In determining longevity, it is the one among a standard set of possible points which has certain qualifications (see VIII.1.3). In annual predictions one either directs or **distributes** the longevity releaser, or any one of a number of points for particular topics, or else the degree of the **Ascendant** as a default releaser. Many astrologers direct the degree of the Ascendant of the **revolution** chart itself as a releaser.
- **Sect.** A division of charts, planets, and signs into "diurnal/day" and "nocturnal/night." Charts are diurnal if the Sun is above the horizon, else they are nocturnal. Planets are divided into sects as shown in V.11. Masculine signs (Aries, Gemini, *etc.*) are diurnal, the feminine signs (Taurus, Cancer, *etc.*) are nocturnal.

- **Time lord**. A planet ruling over some period of time according to one of the classical predictive techniques. For example, the lord of the year is the time lord over a **profection**.
- **Victor** (Ar. *mubtazz*). A planet or point identified as the most authoritative over a particular topic or house (I.18), or for a chart as a whole (VIII.1.4). See also *The Search of the Heart* (Dykes, 2011). We may distinguish between procedures that find the most authoritative and powerful planet ruling one or more places (a victor "over" places) or the member of a list of candidates which fulfills certain criteria (a victor "among" places).
- **Whole signs.** The oldest system of assigning house topics and **aspects**. The entire sign on the horizon (the Ascendant) is the first house, the entire second sign is the second house, and so on. Likewise, aspects are considered first of all according to signs: planets in Aries aspect or regard Gemini as a whole, even if aspects by exact degree are more intense. See I.12, III.6, and the Introduction §6.

BIBLIOGRAPHY

Abū Maʿshar al-Balhi, *The Abbreviation of the Introduction to Astrology*, ed. and trans. Charles Burnett, K. Yamamoto, and Michio Yano (Leiden: E.J. Brill, 1994)

Al-Bīrūnī, Muhammad bin Ahmad, *The Book of Instruction in the Elements of the Art of Astrology*, trans. R. Ramsay Wright (London: Luzac & Co., 1934)

Bonatti, Guido, *Bonatti on Nativities*, trans. and ed. Benjamin N. Dykes (Minneapolis, MN: The Cazimi Press, 2010)

Bonatti, Guido, *Bonatti on Basic Astrology*, trans. and ed. Benjamin N. Dykes (Minneapolis, MN: The Cazimi Press, 2010)

Brady, Bernadette, *Brady's Book of Fixed Stars* (Boston: Weiser Books, 1998)

Brady, Bernadette, *Predictive Astrology: The Eagle and the Lark* (York Beach, ME: Red Wheel/Weiser LLC, 1999)

Coley, Henry, *Clavis Astrologiae Elimata: Or, a Key to the Whole Art of Astrology* (London, 1676; reprinted by Renaissance Astrology Facsimile Editions, 2004)

Crane, Joseph, *A Practical Guide to Traditional Astrology* (Reston, VA: ARHAT Publications, 1998)

Cunningham, Donna, *An Astrological Guide to Self-Awareness* (CRCS Publications, 1994)

Dorotheus of Sidon, *Carmen Astrologicum*, trans. and ed. David Pingree (Abingdon, MD: The Astrology Center of America, 2005)

Dykes, Benjamin, trans. and ed., *Works of Sahl & Māshā'allāh* (Golden Valley, MN: The Cazimi Press, 2008)

Dykes, Benjamin, trans. and ed., *Persian Nativities I: Māshā'allāh and Abū ʿAlī* (Minneapolis, MN: The Cazimi Press, 2009)

Dykes, Benjamin, trans. and ed., *Persian Nativities II: 'Umar al-Tabarī & Abū Bakr* (Minneapolis, MN: the Cazimi Press, 2010)

Dykes, Benjamin, trans. and ed., *Persian Nativities III: On Solar Revolutions* (Minneapolis, MN: The Cazimi Press, 2010)

Dykes, Benjamin trans. and ed., *Introductions to Traditional Astrology: Abū Ma'shar & al-Qabīsī* (Minneapolis, MN: The Cazimi Press, 2010)

Hermann of Carinthia, Benjamin Dykes trans. and ed., *The Search of the Heart* (Minneapolis, MN: The Cazimi Press, 2011)

Ibn Ezra, Abraham, *The Beginning of Wisdom*, trans. Meira Epstein, ed. Robert Hand (Reston, VA: ARHAT Publications, 1998)

Gansten, Martin, *Primary Directions: Astrology's Old Master Technique* (The Wessex Astrologer, 2009)

Hermes, Martien, "On Profections, a Traditional Method of Prediction," in *The Astrological Journal*, Vol. 44, No. 6 (2002), pp. 51-60, and Vol. 45, No. 1 (2003), pp. 21-27.

Hermes Trismegistus, *Liber Hermetis*, ed. Robert Hand, trans. Robert Zoller (Salisbury, Australia: Spica Publications, 1998)

Hand, Robert, *Night & Day: Planetary Sect in Astrology* (Cumberland, MD: The Golden Hind Press, 1995)

Hand, Robert, *Whole Sign Houses: The Oldest House System* (Reston, VA: ARHAT Publications, 2000)

Holden, James H., *A History of Horoscopic Astrology* (Tempe, AZ: American Federation of Astrologers, Inc., 2006)

Houlding, Deborah, *The Houses: Temples of the Sky*, 2nd edition (Bournemouth, England: The Wessex Astrologer Ltd, 2006)

Al-Kindī, *On the Stellar Rays*, trans. Robert Zoller and ed. Robert Hand (Berkeley Springs, WV: The Golden Hind Press, 1993)

Lang-Wescott, Martha, *Derivative Angles* (Treehouse Mountain, 1992)

Lehman, J. Lee, *Classical Astrology for Modern Living: From Ptolemy to Psychology and Back Again* (Whitford Press: Whitford Press, 2000)

Lilly, William, *Christian Astrology* Vols. 1-2 (Abingdon, MD: Astrology Classics, 2004)

Louis, Anthony, *The Art of Forecasting using Solar Returns* (The Wessex Astrologer, Ltd., 2008)

Manilius, Marcus, *Astronomica*, trans. G.P. Goold (Cambridge and London: Harvard University Press, 1977)

Maternus, Julius Firmicus, trans. James H. Holden, *Mathesis* (Tempe, AZ: American Federation of Astrologers, Inc., 2011)

McCullough, Nance, *Solar Returns Formulas & Analysis* (Namac Publishing, 1998)

Morin, Jean-Baptiste, *Astrologia Gallica Book Twenty-Three: Revolutions* (2nd edition), trans. James H. Holden (Tempe, AZ: American Federation of Astrologers, Inc., 2003)

Morin, Jean-Baptiste, *Astrologia Gallica Book Twenty-Four: Progressions and Transits*, trans. James H. Holden (Tempe, AZ: American Federation of Astrologers, Inc., 2004)

Morin, Jean-Baptiste, *Astrologia Gallica: Book Eighteen, The Strengths of the Planets*, trans. Anthony L. LaBruzza (Tempe, AZ: American Federation of Astrologers Inc., 2004)

Morin, Jean-Baptiste, *Astrologia Gallica: Book Twenty-One, The Morinus System of Horoscope Interpretation*, trans. Richard S. Baldwin (Tempe, AZ: American Federation of Astrologers Inc., 2008)

Paul of Alexandria, trans. Dorian Gieseler Greenbaum, *Late Classical Astrology: Paulus Alexandrinus and Olympiodorus* (Reston, VA: ARHAT Publications, 2001).

Ptolemy, Claudius, *Tetrabiblos*, trans. F.E. Robbins (Cambridge and London: Harvard University Press, 1940)

Al-Qabīsī, *The Introduction to Astrology*, eds. Charles Burnett, Keiji Yamamoto, Michio Yano (London and Turin: The Warburg Institute, 2004)

Robson, Vivian, *The Fixed Stars & Constellations in Astrology* (Abingdon, MD: Astrology Classics, 2003)

Rochberg, Francesca, *The Heavenly Writing: Divination, Horoscopy, and Astronomy in Mesopotamian Culture* (Cambridge: Cambridge University Press, 2004)

Schoener, Johannes, *Three Books on the Judgments of Nativities* Vol. 1, trans. Robert Hand (Reston, VA: ARHAT, 2001)

Volguine, Alexandre, *The Technique of Solar Returns* (ASI Publishers, Inc., 1980)

Zoller, Robert, *The Arabic Parts in Astrology: A Lost Key to Prediction* (Rochester, VT: Inner Traditions International, 1989)

Zoller, Robert, *On the Fifth House* (Mansfield, Notts: Ascella, 1997)

Zoller, Robert, *Foundation Course in Medieval Astrology* (London: New Library Ltd., 2000)

Zoller, Robert, *Tools and Techniques of the Medieval Astrologer Book 1: Prenatal Concerns and the Calculation of the Length of Life* (London: New Library Ltd., 2001-02)

Zoller, Robert, *Diploma Course in Medieval Astrology* (London: New Library Ltd., 2002-03)

Zoller, Robert, *Tools & Techniques of the Medieval Astrologer: Book Two, Astrological Prediction by Direction and the Subdivision of the Signs* (London: New Library Ltd., 2002-03)

Zoller, Robert, *A Medieval Astrologer Looks at Rantzau's Nativity* (Privately published, 2004)

ABOUT ASTROART:
THE SCHOOL OF ASTROLOGY

The School of Astrology has been established with the aim of contributing to teaching and developing astrology in Turkey and providing sound knowledge for astrology lovers. The training program begins with the Traditional Astrology classes and expands to modern techniques. Following the Beginner and Intermediate Levels, sophisticated courses like Horary Astrology and Electional Astrology are made available.

In the School of Astrology, our goal is to teach practical astrological information, not only theory. Those who complete the training can use astrology in practical life and for their own personal developmental process. The School of Astrology also hosts numerous events on personal development techniques and astrology seminars, in addition to individual and corporate astrological consultancy services.

As the training is a serious process for us, the course contents are prepared in fine detail. The lessons are enriched with examples to help improve understanding. Our training style is not dogmatic; we do our best to pay attention to a variety of astrological approaches. We both encourage open communication of ideas and we preserve the principles of astrology.

Astrology Course Categories:

Our training is composed of three categories:
1. *Beginning Level (36 weeks)*
2. *Intermediate Level (36 weeks)*

These two training programs are linked to each other. Before attending the Intermediate classes, the Beginner course should be completed.

3. *Advanced Level*
   a. Horary Astrology
   b. Electional Astrology
   c. Astro-psychology
   d. Mundane Astrology
   e. Medical Astrology

The classes in the Advanced Level are independent, so students can attend whichever class they prefer. Completing all modules is not obligatory.

In addition to these main courses, Sufism and Astrology, Esoteric Astrology, Indian Astrology, Chinese Astrology and Mayan Astrology classes are also available. Also, many seminars are held during the year on specific astrology topics.

Course Materials

We provide detailed and adequate materials, but we do advise you to have certain crucial books and reference guides. Students should also read articles about each subject and exchange information with others who are at the same level of knowledge.

Lessons are designed based on a self-guided, step-by-step educational method. The aim is to let students develop their own styles and use their knowledge by expressing themselves clearly instead of just memorizing data. By enrolling the classes, you can enter into a systematical learning process.

The courses are easy to understand. However, students should always be well focused on the lessons. We understand that learning is a difficult process. For that reason, we are flexible and do our best to answer all of your questions; conversely, we do ask you to make a sufficient effort.

Completion and Certificates

To be a master in any profession, one needs great experience in addition to knowledge: experience makes the difference between a master and an apprentice. Whether you learn astrology for your own individual development or in order to be a professional, your instructor will guide you so as to help you achieve your goals.

After completing the Advanced Level, one may move to a Master's Project.

Contact Information:

AstroArt Astroloji Okulu
www.astrolojiokulu.com/eng
http://www.onerdoser.com/eng/
0 216 386 73 96 / 0 216 358 12 23 / 0 532 284 89 79